WOMEN AND URBAN CRIMES

Dr. Doel Mukerjee

Publications

KALPAZ PUBLICATIONS

DELHI—110 052

WOMEN AND URBAN CRIMES

(Women, Crime)

Rs. 870

ISBN: 81-7835-406-3

Published in 2005 in India by
Kalpaz Publications
C-30, Satyawati Nagar
Delhi-110 052
E-mail: kalpaz@hotmail.com

Laser Typesetting by: Varsha Graphics, Delhi
Printed at: Salasar Imaging System, Delhi

WOMEN AND URBAN CRIMES

Dedicated to My Loving Mother

Contents

Preface

A woman belongs to an endangered species, leading the life of a dependent, both emotionally and financially from birth to death. There are chances that a female life may be snuffed out before she is born or she may be abandoned after birth or remain as a neglected member of the family. She is the target of all types of assaults both at home where she is born as well as at her marital home. This is a universal feature.

Being a woman it was but natural for me to research on this endangered species. Hence, I started this endeavor to gain an insight into the various aspects of crimes against women. In the process I realized that the world of protection that is created by the male counter parts is nothing but a myth. For within the four walls of the home there are wails and deep sighs of tormented women. These do not reach books on facts and figures. A common complaint made by victims are that their cases are not taken seriously by their families or the police are known to handle them insensitively, be it in the Developed World or in the traditional environment of the Developing World. Through research I realized that victimized and traumatized women come from all types of backgrounds just as the wife batterers and molesters.

In course of this study I was able to meet women who were assaulted, battered and wronged both in India and Canada. The stories were the same; only the time, place and situations were different. However, with education, more liberal views and some amount of awareness women are finding the courage to report offences. Though, law enforcement agencies are often unable to handle such cases of battery and rape in a sensitive manner and making the victims develop an apprehensive attitude towards reporting to the police. Infact victims all over the world prefer to report a crime to an NGO or a social welfare organization, rather than report the offence to the police. Often the long drawn process of accessing justice by reporting to the police, followed by incessant questioning and then the trial process, which is often lengthy leading to the acquittal of the suspect further, traumatizes a victim. Today, the number of cases reported to the police have increased, though this is in no way the actual picture of crimes against women, it is only the tip of the iceberg.

Crime against women is not limited to a particular class of people. It is a universal feature. I realized this only too soon that there is no escape even for those who are educated. On 21st March 1997, I was a witness to a case of molestation at the Jawaharlal Nehru University campus. There were ten to twelve odd men and women who witnessed the incident, but not a single person came to the victim's rescue. The incident was reported within 10 minutes of its occurrence at the Vasant Vihar Police Station. We were received by an unhelpful staff who claimed that the day's work was over and so the station diary, the paper and registration forms etc were all locked. However, good sense prevailed on us and we were able to put in a complaint on some plane paper stating the time, the place and the description of the molester and his vehicle. The application was made out on two copies and one was received. However, no receipt was given in lieu of the application. After a week when the victim enquired about the case, she realized that the application was missing. The victim was told very politely to forget about the small incident and get on with her life. I realized at this stage that accessing justice is difficult for woman.

As I completed my research both in Kolkata and Toronto, I was able to not only see the darker side of society but also discovered the humane side of humans. Our cities are made up of all kinds of people coming from a maze of traditions and cultural diversity, which have a tremendous effect on the society. The city makes people lose their bonds, bindings and sometimes their mind. This leads to heinous incidents.

But it would be wrong to say that rural areas have few crimes against women. There is less reporting in the rural areas due to lack of knowledge, awareness, distance of police stations and the immobility of the women outside their homes leading to practically non-reporting of incidents. The women find it difficult to come out of the social bonds, the close-knit families to report their cases, as it is a taboo to discuss. And this was also one reason why I chose to research on this phenomenon.

As I complete this research, I would like to end by adding yet another dimension of human nature ... the dimension that can show gratitude to the "humane side". After all, it was because of these facets of the human nature that it became possible to see the dimension first mentioned, i.e., the criminal nature in a negative light.

The study has taken its present shape due to the constant guidance, support and active interest of my philosopher and guide Prof. R.C. Sharma. I am indebted to him, as he has extended a helping hand in not only while I was his student but also has taken a keen interest in my career. My travel to Toronto was possible as I was able to receive a timely fellowship grant from the Shastri Indo - Canadian Institute, for six months and was able to be closely associated with the University of Toronto.

In Toronto I was made to feel at home with the timely assistance of Prof. Rosemary Gartner and Prof. Anthony Doob of University of Toronto (UOfT), Department of Criminology. Many thanks to Dr. Kim England (UOfT) Department of Geography for helping me out with the initial reading list as well as finding a comfortable work- space in the Department. I am much obliged to her kindness. Meeting Ranu Basu and Richard Massie was a boon to me and a nightmare for them. Through their active cooperation I was able to meet another wonderful Canadian Professor John Miron who opened the world of MapInfo techniques to me. Mr. Siegfried Schulte was another of my victims in the Department of Geography at UOfT. Many thanks to him and his patience. Donna the Secretary of the Department of Geography at the UoFT (with a big heart) helped me to mail all the documents I had collected over six months back home. Professor David Wood and Prof. Robert Murdie of York University gave valuable suggestions on the chapter on Toronto.

The police is a closed system, they are said to be ruthless, brutal and unfriendly. But all my apprehensions proved wrong as I was able to gain access to all documents due to the friendly support of Kristina Kijewski (Director Corporate Planning) of the Toronto Metropolitan Police Service. The man behind the wings, Hans Peterson of the Statistics Department did a great job by compiling all the data on crimes against women in Toronto. I was also able to receive support from Police Chief David Boothby's office and Ray Desjardines. The study on India started way back in 1993. It took a while to build contact with the Police Headquarters. The first visit to them had not proved fruitful, till Mr. S.N. Menon the then Secretary to Chief Minister of West Bengal took interest in the research. Through him I was able to meet some wonderful policemen. My sincere thanks to Mr. Gautam Chakraborty (then the Joint Commissioner of Police, Lalbazar), Inspector Niharendu Roy and Sub Inspector Sujit Bhattacharya for their precious time and information they provided.

Perched on the attic of the Statesman House, Kolkata, were two men, Ajay Datta and Nimay Ganguli who inspite of all the dust of the Records Room always maintained their cool and very efficiently helped me in collecting information on atrocities on women - for which I am obliged to them. Data processing is as difficult as data collection. The 70000 odd records of the Toronto Police was organized by Mr. Akhilesh Kumar of PPCL at (Amjhor, Rohtas - Bihar). At this stage I would also like to thank the NGO's and the police personnel who kindly gave their views on the subject. My deep gratitude also goes to my publishers who were patient with the whole process of finalizing the book. I would also like to thank my husband for providing constant encouragement.

While we are on the subject of human nature, it is well known that to err is human and so many errors might have been inadvertently left in this work. I owe full responsibility for all such shortcomings and mistakes.

Doel Mukerjee

1
Introduction

Setting the Stage

The study of human relationships in the urban environment vis–a–vis the incidences of crimes against women over geographical space has been dealt with in this study through an understanding of two different environments, that of the developing and the developed world. Crimes against women is not only limited to being a social problem but more and more it is being taken into consideration by departments other than the law enforcement while formulating policies: while planning cities, planning out policies on health and other fields. Burgess and Theodorson (1982) found a close connection between zones of vice and crime in a city where these areas of mobility are also the regions in which there is maximum juvenile delinquency, gangs, crime, poverty, wife desertion, divorce, abandoned infants etc. The zone of transition, when compared to the other concentric zones of the urban community, has very high crime rates and the safety for women is very low.

The present research probes into crimes against women and its correlation to the geography of urban space and time. The issue of domestic violence legislations has also been looked into in the two countries, which proved that this has been a subject for the back burner for legislators all over the world. National economy, religion and various world events take up much of the time of the policy makers irrespective of the fact that 50% of the population needs better laws to lead decent lives. The media has to a large extent been able to get news of atrocities from within the four walls of a home out in the open and has thereby added strength to the voices of the weak. With awareness, education and with greater advocacy efforts by different critical groups, crimes against women and especially domestic violence is being recognized world over as a serious malfunctioning of society which needs to be addressed. Even a quarter century ago, people did not discuss these issues openly as it was a social stigma. At the Fourth World Conference on Women in Beijing, the United Nations Secretary-General, Boutros Boutros-Ghali, expressed the gravity of the situation on violence against women, that it is a universal problem that must be universally condemned. But he said that the problem continues to grow. The Secretary-General noted that domestic violence alone is on the increase as studies in 10 countries have projected that between 17 per cent and 38 per cent of women suffered physical assaults by a partner.

The core document prepared by the Platform for Action at Conference declared that "violence against women constitutes a violation of basic human rights and is an obstacle to the achievement of the objectives of equality, development and peace".

No doubt crime against women is a reality, which has to be recognized and tackled with sincerity. Advances and assaults by men are often ignored and go unreported, as the women fear that the police may further victimize them. However, it must also be recognized that crimes against women has existed over the ages both in the form of criminal violence, domestic violence and social violence. Crimes against women are neither culture specific nor region specific. It is uniformly distributed in every society. The difference in statistical figures on crime against women in every country is in degree and scale only.

However, the forms of violence such as wife beating, harassment, dowry death, infanticide, female genital mutilation, honour killings etc. are culture specific. In Canada, Indian women immigrants are known to face dowry related harassment. On the other hand offences such as stalking is a menace throughout Canada and North America as the laws are not properly worded to tackle such a problem. Violence worldwide can be shown in three spheres:

- In the family (including domestic violence, traditional practices and infanticide);
- In the community (including rape, sexual assault, commercialised violence such as trafficking in women, labour exploitation, female migrant workers, etc.);
- By the State (including violence against women in detention as well as violence against women in situations of armed conflict and against refugee women). There have also been incidences of state sponsored violence against women belonging to vulnerable groups.

Discrimination against women is not limited to any one particular walk in life. According Krishna Ahooja Patel (1978), " women account for more than one – half of humanity and they work for nearly two – thirds of all the working hours but they receive only one – tenths of the world income, and own less than a bare one percent of world's productive assets." The World Bank reports have shown a marked disparity in the economic status of women in different countries. The Gender Development Index (GDI) of Canada has been at the very top while India has been amongst the low Gender Development countries. In this century the traditional role of women has somewhat been replaced due to economic decentralization within families and globalisation where there is information transfer, empowerment, emancipation, better legislations etc. however reporting of incidences on crimes against women still remains illusive. The high crime rates against women in Toronto as compared to the low projection of crimes against women in Kolkata suggest that the truth is concealed. The relatively large statistical evidences in Canada are due to the large number of reporting of cases due to greater awareness levels of the women, the society and the law enforcement. The contrary is the case in India where reporting is restrained as people do not want to come to terms with offences which are not discussed both within families and the community as it is a social stigma, making the offences go unrecognized.

However, in the recent years, women have been able to garner support from certain sections of civil society, the commitments made by governments at the Beijing Summit to adopt and implement national legislation to end violence against women and to work actively to ratify all international agreements that relate to violence against women. There are more shelters, legal aid and other services for girls and women at risk, counselling and rehabilitation for perpetrators. But the most important part in strategic planning is that attempts are necessary to bring in a policy of zero tolerance to violence of women giving emphasis to registration of cases, which is the first cornerstone of starting the wheel of the criminal justice system.

Background

There is enough literature on status of women, legislations and country reports that are prepared by Governments, civil society groups and concerned individuals. However, specific literatures on spatial and temporal analysis of crimes against women are few. Three thematic areas were reviewed through examination of literature:

- Crime in spatial-temporal context
- Crimes a social construct in India
- Crime a Social Problem in Canada

Crime in spatial-temporal context

Crime is an outcome of the negative effects of society. A framework for the present study was worked out with the help of the literature survey.

Carolyn Rebecca and others (1995) established the fact that crime especially lethal street violence could be avoided by proper patrolling techniques. In this case planning through mapping techniques could solve several social evils. Through observations of spatial crime patterns, crimes can be detected and curtailed, as there is an area correlation between crime pattern and other social phenomena. Through the observation of Carolyn Rebecca Block and others, it is evident that crime and its prevention are possible by controlling the various negative phenomena in areas, which are more prone to crime. The study on crime against women, with emphasis on Kolkata and Toronto, draws much information from the above study, and credit goes to the modern methods of computer mapping and its techniques.[1]

Cohen's paper (1941) entitled "The Geography of Crimes" explains how climate and seasons affect the crime rate. He found that crimes against individuals such as assaults, homicide are more numerous during summer, while property related crimes are reported more during the winters. The weather operates directly upon the emotional and physiological activities of the individual.[2] Cohen's study highlighted that geography of space plays a sufficient role on crimes in general. The phenomenon of weather has been used in the study to understand occurrence of crimes against the vulnerable groups.

The study by Herbert and Smith (1979) has explored the empirical identification of the spatial incidence of social problems. Problems arise only when social reproductions are frustrated, retarded or prevented. The focus should be on the entire economic and social formation as it is only in this context that problems can be identified and understood.[3]

Gordon Young's article (2003) in Computeredge[4] focused on crime profiling through mapping techniques and the use of Geographical Information Systems (GIS). The study focuses on the place of residence of the accused and how crime profiling helps in locating the criminal as they share certain common attributes. Gordon found that serial criminals usually operate inside a personal "comfort zone," a turf where they feel safe, powerful, and know their way around. This might be their own city neighborhood, a woodland where they've vacationed, the commuting route they take to work and back, or a type of area they know well —a university campus or strip mall, for example. Godwin's research has shown that, growing bolder and more experienced with each crime, they tend to operate closer and closer to home, inadvertently giving away the information needed to zero in on them.

Another study which has used the concept of geography and projected crime as a social problem is Valentine's "London's Streets of Fear" (1992) which deals with the issue of mental mapping that women create in their minds of places which they feel would be dangerous. In fact most girls have mental images of places where strange men may approach them instilled at an early age.[5] In fact the, study lays stress on the concept of use of space by women, both in the context of fear and the constrained space which is available to her, due to patriarchy. The study has used London as a case study.

Evans and Herbert (1989) emphasized on the inverse relationship between assault and socio – economic status, but the hypothesis that a threshold of discomfort could be reached beyond which all activities including crime, ceased could not be confirmed. There are place variations with differences between types of residential areas, time variations and people variations with specific types of people at greater risk.[6]

Another study, which has emphasized on the spatial context of crime, is a set of essays in environmental criminology edited by D.J. Evans and others (1992). The article deals with the explanation of crime and place. The framework of approach deals with the intimate relationship of social relations and spatial structures in crime. The article lays emphasis on the Chicago theory of social disorganization and the structuration theory. These two theories are the primary theories used in environmental criminology.[7] The Chicago Theory has been used in the present study to understand the nuances of social conflict in a city.

Vold (1941) used the example of Chicago to deal with the core – periphery concept of crimes trends in a city. Vice, gambling, crime and other institutions of degeneracy are more characteristically to be found in cities than in rural areas. In fact, the difference in the rural and urban atmosphere is the difference in the culture, which involves both in the sociological as well as in the anthropological sense in the mode of life of the people.[8]

C.F. Schmid (1960) elaborated on the idea of Vold and made a detailed study on the Chicago theory elaborating further on the core – periphery model. The study on Seattle through the use of quantitative techniques emphasized the tendency for crimes to decrease in direct proportion to the distance from the center of the city.[9]

More recent literature[10] on crime mapping elaborate on its usefulness and taking into consideration reference points in a city which act as either crime generators or crime suppressors. The study also analyses hotspots to show the frequency and sequence of crimes.

Just as crime has both spatial as well as temporal characteristics, there are certain regional dimensions as well. Buendia (1989) found that economic development generated massive urbanization, social as well as occupational changes that can erode the cohesiveness in traditional societies. One result is that in many societies economic growth correlates to increasing crime rates. Yet, urban crime is seldom considered in national development strategies and government policies. So these policies prove to be inadequate, underfunded and poorly administered. The book presents several case studies of eight cities, Bangkok, Bogota, Lagos, Nairobi, San Jose, Singapore, Tokyo, Warsaw. For each a detailed analysis of crime trends, policy measures and control of how criminal justice systems function and the situation of juvenile delinquency is presented.[11]

Marshall B. Clifford and others (1973) wrote about crime in developing countries. They contemplated that certain sociological theories on crime apply in developing countries. It is felt that crime is learned in association with others, while differential access to resources or goals in society and the illegitimate means to achieve these goals accounts for crime. The theories of differential association and differential opportunity are at work on most occasions. Clifford felt that crime in the less developed countries is currently at a stage that provides a reflection of England, the U.S. and other developed societies, as they were at the time of rapid industrialization, urbanization and development in the early 19th century,[12] a pertinent observation for global crime theories.

D.M. Smith and E.S. Kuchta (1993) emphasized on the gender issue in crime, dealing particularly with violent offenses between 1973 to 1989.The study explores trends in violence in relation to the low victimization rates. The trend is more towards greater representation of women as the victimized population primarily due to more pronounced decrease in victimization rates for men. The study used the example of decline in incidences of rape in the United States as a part of the study.[13] However, this study was contrary to what was found in the case studies of both Kolkata and Toronto.

A social problem such as crime is identified over space in correlation to various social variables. The primary being the economic variable as mentioned by M.D. Smith and others (1992). The study has explored the age and race specific rates of unemployment and corresponding rates of arrests for homicide, robbery and burglary in United States during the period 1959 – 1987. Through the study, a negative criminal opportunity and positive criminal motivation related effects are found at the aggregate level, but these vary among age groups and are more evident in the arrest rates. Hence, unemployment, which is also related to ethnic factors of a population, is correlated to the crime in a region.[14]

Crimes a social construct in India

Various amounts of literature on the sociological reasons for crimes in India have helped to contribute to this study. Crime against women is an impact of the social milieu in families and the close knit traditional community of the country.

Spatial studies on crime are few and those on crimes against women are negligible. Some of the major studies have been consulted, as Kelkar's (1992) reconceptualiation of the issue of violence against women which has emerged particularly in relation to intra and extra family gender relations and the role of the state in reinforcing patriarchal oppression. The paper gives an overview of the approach of women's movement in India to the problem of violence against women. Emphasis has also been placed on civil society involvement in places like Delhi to deal with such problems. Women's collective actions have effect on male violence and cultural control within the intimate terrain of the family. According to him, violence against women has to be studied in the socio – economic and political context of power relations.[15]

There have been a few empirical studies as M.K. Singh's (1984) study on "A Decade of Crime – A Sociological Analysis", which discusses the rate of increase of crime is more than the increase in population. Statistical evidences in the study also prove the hypothesis, which is based on Maharashtra that inspite of development the levels of crime have increased. This is contrary to a few of the studies which have been referred to earlier. Singh suggests that growth in crime and economic change are related as both show an upward trend.[16]

There have been a few empirical studies on cities as the "Town Size and Crime" by Sivamurthy (1986) based on Madras, where he advocated that rising crime rate in developing countries is not related so much with social change but it is related to the complexity of urbanization and industrialization. The size of the population and the size of a city are factors for violent crimes. A high degree of positive correlation is found between size of town and occurrence of crime. The study on media reflects the urban way of life is characterized by extensive conflicts of norms and values, rapid social change, increased mobility of population, emphasis on material goals and individualism. Heterogeneity is a striking characteristic of large cities and naturally exposes the great diversity in norms and values. This moral decay in the crowded towns results in the break – down of law.[17]

Dealing exclusively on the North Indian context, Dutt and others (1979), in the article "Is there a North – Central subculture of violence in India", showed the seasonal rhythm of dacoity in North – Central India where the maximum numbers of cases are reported in September till harvest time as the crops provide excellent cover for the dacoits to hide and escape. Dacoity is minimum in autumn as most of the fields are water logged and the roads are difficult to commute due to slush. The study gives a micro level insight at the districts examining the factors that promote violence in North - Central India. Significance is placed on both the urban and rural environment especially areas which are degenerated such as physically dilapidated neighborhood setting, historic circumstances and high population densities.[18]

Sivamurthy (1982) in "The spatial – temporal variation in the incidence of theft in Madras city" pointed out that property crimes originate in areas where there are upwardly mobile and higher income populations suggesting that occurrence of property crimes is a function of physical characteristics and economic prosperity of an area.[19]

Ahuja's (1987) empirical observations on rape, kidnapping, dowry death, wife battering and murder defined power and authority as motivations for violence against the vulnerable groups. To prevent abuse of women in society, it is necessary to socially redefine violence, strengthen women's organizations, and encourage a humanistic approach.[20]

Nayar (1975) deals with the National Trends in Crime, 1953 – 70 which is an empirical investigation into the subject of violence and crime. To a certain extent, the incidence of violence and crime in a state may be described as an attribute of the culture of a state or in the case of political violence such as riots an element in the political culture of the state. As far as the regional distribution is concerned it is evident that the eastern part of the country is most prone to political violence. Crimes against women and against individuals are mostly prevalent in Madhya Pradesh and the Northern belt covering the states of Delhi, U.P. and Maharashtra.[21]

The problems of crime and delinquency was also dealt by Kerawalla (1959) where research was confined to the problem of crime in Bombay. Empirical observations on age, literacy, religion, occupational hazards emphasize on crime in urban areas which differs from those in contiguous rural areas.[22]

Jean Racine's study (1990) on Kolkata is one of those few studies, which have dealt with the population problem in a holistic manner. The study through maps and figures have traced the history of the city from the colonial period to the present day along with its multifaceted ethnic areas which have been demarcated by various socio – economic variables which are active.[23]

Another article, which deals exclusively with the urban problem of Kolkata is by Roy and others (1992), dealing with the environment of the shanty settlements of Kolkata. The article deals exclusively with the social problems that emerge due to the economic conditions of the bustees.[24] The article has identified the major "bustees" and resettlement colonies of the city.

Flavia Agnes (1992) dealt with pro women legislations of the country. There have been several loopholes in the laws. In the 1980's the campaigns for women's rights and liberation were aimed at protection of women's lives. However, these had little impact. The article reviews laws on Dowry, Rape, Domestic Violence, Prostitution and Indecent Representation of Women, Sati and Sex Determination tests. All these reforms came about after 1983. There is an urgent need to not only bring in more progressive laws for women but also there is an urgency to change the long delays in the criminal justice system so that there are speedy trials and there is access to justice for all.[25]

Crime as a Social Problem in Canada

A large amount of literature is available on crime as a social problem in Canada. This section has been reviewed as "Crime as a Social Problem" as the literature has focused on social factors and sex–role stereotyping which leads to the criminal acts. Socio – spatial studies on crime however have been few.

McLaren ed. (1988), through a series of articles on various social problems faced by women in Canada underlined the position of women in society. Battered women in a traditional nuclear family unit suffer isolation both from within the family as well as the society. This is due to both social as well as psychological reasons. Like wife battering, sexual harassment is also a method of social control by those who want to use power. When society suffers from economic hardship, it is important to coordinate with unemployed groups of workers as the most vulnerable group for their vent to frustration are the women.[26]

Silverman and others (1990) showcased crime as an urban phenomena. There has been an association between urban location and crime, both theoretically and empirically proved in criminology. The study found large concentrations of heterogeneous population leads to weakening of interpersonal ties, primarily social relations and normative consensus with the ultimate consequences of individual alienation, anomie and an increased prevalence of deviant behavior. Unemployment and deprivation are taken to be the key indicators of crime. Through empirical observations, the hypothesis have been verified both for violent as well as property crimes.[27]

The Chicago School of thought dealing with Environmental Criminology and the socio- economic reasons for sexual assault and prostitution have been studied by I.M. Gomme (1993). The legal framework for rape and sexual assault laws have been elaborated on. The Canadians had traditionally viewed rape, indecent assault and child molestation as heinous crimes committed by psychopathic strangers. However, with the heightening of women's movements and several in-depth studies, criminologists have realized that strangers attacking women is a myth. The study has taken various case studies and variables to establish the socio – economic background of both the victim and the assailant.[28] This is a well-defined study on crime in Canadian literature.

L.S. Bourne and Olvet (1995) gave a detailed account on urbanization and regional development. The study draws details from data to describe the urban trends. The paper concludes with a summary of some of the policy and research challenges that flow from these trends.[29]

Another detailed study was made by L.W. Kennedy and V.F. Sacco (1999) on Canadian crime trends and referred to crime as a social incident. Reference to surveys on crime such as the Uniform Crime Report Survey in 1961 and other General Social Survey and Violence Against Women Survey (1993) have been made. The General Social Survey was initiated by Statistics Canada giving details of the socio – economic fabric in society. While the Violence Against Women survey was the first reliable survey of violence against women. The study gives large amount of information on the surveys, their techniques and some of the laws in the criminal code dealing with crimes against women and children etc. The authors are of the opinion that the surveys and awareness programs were instrumental in removing stereotyping to an extent.[30]

According to Valentine (1992), women perceive themselves to be at risk from male violence in public space inspite of the fact that they are more prone to assaults at home. According to her, women develop certain notions of fear from strange men attacking, mostly in dark alleys. Crime statistics also suggest that women are more at risk at home and from men they know. However, women still perceive the home to be a haven. This article discusses the spatial nature of the perception of fear and the utility of public space by women during specific time periods.[31]

Whitzman (1992) analyses Toronto over the past ten years and how its public policy was designed to prevent violence against women in public space. The city planners and civil society groups shared a common platform and translated the needs of women to a feminist campaign in the city. First they treated crime and fear of crime as a gender related problem and as part of this they adopted the fact that public places may be harmful for women. This could be dealt by the group in society who are endangered, so they can bring about solutions to the problem. In the case of Toronto, safety audits were proposed which were initiated by organizations such as METRAC. In the past 10 years, individuals, community groups and government agencies in Toronto have developed ways and means of promoting women's safety in public spaces.[32]

United Way of Greater Toronto's (1997) research is a comprehensive analysis of community requirements and social trends in Metropolitan Toronto. The major socio – economic variables such as demographic details, the economy such as employment, social and funding trends have been explored. The report was to meet the urgent needs and improve the social conditions in the city.[33]

A media scan on violence against women accounts for an absence of feminist perspectives in newspaper coverage as remarked by Stone (1993). The press has not treated for the most part violence against women as a social issue but reporting have been more descriptive with details on arrest and proceedings of court cases. Crime news is often titillating and entertains the non-serious reader. Indeed, the crime beats are a crucial part of newspapers, and newspapers have long been sold on the basis of this kind of product. This aspect of newspaper production represents an important systemic constraint to mitigate the likelihood of feminists inserting radical messages into routine crime news.[34] A content analysis of the Toronto Daily Star for the study on Toronto reiterated that newspaper coverage was maximum on sensational crimes. This distorts ways and means to combat crimes against women.

The report by METRAC gives in detail the methodology in conducting and planning personal safety audits. The scheme can be executed through a three-pronged approach by identifying the area, identifying the group and the way to organize a meeting. Between the meeting and the actual audit, the report acts as a guide, taking the women step by step on how to fulfill their goals.[35] This report is a practical manual, which can be used by a group of people who can solve their problems on their own. As women who face danger or threat, are involved in the safety audit, they are in a better position to take care of the special problems of the area.

"Safe City" is an extension of the previous article by METRAC on safety audits. The article emphasizes that although Toronto is a relatively safe city, yet women feel unsafe. This article reflects the same thought as expressed by Valentine in several of her articles and acknowledges most cases of violence against women occur in private spaces. The community has an obvious stake in preventing all forms of public violence. While the strategies as safety audits put forward preventive measures by focusing on the critical group, the benefits from their implementation accrue to the general community, particularly those who feel most vulnerable to public violence including seniors, children and the disabled.[36]

England (1994) taking clue from David Harvey's "Social Justice and the City", described the contemporary women's movement in the early 1970's which was ignored earlier. In the 1990's feminist writers took up women's movement with enthusiasm and issues, which were thought to be private, were brought out in the public domain and formed part of the Municipal Agenda. Toronto's exemplary women – friendly safety audits is a learning exercise for many other cities in Europe. Often assaults in public spaces are crimes of opportunity due to the urban built environment. In 1984 Metro established and funded the advocacy agency METRAC (Metro Action Committee on Public Violence Against Women and Children) to carry forward the recommendations of its Task Force. METRAC was a catalyst for eradicating public violence against women through its joint projects.[37]

Other contemporary literature on crime mapping as[38] the Spatial Analyses of Crime and Criminal Behavior: An Overview of Current Research Applications which gives an overview of the work of the Crime Mapping Research Center at the National Institute of Justice provides a summary of some current research applications of geographic information systems in criminal justice.

The studies and articles helped to gain an insight on the status of women in both developing and developed countries, as well ascertained the socio – economic conditions prevailing in each country. The present study has taken sufficient information from the above-mentioned sources. The study is based on both qualitative and qualitative research, which has helped in establishing the hypotheses. As noted earlier, there has been little research on the spatial analysis of urban crime against women and little effort has been made to help the law enforcement agencies to formulate policies to combat crime. The technique of crime mapping which is the crux of this study helps in channeling limited resources and helps the community to understand their weaknesses. Modern GIS systems for personal computers have made automated pin mapping an easy task for police departments to adopt. Improved crime analysis techniques will require greater use of criminological theory. Use of theories drawn from environmental criminology for informed crime analysis is illustrated using the Crime Pattern Theory and the Chicago Model. The present study gives empirical evidences along with the necessity to know the socio – economic variables to arrive at the conclusion that it is important to design and manage the public policy of a town or city taking into consideration the aspirations and requirements of the people.

It was also realized that social, ethnic and spiritual values that binds society, often fails to do so in the urban space. Vice rears its ugly head in the highest places as seen in the case study of Kolkata. Kolkata and Toronto although projecting different levels of development showed that most cities have much in common; that common socio-economic factors lead to different types of crimes against women. Through the objectives of the study, it is also possible to see the various nuances that play on incidents of crimes against women.

Objectives

There is a clear geographical expression of prevalence of urban crime against women, which is deep rooted in the socio – economic fabric of the cities. The concept of place has a special meaning in geography. Places can be seen as subjective, underpinned by ideas such as sense of belonging, shared values and images and common concerns. Social ecology especially used in crime studies provides some kind of basic framework, as crime consists of the four dimensions of law, the offender, the target and the place. All of these have essentially to be integrated into an overall understanding of crime against women, but each is capable of focussed study in its own right. As there are wide geographical inequalities in this socio – economic base between the cities and in different areas within a city, thus urban crimes against women show spatial variations. The urbanization process or urbanism leads to several social problems in million plus cities, which ultimately has an impact on women and their status as well.

Geography of crime against women in cities have close bearing with the population density, residential segregation and urban social deprivation, etc. within a city. With the wide variations of geographical inequality within a city, there are also different types of crimes. Thus social problems in cities have clear spatial expressions. Thus, it can be hypothesized that the total crime against women will be high in low residential areas, in relatively high population density areas and areas having widening social deprivations. Similarly, total crimes against women may be more in the urban periphery than the core of the city. This is primarily because of poor socio – economic conditions, more rural and semi – urban characteristics in the urban periphery on the one hand and poor enforcement of law, lack of strict vigilance, access to the police station being difficult due to distance etc. as compared to the city center. Hence, within a city a micro study is equally needed.

The study areas, namely Toronto and Kolkata are appropriate for a comparative study on crime as both cities are multi – cultural with large numbers of immigrants populations and is also the threshold city in their respective regions. Toronto is the largest industrial center in Eastern Canada, with the largest populations, while Kolkata acts as the break even point to the States of Eastern, North – Eastern India and Bangladesh. The interesting feature is that most immigrant populations live on the peripheral parts of the city in both the cities. The social legislation on crime against women was studied to understand the process of registration of offences and the scope for access to justice of the vulnerable population in the two countries. The study on Toronto and Kolkata are antipodes as one represents the developed world- a place of abundance, while the other, the developing world, where resource allocation is lopsided and opportunities are few.

Hypothesis

For a more clinical examination of the study, several hypotheses have been used:

- Faster the rate of development and urbanization, the greater the crime against women.
- Areas with higher density population and with greater urban deprivation show higher rate of total crimes against woman in the city than low – density

areas.

- The rate of total urban crime is more in the low residential areas than in the high residential areas within the city.
- Higher the male population, in a city, greater will be the number of crimes.
- Types of crime against women are more prominent in specific areas of the city. However, the total crimes against women are more in the urban periphery or suburbs than in the city core.
- A correlation was used between time and the seasonal variation of crime. Through the study, it was possible to see that a universal phenomenon prevailed in most countries regarding the seasonal nature of crime.
- Between crime and conviction another important phenomenon are the laws in each country that are available to the victim. Better laws and their proper use could make the life of the victim much easier and improve the overall status of women.

Methodology

The research design for the study is based on the following:

- An in-depth study of crime against women in two jurisdictions taking into consideration multiple variables depending on the legal framework of the country, which was further, confirmed by expert opinion.
- Primary and secondary sources of information and data were looked into.

The data collection was from various sources:

- Literature review

- A structured interview schedule with critical groups.
- A study on the legal framework
- A media scan covering five years in both countries
- Crime statistics from the police headquaters in Kolkata and Toronto

A detailed look at the primary and secondary sources of information are as follows:

The primary sources in India: are the registered cases from the 33 police stations in Kolkata over five years from 1991-1996. Although the data is old, the trend and the sequence of crimes are the same even today. This was verified from Crime in India[39] over 2000 and 2001. Crime in India, however is not a very detailed report for crimes as small unit areas as police stations are not projected. Data regarding the socio – economic variables such as literacy, employment amongst male and female population etc. have been taken from the District Census Handbook of Kolkata, 1991, published by Government of India. The maps used in the study on Kolkata have been compiled from various sources. The map of Kolkata City showing the boundaries of police stations have been taken from police headquarters, Kolkata. The ward boundaries, which were converted to police station boundaries for socio – economic variables were taken from the map published by Kolkata Municipal Corporation. The population density map of Kolkata showing police station boundaries is also based on the map published by the 1981 District Census Handbook and 1991 Kolkata Municipal Corporation map. It is important to note here that the data from the District Census Handbook for the year 2001 is yet to be published. To keep conformity with the crime statistics and the social variables the present study has taken its shape.

Another primary source though not extensive were a set of 50 interviews which were conducted amongst persons from various walks of life who are closely involved with gender related issues: police personnel, coordinators of women's organizations, media persons etc.

Primary Sources in Toronto

Just as the study on Kolkata, data was collected both from primary as well as secondary sources for Toronto. The primary sources involve, data provided by the Metropolitan Toronto Police for the years 1991 to 1996, with emphasis on details such as time, date, patrol area, age of the victim involved in each incident. Along with this data, the Department of Corporate Planning of the MTPS also provided a detailed street map with the patrol area boundaries. With the help of this it was possible to create the crime map of Toronto for the years 1991 and 1996. Another primary source for the creation of the map on incidences of crime against women as per patrol areas is from 1991 census map of Canada demarcating census tract boundaries. This helped in coordinating the socio – economic variables such as percentage of immigrant population, unemployment, level of schooling etc. with the crime map.

Sets of 50 interviews were also conducted involving people from various walks of life, working on women's issues and town planning. Besides, these primary sources, at several instances, data and information were supplemented by secondary sources.

Secondary Sources

The secondary sources used in Kolkata were a content analysis of the Statesman newspaper, which is popular in the city for the years. A database was made using the newspaper reporting of 1991-96 and processed into various graphical details. The chapter on social legislation led to detailed study of the Indian Penal Code, 1860 and various subsidiary directives given by the Supreme Court and the National Human Rights Commission. Other secondary sources include books and journals.

The major secondary sources used for Toronto are:

- Canada: Statistics on Vilence Against Women, by METRAC (1997)
- Canadian Crime Statistics 1983,1991,1993,1995 published by Statistics Canada.
- Census directory 1991 published by Statistics Canada.
- Profile of Census Tracts in Toronto-Part A published by Statistics Canada.
- Profile of Census Tracts in Toronto-Part B published by Statistics Canada.
- Annual Report published by Metropolitan Toronto Police Service from 1994 to 1996.
- A content analysis of the Toronto Daily Star for 1991-1996, with the help of which a database was prepared.
- Maps and data from CD-ROM, The "E – Stat" prepared by Statistics Canada.
- Details of Victimization Survey and the General Social Survey of 1993, from the Website.
- Women in Canada: A statistical Report, 3rd edition (Target Groups Project) published by Statistics Canada, 1995.

The chapter on social legislation made an in-depth study on Martin's Annual Criminal Code, 1997 with annotations by E.L. Greenspan and M. Rosenberg published by Canada Law Book Inc., and " Learning Canadian Law" 5th edition by D. Stuart and R.J. Delisle (1995). Other than these books and journals were also consulted.

Limitations of Study

The study is based on empirical sources and this itself is a limitation as statistics do not project the true picture of a place especially as it deals with crimes at home, at workplace and within close-knit societies. Mindsets, stereotyping and traditional roles demarcated for women are impediments in society for empowerment of the vulnerable groups.

As a large part of the study is based on data from police stations this does not project the correct crime statistics as there is under reporting and non- registration of cases by the victims and the police personnel respectively. There are instances where the law enforcement agencies act as mediators and cases are not registered. On the other hand, newspaper reporting has been high, although only highlighting sensational cases leaving little scope for projecting the gravity of the crime situation.

Details on each case have been read with care and it became evident that some murder cases were due to dowry harassment; at other instances suicides and accidental deaths were also due to harassment and pressures in the marital home. These cases have been recorded in the study with duc caution. Official statistics on cases on kidnapping and abduction are often incorrect. The incidents even if reported are not registered as criminal offences unless the culprits are named or the circumstances of disappearance clearly established that an offence has occurred. Due to lack of knowledge and burking of offences such cases are treated as cases of missing persons and closed after nominal inquiries. It is only when a child is recovered or when physical abduction is established through impeachable evidence that offences are registered and investigated with some semblance of vigor.[40] Cases of rape are least reported criminal offence in India, not because of their low incidence, but because of the reluctance of the parents to publicize. In addition to this, the various caste loyalties, traditional inhibitions, under reporting due to reconciliation measures taken by the police officers lead to distortion of the crime statistics. This distortion is done deliberately to restore confidence in the public and to project a positive image of the state and government.[41]

Another limitation to this study has been the interviews, which were few and were limited to perceptions of a limited number of people, which has been used in the study. Being comparative study seven crime parameters were included in India and 22 depicting crimes against women.

Conclusion

The next chapters deal with urbanization as a social problem and how it has had an impact on women in society both in the developed parts of the world as well as in the traditional society. The chapter also justifies the reasons for taking up the study on India and Canada and the two case studies of Toronto and Kolkata.

References

1. C.R. Block and others, *Crime Analysis Through Computer Mapping*, (Washington, 1995).
2. J. Cohen, The Geography of crime, *Annuals of the American Academy of Political and Social Sciences*, Vol. 217, Sept. 1941.
3. D.T. Herbert and D.M. Smith, *Social Problems and the City: Geographical Perspectives, (*Oxford University Press, 1979).
4. Gordon Young, Mapping Mayhem: The Geography of Crime, *Computoredge* August 2003.
5. G. Valentine, *London's Streets of Fear*, p. 90 – 102 (Routledge, 1992)
6. D.T. Herbert, *The Geography of urban crime*, (1982).
7. D.J. Evans and others ed. *Crime, policing and place: Essays in Environmental Criminology,* (Routledge, 1992).
8. G.B. Vold, *The Annuals of the American Academy of Political and Social Science,* pp. 38 – 45 (Philadelphia, 1941).
9. C.F. Schmid, *American Sociological Review,* (Washington , 1960)
10. John Markovic and Christopher Stone:Crime mapping and the policing of democratic societies; Vera Institute of Justice, March 2002.
11. H.E. Buendia, *Urban Crime: Global Trends and Policies,* (Tokyo,1989).
12. M.B. Clinard and D.J. Abbott, *Crime in Developing Countries: A Comparative Perspective,* (1973).
13. M.D. Smith and E.S. Kuchta, *Social Science Quarterly,* Vol. 74 (Texas 1993).
14. M.D. Smith and others , *Sociological Perspective* , Vol. 35, (1992)
15. Govind Kelkar, *Violence Against Women: Perspectives and Strategies in India,*(New Delhi, 1992).

16. M.K. Singh, *Indian Journal of Criminology*, 12(2) July 1984.
17. A. Sivamurthy, *Indian Journal of Criminology*, 14(2), July 1986.
18. A. Dutta and others,"Is there a North- Central subculture of violence in India", *The National Geographical Journal of India*, 25(1979).
19. A. Sivamurthy, "The spatio – temporal variation the incidence of theft in Madras city", *Indian Journal of criminology*, Vol.10, No. 2, July 1982.
20. Ram Ahuja, *Crime Against Women*, Jaipur 1987.
21. B.R. Nayar, *Violence and Crime in India: A Quantitative Study*, (Delhi 1975).
22. P.C. Kerewalla, *Study in Indian Crime*, (Bombay 1959).
23. Jean Racine ed. *Kolkata 1981: The City its Crisis and the Debate on Urban Planning and Development*, (New Delhi 1990).
24. P. Roy and others, Measuring Bustee Environment in Kolkata, *Social Change* Vol.22(1),1992.
25. F. Agnes, Protecting Women Against Violence?: A Review of a Decade of Legislation 1980 – 89, *Economic and Political Weekly* 27(170), 1992.
26. A.T. McLaren ed. *Gender and Society: Creating a Canadian Women's Sociology* (Toronto 1988).
27. R.A. Silverman and others ed. *Crime in Canadian Society*, (Toronto 1990).
28. I.M.Gomme, *The Shadow Line: Deviance and Crime in Canada* (Toronto 1993).
29. L.S. Bourne and A.E. Olvet, *New Urban and regional geographies in Canada:1986 – 91 and Beyond*, (Toronto 1995)
30. L.W. Kennedy and V.F. Sacco, *Crime Counts: A Criminal Event Analysis*, (Toronto, 1996).
31. G. Valentine, "Images of danger: Women's Sources of Information about the Spatial Distribution of Male Violence, *Area*, 24(1),1992.
32. C. Whitzman, "Taking Back Planning: Promoting Women's Safety in Public Places – the Toronto Experience," *Journal of Architectural and Planning Research*, 9(2) 1992.
33. *Metro Toronto: A Community at Risk*, United Way of Greater Toronto, 1997.
34. S.D. Stone, Getting the message out: Feminists, the press and violence against women, *The Canadian Review of Sociology and Anthropology*, 30(3) 1993.
35. Report by *METRAC*,(Jan.1994).
36. *The Safe City: Municipal Strategies for Preventing Public Violence Against women*, (Toronto 1988).
37. K. England, From Social Justice and the City to Women –

Friendly Cities? Feminist Theory and Politics, *Urban Geography*,(1994).

38. Nancy LaVigne, (Crime Mapping Research Center, NIJ, Washington, DC), *Western Society of Criminology,1999 Meeting Proceedings.*
39. Published annually by the Ministry of Home Affairs, National Crime Records Bureau.
40. Mary Jos. *A Socio – Spatial Analysis of Crimes in India: A Case Study of Delhi*, CSRD, JNU,1988, p.37.
41. Also known as burking of crime.

2

Million Plus Cities and Social Problems Faced by Women

Introduction

Violence against women is an all-pervading issue, which crosses all boundaries. This issue had never been an important agenda of any United Nations Conference on women, till the Fourth World Conference on women at Beijing in 1995. In the Platform for Action adopted at the Conference, violence against women and human rights of women were two of the twelve critical areas of concern identified as the main obstacles to the advancement of women. Because of publicity given at the Conference and the follow up actions taken by a few countries, violence or any form of crime against women is no longer considered a back burner issue in development.

The issue of advancement of women's rights has concerned the United Nations since its inception. Yet the alarming global dimensions of female-targeted violence were not explicitly acknowledged by the international community until December 1993, when the United Nations General Assembly adopted the **Declaration on the Elimination of Violence Against Women.**

Until that point, most Governments tended to regard violence against women largely as a private matter between individuals, and not as a pervasive human rights problem requiring State intervention. In view of the alarming growth in the number of cases of violence against women throughout the world, the Commission on Human Rights adopted

Resolution 1994/45 of 4 March 1994, in which it decided to appoint the Special Rapporteur on the violence against women, including its causes and consequences.[1]

The United Nations "reaffirms faith in fundamental human rights, in the dignity and worth of the human person and in equal rights of men and women. " Articles such as 1,6,16 and document 18 fully support the dignity of the women as well as the well being of a family, of which the woman is a key member. Inspite of this, the women as a respected group in the historical-traditional context is a myth.

With large-scale urbanization, there has been modernization of agriculture, which in turn has resulted in altered decision of labour between the sexes, increasing women's dependent status as well as their workload.

Large population and urbanization often leads to squalid congested settlements and sets in urban decay. Such settlements have large levels of unemployed and underemployed population, which in turn leads to poverty, low social status, crime and other vices. Urbanization represents a complex socio-economic and political force as well as a distinct local culture and history, which portray the inferior status of women.

Rapid global urbanization leads to lack of space, unequal resource allocations, fewer access to opportunities etc. Cities with relatively high resource opportunities gives way to urbanism. With that comes in the negative growth of a city. For the people coming into these cities in search of employment, they come in and take up jobs with small pay packets leading to underemployment. Most of these people are in their prime and with no close bonding like family or relatives there is anonymity, which releases a person from social conformity.[2]

The status of women improves with urbanization but discrimination against all vulnerable groups does not disappear. In the city, women play roles of that of a housewife and a wage earner. She takes on both traditional tasks and

Diagram 2.1
Percentage Share of Urban Problems

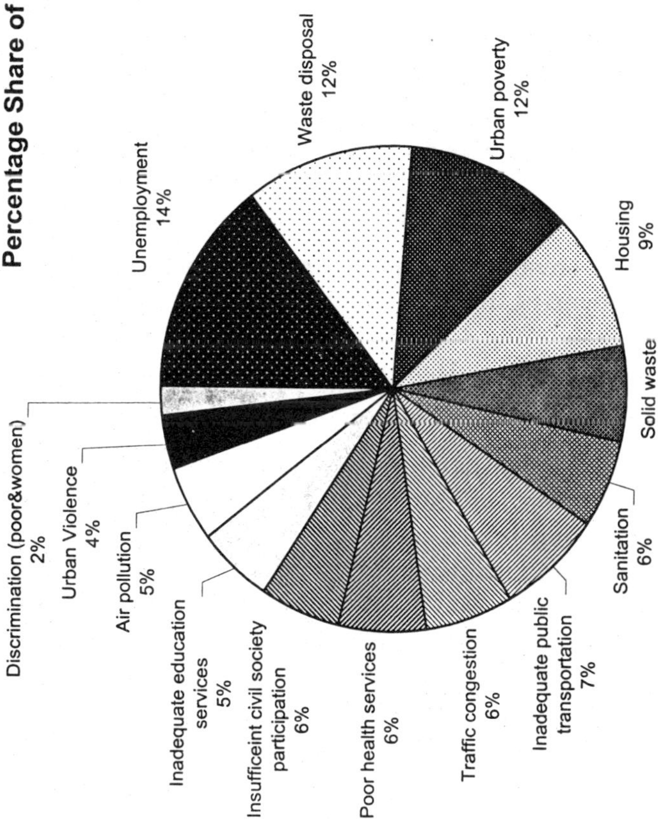

Source: Compiled from 1997 UNDP Survey.

the newly found empowerment gives her scope to venture out. However both within the four walls of the house and outside the women are considered to be weak as she battles with over crowding, congestion, deviant behaviour and other vices in society as crime, alcoholism, drugs and trafficking in human beings etc. In these circumstances the status of women becomes vulnerable, as she is the target of attack for assaults and discrimination getting rid of the myth that women living in cities are safe.

Social Problems in the City

UNDP on the occasion of the International Colloquium of Mayors held in July 1997, corroborated that unemployment is the world's number one urban problem which is followed by insufficient waste disposal, poverty and housing. Of a total list of 14 categories of problems (diagram 2.1) it is surprising to find that violence and personal safety are ranked as the least severe urban problems.

It is obvious that all the major problems stem from unemployment in cities all over. The Mayors from United States attending the colloquia claimed that crime is a serious problem in their cities as well.

Urbanization and Human Development

Social scientists have not yet reached a satisfactory conclusion on the definition of urban places or urban systems. They take a variety of forms in different countries and diverse definitions of "urban" are used for census purposes. This variability makes comparisons rather difficult.

International definitions usually encompass an urban place as an administrative unit with large concentration of population who are in the non-agricultural sector and who can avail of infrastructure facilities like post offices, roads, electricity etc. Historically it was relatively easy to define the differences between urban and rural settlements as cities were surrounded by walls. The removal of the walls and the rapid territorial expansion of cities during the modern period as well as the changing nature of agriculture has blurred the distinction between the physical differences between cities and urban areas. Inquiries on urbanization have led to a good deal of discussion on topics as rural-urban "dichotomy" and "continuum". To put it simply, to understand urban and social problems, it is necessary to understand the extent of the city. The "dichotomy" hypothesis assumes a distinctive differentiation of urban place from rural places and the term "continuum" refers to an environment neither completely rural nor completely urban but rather as occupying a position somewhere between the two extremes.

The use of space is important in urbanization as the fundamental purpose is for effective population distribution, which is due to ecological reasons and not purely for economic purposes as clarified by Dr. Mookherjee (1973). Often the behaviour of an individual or group is determined by space-related activity. The urban population is growing at a much faster rate than the population as a whole and by larger annual increments than ever before. Mookherjee's claims that by the early years of the next century, most of the people in the world will live in urban areas. In most developing regions the proportion of people living in the largest cities is also increasing. Cities are intimately tied to national prospects for sustained economic growth and development.

Like people, cities also have personalities. Each represents a unique form of history and natural setting, cultural pattern and lifestyles.[4] According to the United Nations, the majority of the world population will be urban by 2005. In the less developed regions, total urbanization will be achieved in 2015. Today's current world urban population is 2.6 billion of which almost 1.6 billion are in the

Diagram 2.2

TRENDS IN WORLD POPULATION DISTRIBUTION

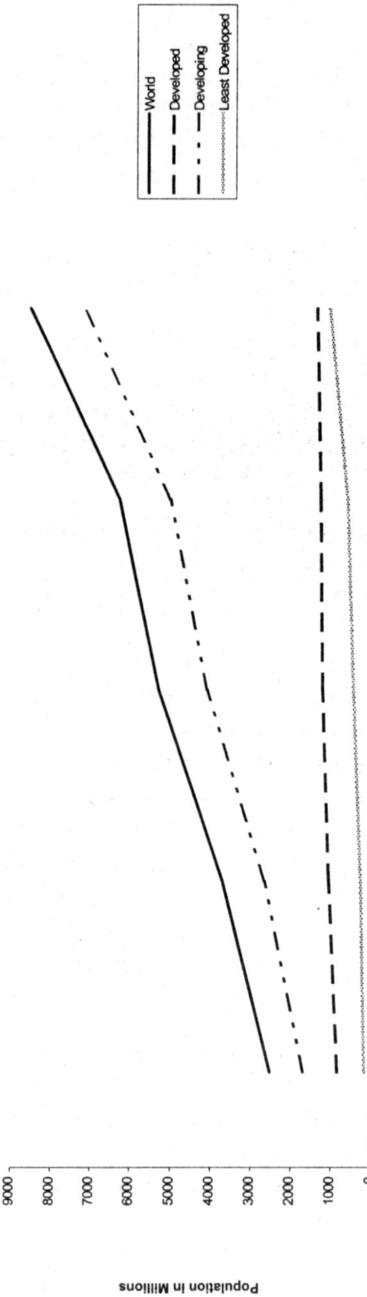

	1950	1970	1990	2000	2025
World	2516	3698	5292	6260	8504
Developed	832	1049	1207	1264	1354
Developing	1684	2649	4086	4997	7150
Least Developed	169	263	444	595	1039

Year

Source: World Population Prospects, 1990 (UN Publications)

less-developed countries. "These regions will include 3.2 billion out of 4.1 billion urban people world wide in 2015 and over 4 billion out of 5.1 billion in 2025."[5] It may be concluded that the rate of urbanization is very high in the less-developed countries while the levels of urbanization is higher in more developed countries as in table 2.1.

Diagram 2.2 projects the future trends in growth of world population where we find that the developing countries have a faster population growth as compared to other regions in the world.

In table 2.1 there is an accelerated growth in world population and in each of the regions. However after the 1990's in all cases there is a slight fall in the percentage increase, as decay in growth has set in. As mentioned earlier, the rate of urbanization is much higher in the Developing as well as the Least Developed regions due to their birth rates and rural to urban migration.

Table 2.1
Percentage Increase in Population

Year	*World*	*Developed*	*Developing*	*Least developed*
1970	31.96	20.68	36.42	35.74
1990	30.12	13.09	35.16	40.76
2000	15.46	4.5	18.23	25.37
2025	26.38	6.64	30.11	42.73

Source: World Population Prospects, 1990 (UN Publications)

In Developed countries, the urban population doubled between 1950 to 1990 from 448 million to 875 million. The urban population in Developing countries more than quintupled over the same period, from 285 million to 1.6 billion by 1990. In 1990 the number of urban agglomerations ove million was 34; 22 of them in Developing countries. By the year 2000, about three-quarters of populations in urban agglomerations will be in Developing countries.[3]

The diagram 2.3 shows that world population in urban areas has been more or less on the rise. While table 2.2 gives a detailed picture on urbanization in countries, having a high human development index and low population growth rates as compared to countries with lower human development indexes but with phenomenal growth rates. In recent years Argentina and Mexico have been good case studies in the developing world.

Diagram 2.3

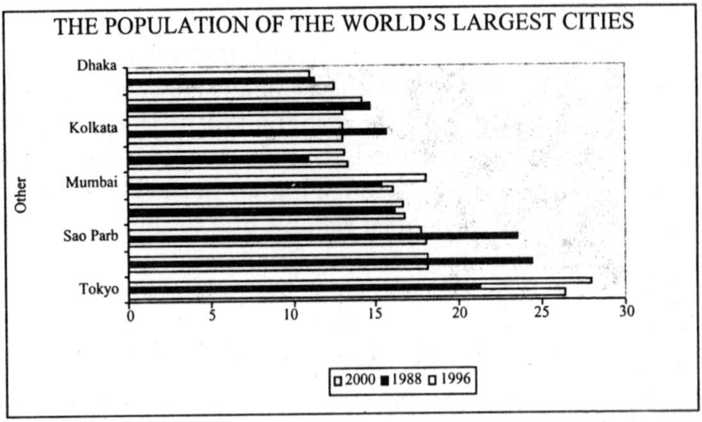

Source: Population Division, Department of Economic and Social Affairs, United Nations Secretariat, New York.

Countries with high human development index also naturally projects a high gender development index[6]. The HDI value for each country indicates how each country is achieving an average life expectancy, education and standard of living. The HDI was constructed by the U.N.D. P. by measuring a country's relative achievement in each of the three basic variables and taking a simple average of the three indicators ..... of the 174 countries for which the HDI was calculated 57 are in the high human development index, 69 in the medium category and 48 in the low category. It has been agreed upon that the HDI values are averages and can be misleading. There have been attempts to desegregate the HDI at a level below regions or provinces, as for districts in Madhya Pradesh, the results show enormous variation in the level of human development among the 95 districts in the state. Indore (0.619) and Bhopal (0.609) which are more developed have a HDI four times as high as those of the backward districts such as Tikamgarh (0.156).[7]

Table 2.2
Demographic Trends and Urbanisation

Country	*Rank*		*Total Population (million) 2000*
	High HDI	*GDI*	
Canada	3	3	30.8
USA	6	4	283.2
France	12	11	59.2
Hong Kong	23	23	6.9
Argentina	34	33	37
Mexico	54	49	98.9
	Low HDI		
India	124	105	1008.9
Pakistan	138	120	141.3
Bangladesh	145	121	137.4

Source: World Population Prospects 1950-2050, UN 2001

It is also evident that the annual rate of growth of Developing countries is higher than the industrialized countries while the percentage of total urban population is much higher in the developed countries. In terms of total population, Asia accounts for 1.2 billion of the 2.5 billion global urban residents (i.e. about 46 per cent) while Europe accounts for 535 million people. Inspite of this there is a substantial variation in the level of urbanization within regions as seen in diagram 2.4.

Diagram 2.4
LEVELS OF URBANISATION IN SELECTED REGIONS

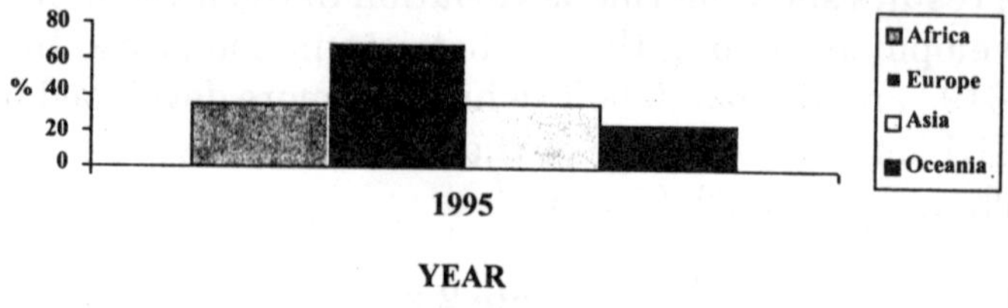

Source: The State of World Population,1995.

Urban growth in less-developed regions is declining, but annual increments will continue to be very large into the next century. The global urban population is growing by 2.5 per cent per year (3.5 per cent per year in the less developed regions and 0.8 per cent in the more developed regions).[8]

Globally it has been found that natural increase in population always results in higher levels of urbanization. When there is economic stability, there may be growth in migration. Between now and 2010, Asia's share of the 15 largest urban agglomerations will grow from nine to eleven; Africa's from zero to one. Latin America will decrease from 4 of the 15 largest cities to 2 and North America from 2 to 1.[9]

In the less developed countries, high population growth rates in the rural areas help fuel migration. Many of the migrants are in the prime reproductive years and their children add on to the city populations. Migration is mainly concentrated between the ages of 15 and 24. Recently, a trend among women towards migration at younger ages has developed concentration between 10 and 20 years age group. There is also a secondary peak among women in their late 50's and 60's into commonly highroad moving frequently than men in the same age group. They are often widows and divorcees moving to join their children or childless women. The absence of a son or a husband can deny elder women status in her own community, forcing her to seek the interaction of other family members or to strike on her own.[10]

In Asia and other less developed regions, often the young women might support a family in the rural areas. Many women and migrants report that they moved to a company or follow a spouse or other family members. Globally, women make up about 29 per cent of migrants (16 per cent accompany their family and 13 per cent for marriage). The growth of cities is not only a shift in its economy and culture but also it is due to ecological reasons as well, mentioned earlier in the chapter.

Urbanization in Developing countries gives rise to several problems. Brazil, China, Mexico, Taiwan etc. are amongst the world's largest producers of manufactured goods. Their manufacturing plants are in urban areas. Hence there is pollution, congestion, poverty. Infact most developing countries have become the hub of overpopulation and poverty. While on the issue of developing countries, the key arguments underpinning the notion that urbanization in developing countries is abnormal is that an unusually small industrial labour force supports their urban populations. Bert Hoselitz, who compared current industry - urban relations in developing countries to those in low developed countries during the late 19th and early 20th century, solidly established this point in the 1950's.[11] Due to over population and congestion in the urban areas, several social problems arise which affects different sets of people in diverse ways.

Social Problems versus Urbanization

Before dealing with the types of social problems, it is important to understand the reasons behind them. Francis E. Merril (1956) has described a social problem as something that is related to a social organization. It must substitute a threat to or an infringement upon established social values. The term social disorganization has unfortunately misleading implications. Disorganization does not mean that there is no social organization rather, it means that some elements in the existing social organization are not functioning as well as would be desirable or is functioning in such a way as to jeopardize social welfare.[12] Merril maintains that social problems and social disorganization are complementary ways of describing the same thing, through the relationship between the two concepts may be simple.

A social problem according to Clarence Marsh Case in (1956), is a state of the social mind. This does not, of course, imply that the social mind exists as an entity. A social problem is not a purely objective situation, which will be apparent to an outsider. However, no social problem exists unless a considerable number of competent observers are aware of it. There is no definitive yardstick for determining the competency of observers and in similar vein, awareness is relative. These terms gain meaning, however, when considered with reference to real situations.[13]

A social problem is hence a part of the social mind and hence not purely a matter of unfavorable objective conditions in the physical or social environment. For example in an Asian country social problems may arise out of unfavorable physical environment, population distribution or conflicting social values as cherished by different classes or groups within the society. In most countries, social problems are both historically and culturally specific. Like the city itself they reflect the prevailing values, ideology, and structure of the existing social formation. At the most general level they will reflect the nature of the urban environment at a particular stage of development achieved and the way in which the people perceive conditions of life within them. More significantly, they will relate to the level of development of the economy, its capacity to support social services, the degree of cohesion or conflict within the population, the prevalence for behavior that might be considered deviant or threatening to the existing social order, the strength of social contact and so on.[14]

While dealing with social problems it is important to understand the characteristics of the city, its population density, spatial mobility, ethnic and class heterogeneity reduced family functions and greater autonomy. The usual explanations as to why a city has more crime than its rural areas is that the number of possible targets are more, there is more vulnerability of people who are unemployed, accessibility to criminals, more freedom and an impersonal life, coupled with the harsh environment of the slums.[15] Earlier in the chapter anonymity has been cited as an important characteristic of urbanism. This in turn reduces ones responsibility to the society and often makes a person's life unaccountable which finally reduces the value system.

Social indicators like individual perception of well being are such obvious conditions as income, housing quality and health, which figure, prominently in the more objective approach to social indicators. There are certain things in life, which are necessary for personal well-being or satisfaction in life. This can range from love, care, and affection to achievement and privacy etc. Dalkey and Rouke (1973) conducted a survey of American Students and formulated a list of components of quality of life. This was identified as a subjective approach where if the basic amenities are cut, then how people may react differently to situations.

The ecological approach on the other hand deals with empirical evidences. Cause and effect relationship may be sought via ecological correlation or by relating to frequency of incidents to distance from the city center. This theory is a part of the Chicago School of Urban Sociology. According to D. M. Smith (1979)[16], problem areas can be identified in cities with the help of a sensibly guided criteria chart which was set by the United Nations to understand human well-being.

Components of Level of Living

Health Including Demographic Conditions
Food And Emotion
Education, Including Literacy And Skills
Transportation

Housing, Including Household Facilities
Conditions Of Work
Employment Situation
Aggregate Consumption and Savings
Clothing
Recreation and Entertainment
Social Security

Smith has used the hypothesis in the case study of London that "social deprivation or need falls away from the inner city to suburbs, in a close approximation to concentric rings.[17] It may be said that the core-periphery concept is prevalent in case of deprivation and social problems. The core are the areas with maximum benefits and the periphery zone forms the zone of vice. When a social problem like crime increases by leaps and bounds, Reckless (1967) pointed out that most people felt that the problem lay in the socio-economic condition rather then the inefficiency of law and order situation. Often an individual cannot cope with the new urban culture, which moves on a fast track leading to anonymity and dislocation of a person from his roots. This isolation and "social deprivation" leads to criminal tendencies. Reckless (1967) emphasized that crime in such society especially the developing countries as a natural process, as there is a clash with the traditional and the modern cultural environments.

In India it has been observed that women living in low cost living spaces are unwanted and struggling to stay alive. A report by the World Bank on women's health in India concludes that poverty and deeply etched social attitudes have produced a kind of hidden holocaust on the country's female population. For every 1000 men in India there are only 927 women, which means that the country has 35 million fewer women than it should have. The World Bank report is technically a survey of female health problems in India.

The question of missing women is so severe, widespread and inextricably tangled with ignorance and social custom that it ends up as a murder mystery: someone or something is killing or murderously neglecting the girls and the young women of India. One of the culprits is the dowry system, which makes the daughter a family burden and a son who collects the dowry an asset. But there are many other aspects such as low level of education in the villages, which leads to a significant gender bias.

Crime Verses Urbanisation

As mentioned earlier causes of world crime is due the lack of basic necessities in life; similarly crime as a social problem and its understanding is where there is poverty, there is a possibility of crime. A question that is frequently asked is whether the poor commit more or less crime than the rich when it comes to considering the human condition. It is more important to consider the context of life within which this crime may occur, and who may suffer.[18] Taking clue from the question it is difficult to say if there is a relationship between development and crime as expressed by Graeme Newman (1990). It is often assumed that the increase in crime that results from economic development occurs among the poor, since it is the poverty that is most often the direct product of economic development.

In research on world crimes, the United Nations Interregional Crime and Justice Research Institute found that the less developed countries were more prone to violence, where as property related crime go up with economic stability and prosperity. The study also found that the violent crime rates for less developed countries is similar to the Developed countries, and the property crime rate for the less Developed countries is considerably less than the developed countries, though slightly higher than the developing countries. The study made an important contribution "that as development increases, the impact of crime may be less even though the rates themselves increase...In developed countries, increases in crime rates are essentially increases, that have affected the lower strata of the societies concerned. The expected "price" that developing countries may be expected to pay for increases in economic development is therefore that the growth in crime will be shifted more and more to the lower state of their societies. This is cause for considerable alarm, because it suggests that as development continues, the lower strata becomes more and more cut off from its "mainstream". It is this class that absorbs the major impact of the increase in crime. In other words, as development continues, a clearly identifiable underclass emerges...The costs of crime are far outweighed by the other benefits in development.[19]

Several studies have been conducted showing a correlated between crime and urbanization. Infact theft rates may correlate more highly with urban growth than with community sizes.[20] Also, the levels of crime have been found to correlate with delinquency, alcohol consumption and to standards of living etc. Hence, there are several circumstances in which urbanization does lead to social problems both is the developed as well as the developing part of the world.

In diagram 2.5 the crime and the population projection for the year 2000 in a few cities of the world shows that where there is less population and more development and amenities there is more awareness which leads to more reporting of cases and higher registration of cases.

Diagram 2.5

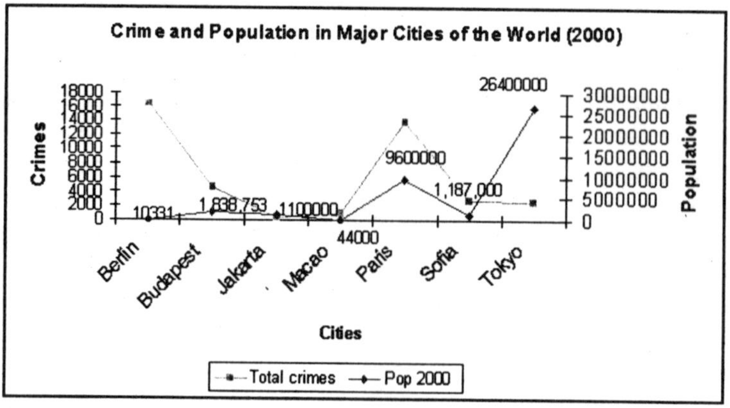

Source: Compiled by Author.

From the above diagram it is certain that where there are high populations there is high incidence of crimes. However, there are variations in each city due to the social and economic dynamics that are working simultaneously.

Status of Women in Developed Countries

Urbanization and modernization has led to better health and modern techniques for all classes of people.

However, violence, which has been chalked out as a major social problem, is on the rise amongst the women. Violence is widespread in all cultures, age groups and incomes amongst women. Its consequences include unwanted pregnancies, infection with STD, miscarriage, partial or permanent disability, psychological problems etc. Recent World Bank estimates indicate that in both industrial and developing countries domestic violence and rape cause women of reproductive age to lose a significant percentage of healthy days. Domestic violence appears to be an example of how the relatively weaker bargaining power of women and the paucity of options for them outside the house can affect the intra household distribution of welfare.[21] The World Bank also gives other harrowing details as the first chance comes when a wife is pregnant. Amniocentesis and ultrasound techniques that allow couples to learn the sex of their unborn child arc becoming common in the cities in India. As in other Asian countries, in India many families choose abortion when the foetus is of a female. Although statistics is hard to gather, a 1990 study conducted by a hospital in Mumbai found that 96% of abortions were the after effects of amniocentesis. The World Bank estimates that such abortions could equal 1% of female births. More recently a study by the Institute for Development and Communications in Chandigarh through a study has found that women with 'autonomy' may yet make informed choices of sex selection in favour of male children. Shaping of 'interests' is a function of ideology in a specific socio-historical context, and to challenge gender hierarchies, the power imbalance in social positions has to be transformed rather than 'empowering a conglomeration of individuals or changing institutional practices.

More than 80% of India's population living in rural areas adopts common practices of drowning, poisoning or strangulation of the new born girls. In Uttar Pradesh it was found that the infant mortality of the girl child less than five years was 70% higher than that of males. The violence that women face in their life cycles is given in a tabular form in table 2.3. The other forms of discrimination are: daughters are almost always breast fed for shorter periods of time than male children; girls are also given less food for weaning; inoculation rate for boys is higher. If the child survives to be a teenaged girl, she is married off and is expected to give birth to male children which leads to the process of multiple pregnancies that are hazardous.

Table 2.3
The Life Cycle of Violence

Phase	Types of Violence
Pre birth	Battering during pregnancy (emotional and physical effects) on the women; effects on birth outcomes.
Infancy	Female infanticide; emotional and physical abuse
Girlhood	Sexual abuse by family members and strangers; forced child prostitution
Adolescence	Dating and courtship violence; economically coerced sex; sexual abuse in work place; rape; forced prostitution and trafficking in women
Reproductive	Coerced pregnancy; rape; abuse of women by male partners; dowry abuse and murder; partner homicide; psychological abuse; sexual abuse off unmarried and childless women; abuse of women with disabilities.

Source: Toward Gender Equality (World Bank 1995), p. 26.

Through violence, women are forced into a subordinate position. It is a manifestation of unequal power relations, which has led to man's domination through discrimination against women. Such kind of violence is often sociably sanctified where the threats of violence instill fear and insecurity in women and hamper their striving for equality, development and peace. There is not much of a difference in the status of women in developed or developing countries. The only difference is in degrees. To give a brief idea, the table 2.4 gives a detailed on status on women worldwide:

Table 2.4
Status of Women World Wide

- Each year, half million women die from pregnancy complications and 100000 from unsafe abortions.
- A pregnant woman in Africa is 180 times more likely to die than a women in Western Europe.
- In the US, a woman is beaten every 18 minutes and raped every 6 minutes. More women are injured in domestic violence incidents than in car accidents, rapes and muggings put together.
- Reports from France say that 95% of its victims of violence are women and 51% of women are assaulted by their husbands.
- About one fifth to half of women worldwide experience domestic violence during marriage.
- In several countries, testing for genetic defects is used to determine the sex of an unborn child to abort female foet uses.
- Women represent two thirds of more than one billion illiterate adults who have no access to basic education.
- On an average, by age 18, girls receive 4.4 years less education than boys.
- 52% of women with AIDS are of African American origin.
- There are 71% female headed families in America, while 35% in Puerto Rica.
- 42% Native American women had been sterilized as compared to 15% white women.

Source: Complied by author from several websites.

After reading these horrific details it does occur as to why such type of crimes and heinous violence take place?

People implicitly hold women accountable for men's violence against them, whenever they fail to question men's behaviour and focus instead on what women do in response to it. Some of the most popular explanations for women abuse is alcohol, drugs or other external problems for men's violence. Explosive anger is blamed on loss of control or an excess of stress. Another explanation is that men who were battered in their childhood and had seen battery are more prone to become violators themselves. But would such an explanation be acceptable for a petty criminal who may be stealing to earn a living?

Table 2.5
The Crime Situation in a Few Countries

Country	*Crime Rate*		*Rape (100000) Pop.*	
	1991	*2000*	*1991*	*2000*
Argentina	114.05	527.9	0.05	7.6
Austria	6074.3	—	6.4	—
Canada	12735	—	113	—
Egypt	3666.61	—	0.03	6.0
India	594.29	515.7	1.22	—
Netherland/				
Wales	10403	—	11	7.6
Japan	1450	1985	8	17.5
Spain	2482.78	2212.6	4.86	—
Singapore	1629.4	—	2.7	—
USA	5897.8	—	42.3	—

Source: Crime in India, 2002.

It is a universal fact that in no one particular society the women are treated with dignity. Gender equality can be achieved across different income levels, political ideologies, cultures and stages of developments. In case of gender empowerment measures, Norway, Sweden, Denmark and Finland top the list. In this case Canada takes a back seat at number 6th position. Hence, high-income levels do not necessarily make the women more powerful and assertive of their position. It is also important to take a glimpse on crime against women in a few countries to see a close relation between crime and status of women as in Table 2.5.

As seen in Table 2.2 Canada ranks third for both HDI and the GDI list but has a high crime rate and a high incidence of rape cases. Seeing this data it is possible to say that prosperity and development does not play a role in combating crime against women. However, this kind of projection is incorrect, as we will soon see that with prosperity and higher levels of education the women and their families report offenses especially sexual related crimes more in the developed countries.

The dark side of the story of status of women is domestic violence, which is inflicted by a family member in the form of threat, assault, mental trauma, incest, homicide in family, sexual assault and rape and sexual harassment. These offences are normally not reported to the police as most of the time the offences are committed by someone who is known to the victim. Statistics from the criminal justice system and data from rape crisis centers from six countries (Chile, Malaysia, Mexico, Panama, Peru and the United States) have been used to estimate that in more than 60 per cent of all sexual assault cases the victims knew the perpetrator. The statistics on forced sex that are roughly comparable across countries are from surveys among college going women. If attempted rapes are included, the rate of sexual assaults increase to anywhere between 20% and 27%. Data also indicates that sexual abuse is an all too common aspect of a girl's childhood.[22]

Table 2.6
UN Survey on Adult Women Who Have Been Physically Assaulted by an Intimate Partner

Country	*Percentage of assault*
Canada	25
Japan	59
USA	28
Mexico (Mexico City)	34
India (Sn. Karnataka/Jullundhar district)	22
Korea, Rep. of	38
Malaysia	39
Sri Lanka	60

Source: UN Survey by Lori Heise (1993).

Similarly in diagram 2.6 and table 2.6 shows that the women in Asian countries are more prone to domestic violence while sexual abuses are more readily reported in the West.

Diagram 2.6

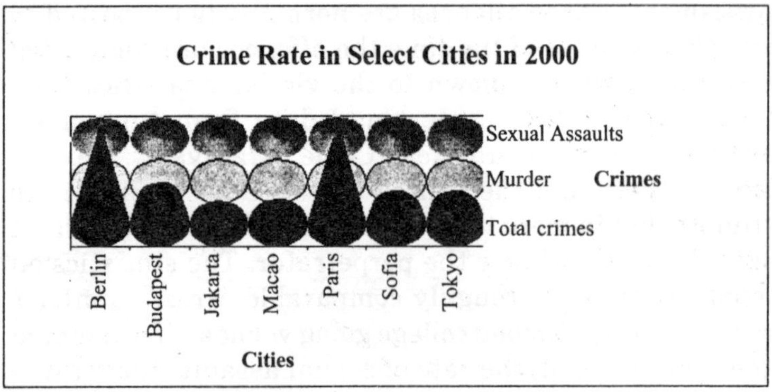

Source: Interpol Data 2000.

Without doubt, violence against women is prevalent worldwide. The World Bank has reported that violence against women is a health issue. The phenomenon has always existed worldwide but only today it is reported regularly. During World War II forced prostitution was imposed by the Japanese Army on Philippine and Korean women to be "comfort women" for the soldiers. The recent war in Bosnia is particularly visible in the atrocities committed against women. Although, the process of development has been positive it has affected women and men differently. Modernization of agriculture has altered the division of labour between the sexes, increasing women's dependent status. However, violence in urban areas are a result of low social cohesion, weak family life and low socio-economic status due to population explosion, congestion and low resource allocation. Crime takes place in areas which suffer from the maximum disadvantages. At the macro-level it is evident that crime and poverty do not necessary go hand in hand especially crime against women as evident in tables 2.2 and 2.9. However, it is true that crime and violence is more in areas, which have disadvantaged sections in society. Crime against women is more or less the same both in the developed as well as developing countries, the only difference being that the types of crime vary.

References

1. Women Aid International, *Women and Violence*, website London.
2. The process through which the cities grow.
3. Ram Ahuja, *Social Problems in India* (Jaipur, 1992).
4. *The State of World Population*, 1996. (UNPF, 1996), p. 23.
5. *Ibid.*, p. 24.
6. *World Social Situation In The 1990's*. p. 102.
7. Human Development Index (HDI – includes life expectancy, incomes and education, while Gender development Index (GDI–includes female life expectancy, education and incomes).
8. *The Human Development Report* ,1996 (UNDP, 1996), p. 30.
9. *The State of The World Population* , (UNDP , 1996) p. 25.
10. *Ibid.* p. 25.
11. J. Gugler, *The Urbanization of the Third World* (Oxford, 1988) p. 23.
12. *Ibid.*

13. John Eric, *Analyzing Social Problems (*1956) p. 46.
14. D.M. Smith (Ed), *The Identification of Problems in Cities:Applications of Social Indicators,* p.14.
15. W. Walter Menninger, M.D., *The Roots of Urban Crime: A Psychodynamic Perspective*, 1970, p. 17.
16. *Ibid.,* p.14
17. D.T. Herbert and D.M. Smith, *Social Problems and The City: Geographical Perspectives*, p. 24.
18. Graeme Newman, *Crime and The Human Condition,* 1990.
19. *Ibid.*
20. Howard Zehr, *Crime and the Development of Modern Society,*1976, p. 57.
21. *Development in Practice* (World Bank, 1995), p. 25.
22. *The World's Women 1995,* Trends and Statistics (UN 1995), p. 159.

3

Urban Crime Against Women in India and Canada : Socio Special Perspective

The perception of fear amongst women is universal. Women in the social fabric occupy occupy a lower position which makes them more vulnerable and in the process she is susceptible to being more terrorized, traumatized and brutalised. These aspects are not region specific. It happens in all parts of the world. Only the degree and scale varies. In the past and in the present day there have been several Draupadi's and Joan of Arc's who have sacrificed their lives, fallen prey to the whims of the patrircal society. They have had very little voice of their own; as society has laid all the rules for her.

In recent times, there has been a steady rise in crime as seen in the previous chapter. As this piece of research deals with environmental criminology, where it is not the offender who has importance from the research angle, but the place where this offender grows and lives is equally important, so also is the place of ocurrence of such crimes needs to be carefully studied to bring down the offences. The subsequent chapters will deal with this aspect of crime in progression first understanding the dynamics of the social and cultural milieu of the State and then the micro space of the city.

As observed in the earlier chapter, places which are urban are more prone to criminal activities and criminals. As society degenerates, places also assume the same characteristics. The three elements in a space which are prone to crime are:

- A motivated offender
- An attractive target
- An absence of protection or "capable guardians"[1]

It is in this urban space that the lives of people become complex with constant pressures to find a suitable living space or an identity. But sometimes the individuals who try to strike out a survival also face internal conflicts, cultural, social and ethnic isolation. The social bonding loosens leading an individual to be anonymous in the urban space.[2] The last criteria of anonymity leads a person to the threshold of vice.

In the developing contries, the application of the theory of differential association can be viewed as crimes learnt in association with others. Another theory also applies in the case of developing countries where differential distribution of wealth and goals in society leads to crime. It is important to find out whether crime in the developing countries is committed primarily by youth, as the fine art of stealing or pickpocketing may be a learned trait from fellow companions. There have been several such deductions made in the past based on research.

Crime according to Durkheim is dissimilar in the developed world from the developing societies, but at the same time are undergoing many similar process (Clinard and Abbott 1973). Crime in the developing countries are similar in the "take-off" stage as in the case of industrial areas. This is the stage the developing countries are going through rapid industrialization, urbanization, and development and along side the squalor, grime, vice and increase in crimes. However in a developing country the urban areas which are "primate" cities have a larger influence on the surrounding areas than in a developed country. Hence in the developing countries, there is a large social imbalance as compared to the developed countries. In all countries the best available index for crime is recorded with the police by the citizens or crimes discovered by them and noted in their records.

Table 3.1
Balance sheet of human development in South Asia during the nineties

Progress	*Deprivation*
Life expectancy	
• Average life expectancy increased from 58 years in 1990 to 63 years by 2000	• The life expectancy in South Asia is still among the lowest in the world second only to Sub-Saharan Africa. • By the year 2000, 95 out of 1000 children on average still died before reaching the age of five.
Health	
• 78 per cent of the population has access to health services.	• The region is host to the highest proportion of underweight, stunted and wasted children in the entire world. • Overall, nearly half of the children under the age of five are chronically malnourished in South Asia.
Food and nutrition	
• The daily supply of calories increased by 10 per cent during the nineties	• Daily calories supply of 2379 still below the average for developing countries at 2663.
Education	
• Adult literacy increased by points during the nineties from 42 per cent in 1990 to 543 per cent in 1997	• The total number of illiterates increased from 366 million in 1990 to 388 million in 1997. • 39 million children lack even primary education.
Income and poverty	
• Income per head grew annually by almost 5 per cent during the nineties.	• South Asia is still home to the largest number of poor people in the world, i.e., 515 million.

	• GDP per capita of $ 2238 much below the average for developing countries at $ 3783.
Women	
• Female literacy rate had reached 42 per cent by the end of the nineties.	• 365 million women are still illiterate in South Asia.
	• Women on average earn only 40 per cent of what their male counterparts earn.
Children	
• Infant mortality dropped by around 29 per cent during the nineties.	• Nearly half of the children under the age of five are chronically malnorished in South Asia.

Source: Human Development In South Asia 2002.

Table 3.1 sums up the challenges that the people in South Asia face-extreme poverty, little or no education for women, malnurishment etc. These challenges of human development facing South Asia increased in magnitude as its population crossed 1.3 million by 2000, up from 1.1 billion at the start of the 1990s (table 3.2).

Table 3.2
Population of South Asia
(million)

	1990	*2000*
India	851	1014
Pakistan	122	138
Bangladesh	108	129
Nepal	19	24
Sri Lanka	17	19
Bhutan	1.5	2.1
Maldives	0.2	0.3

Sources : UN Year Book 1999.

India being the most populous country in the region reached the million mark by 2000, representing 76 per cent of

South Asia's population. It has been estimated that India would surpass China as the most populous country in the world by 2015. The comparision of South Asia's population growth during the two halves of the nineties shows that Bhutan experienced the highest growth in population during 1990-95, whereas Maldives recorded the highest growth of the latter half of the decade. Population growth in Pakistan remained high at 2.3 per cent during both periods of the nineties, as the country had one of the highest fertility rates in the region. Sri Lanka, on the other hand, experienced the lowest rate of population growth in both periods of the decade.

Table 3.3
Poverty in South Asia

	India	*Pakistan*	*Bangladesh*	*Sri Lanka*	*Nepal*
Population below poverty line (per cent) $ 1 a day (93 PPP USS)					
1989-94	53	12	-	4	-
1995-97	44	31	29	7	38
$ 2 a day					
1995-97	86	85	78	45	83
National poverty line					
1990-94	41	34	43	22	-
1995-97	35	-	35.6	25	42

Sources :ADB 2001b, World Bank 2002a.

Towards the end of the 1990s South Asia has become the second most populated region in the world, after East Asia (see table 3.2). It is the most densely populated region with 278 people per sq. km., which compares unfavourably with the population density of East Asia of 115 persons per sq. km. The high level of population growth has put tremendous pressure on the resoures of the regions. The nineties was characterised, in particular, by declining public expenditures on the provision of social services, like health and education to the increasing number of people in South Asia. However, the contribution of non-government organisation (NGOs) and community based organisation (CBOs) in the development of social sectors increased significantly during this decade. This has also helped in the aspirations of the people. Yet it is difficult to say as to how much impact there has been in such development work.

Human Development verses Poverty Nexus

Poverty is one of the most serious challenges facing South Asia in the last decade and will continue to do so in the next decade. The number of people in absolute poverty has risen in making it home to the largest number of poor in the world. Recent data reveals that out of the 1.3 billion poor people in the world 515 million lived in South Asia[3]. In India between 1989-94, more than half the population, 53 per cent, lived on just 1$ per day (table 3.2). This was true in Nepal a well. In Bangladesh, 29 per cent of the population was living below 1$ per day in the early part of the nineties. The poverty situation in Pakistan which was only 12 per cent of the population in the start of the 1980s went up to 31 per cent by the later half of the nineties. In India, on the other hand, this figure has declined by more than 10 per cent in the recent years.

The share of South Asia in global poverty is constantly on the rise. In 1998, 43 per cent of the poor were living on less than $ 1 a day against 39 per cent in the begining of the 1990s.

The UNDP defined poverty in its most common definition as being poverty of income or as seen in terms of consumption. However, poverty is a very broad concept and these definitions do not often capture the other broader dimensions of poverty-the poverty of opportunity. In the context of human development, which is concerned with enlarging people's choices, it is the poverty of opportunirites that creates and sustains poverty. The lack of opportunities available to an individual to lead a healthy and productive life, to be able to make informed decisions about his likes, to enjoy a decent standard of living, freedom and security, would convey all deprivations.

The human development approach to poverty is based on the concepts of both building capability as well as enhancing opportunities, stating that the poverty of life lies not merely in the improverished state in which the person actually lives, but also in the lack of real opportunity—due to social constraints as well as personal circumstances—to lead valuable and valued lives. The 1997 UNDP Human Development Report introduced the Human Poverty Index (HPI) as a more comprehensive measure of poverty, more in line with the human development concept. The HPI mean deprivations in the three basic dimensions of human development, captured in the HDI as :

- A long and healthy life, as measured by life expectancy at birth
- Knowledge as measured by the adult literacy rate combined primary, secondary and tertiary gross entrolment ratio.
- A decent standard of living, as measured by GDP.

Table 3.4
HPI in South Asia

	India	*Pakistan*	*Bangladesh*	*Nepal*	*Sri Lanka*
1997	35.9	42.1	44.4	51.9	
1998	34.6	40.1	43.6	51.3	
1999	34.3	39.2	43.3	44.2	
2000	33.1	41.0	42.4	43.4	

Source: Human Developemnt in South Asia 2002.

India is a typical example of a developing country. The uniqueness is that this is the land of the worship of Shakti or female Goddess. However, in the social structure of the society, there are severe contradictions. Ever since 1954, when "Crime in India" was first published it has become evident that the crime against women has been on the rise. Besides this, the tremendous growth in population since Independence has also led to several social problems in the country. There has been unbalanced growth, which in turn has led to tremendous rural-urban migrations. Migration of unskilled labor to the cities has further led to urban congestion, unemployment and under employment, which is turn, leads to the genesis of crime.

In the Indian context it would be interesting to study the relation between population structure and the rates for different types of crime. It will be interesting to note the change in the crime rates with the changes in population over the last decade; In India, class, caste and ethnicity all play an important role in the various forms of crime. Yet, amazingly crime against women is a uniform feature amongst all.

Crime in India is published by the National Crime Records Bureau which is under the Ministry of Home Affairs (Governemnt of India), brings out national crime statistics each year and also at the district-level and city wise statistics. This helps in studying the magnitude of the problem. It is generally agreed that crimes reported to the police furnish the best crime index. This is obvious from the fact that it is the police who receive and record the first official report of the occurrence of a crime through information furnished by the victim or someone who has knowledge of its commission.[3] Hence, the major bulk of crime statistics is provided by the police, although it is only a statement of under reported crime statistics.

In India, every seven minutes some crime is committed against women in the country, every 56 minutes a women is raped, every 26 minutes one is molested, every 33 minutes some criminality is perpetrated against her and every one hour and 42 minutes, a dowry death takes place.[5] There has been an overall rise in violent crimes (1.1) per cent. The crime rate in Delhi has gone up to 429.7 per cent which is more than double the national average 185.1 per cent. According to the 1995 figures, the incidence of rape has increased by 4.1 per cent over the previous ten years. However, the incidence of crimes against women is highest in Maharashtra. These are some of the alarming features of crime against women. However, when the situation of crime is studied more closely it will be evident that the growth in population plays an important role in the incidence of crime as a whole and against women as well.

Crime Trends in India

The bedrock of our penal system is the Indian penal code (IPC) which is a combination of western scientific outlook and oriental sensitivity. The code covers a vast range of anti-social behavior in relation to the state of society as it was enlisted more than a hundred years ago. The IPC makes a broad classification of crimes against property, person and state.[6]

Table 3.5
Growth in Incidence of Crime IPC in Relation to Increase in Population 1961-2000

Year	*Population ('00000)*	*Incidence of crime (000')*	*Rate of crime ('00000)*	*per cent violent crimes of total*
1961	437.7	626	142.9	8.9
1971	551.2	953	172.8	13.1
1981	690.1	1386	200.8	13.9
1991	849.6	1678	197.5	14.7
1995	916	1696	185.1	14.7
2000	1002.1	1770	176.7	13.5

Sources : Compiled From *Crime in India 1995, 2000.*

In case of crime against women, the National Crime Records Bureau has categorised crimes such as rape, kidnaping and abduction, homicide, dowry death or their attempts, torture- both mental and physical, molestation, eve-teasing, importation of girls, commission of Sati, Dowry, Prohibition, Immoral Traffic (Prevention) and Indecent Representation of Women. Out of these, culpable homicide for dowry, rape, kidnapping and abduction are considered as violent crimes. the other crimes such as Sati, Dowry, Immoral Traffic (prevention), Indecent Representation etc. all come under special laws of the state. Till 1989, data on rape and kidnapping and abduction was only collected as cases of crime against women. A separate chapter on "crimes against women" is included and a more detailed information on "victims of rape" is also covered.

A Snapshot of India shows that :

(1) In 2000, incidence of molestation has shown an increase in trend by 1.9 per cent over the previous year. A total of 32,940 cases were reported in the country. In Madhya Pradesh there were 8516 cases (showing an incidence of 10.6 per cent against the national average of 3.3 per cent.

(2) 64 cases were registered during 2000 of importation of girls as compared to only one case registered in 1999, 40 cases were reported in Bihar alone followed by 13 cases from Orissa, 7 from Tamil Nadu and 4 from Madhya Predesh.

Several reports brought out by the Government of India (such as the National Police Commission recommendations) as well as those reports prepared by non-governmental sources suggest that there are large numbers of cases that go unreported and that is true even for the crimes committed against women.

Crime in India 2000 also published the following details:

- 4.1 per cent increase in crime against women.
- Highest crime incidence in Uttar Pradesh (14.0 per cent)

- Highest crime rate in Rajasthan (24.0 per cent)
- All India crime rate is 14.1 per cent
- 960 per cent increase in cases of buying of girls and prostitution.
- 49.2 per cent increase in foeticide cases over 1999.
- 62.5 per cent importation of girls cases reported from Bihar.
- In 87.4 per cent of rape cases, offenders were known to the victims.
- 30 per cent of the offenders of rape were neighbours.
- 19.3 per cent crimes against children.
- Highest incidence of crime against children in Madhya Pradesh
- 33.7 per cent of child (up to 10 years) are victims of kidnapping from NCT of Delhi.

From table 3.5 it is evident that crime and population are going through an upward trend. Since 1992, there has been a check as regards to the incidence and the rate of violent crimes. It is also evident that there is a positive correlation between population growth and incidence of crime, especially in the case of urban population. It is generally observed that with the increase in population there is an increase in the trend of crime. During 1981 the urban population was 23.34 per cent of the total population and this increased to 25.72 per cent by 1991.

Crime in India suggests that between 1995-1996, the percentage change for magnitude of 0.8 per cent incidences is in 1996 as against 1696 cases in 1995. As for the cases of violent crimes- in 1996 there were incidences (as per Crime in India 1996) of 14.2 per cent as against 14.5 per cent in 1995.

There is a positive correlation between population growth and crime. In the urban sphere, population is increasing due to natural growth, as well as rural urban migration and urban areas being large growth centers attract haphazard settlement leading to congestion etc. It is observed that the lack of opportunities, uneven distribution of incomes, diverse socio-reigio-cultural disparities makes urban areas a breeding ground for criminal activities. The population growth of cities especially the large floating population are major contributing factors for urban crimes. Criminal propensity is also known to be higher in urban industrial areas. Migration of poor, illiterate people having roots in a simple environment consequent to migration suffer emotional instability in the urban setting. They are easily lured into crime. Crime and development are intrinsically linked. The phenomenon of urban crimes is an important feature in metropolitian cities but the pattern varies from city to city. The size and nature of urban center is quite crucial.

There is no demarcation between rural and urban areas as far as the crime statistics are concerned since these are not collected on this basis. But the trend shows that the crimes in urban areas are peculiar and have shown a consistent rise parallel to the population increase.

Recently a newspaper article by the Hindustan Times in Delhi published "Hell for Eves" which placed a consolidated crime statistics of 170 molestation cases and 630 cases of eve teasing in the capital that were reported up till June 30,2003, bringing home a grim truth. The country's capital is not a women friendly city, and unpleasant incidents can happen to anyone, anywhere, any time.But now a change seems to be quietly sweeping through the minds of women in Delhi. "Circumstances can't be changed, change yourself," this new initiative is what young women appear to be adopting after having realised that their safety is largely in their own hands.

- 170 molestation cases have been registered till june 30, 2003
- 630 reported cases of crimes against women

DIAGRAM 3.1
SEX RATIO IN INDIA AND SELECTED COUNTRIES 2001

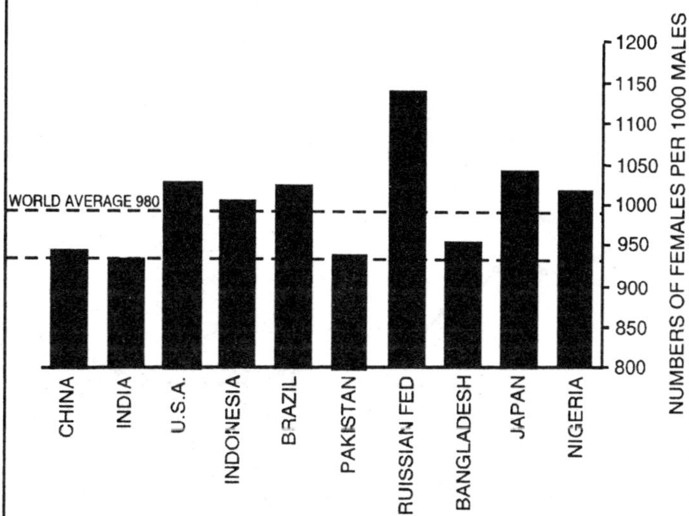

- Women cell is organising training sessions in educational institutions
- Karate and judo techniques are included in the training.

In the urban areas there are a large number of working women with a certain amount of economic independence and higher levels of literacy. However, the social position remains as uncertain and lower than men in the rural areas. Studying the sex ratio also helps in understanding the position of women in society. Male dominated societies (where the male child is sought), neglect their female children and are given less nourishment and this leads to fewer female population as compared to the males. The low sex ratio is seen both in Diagram 3.1 and in more detail state wise in Diagram 3.2.

Diagram 3.2
Sex Ratio in Select States in India

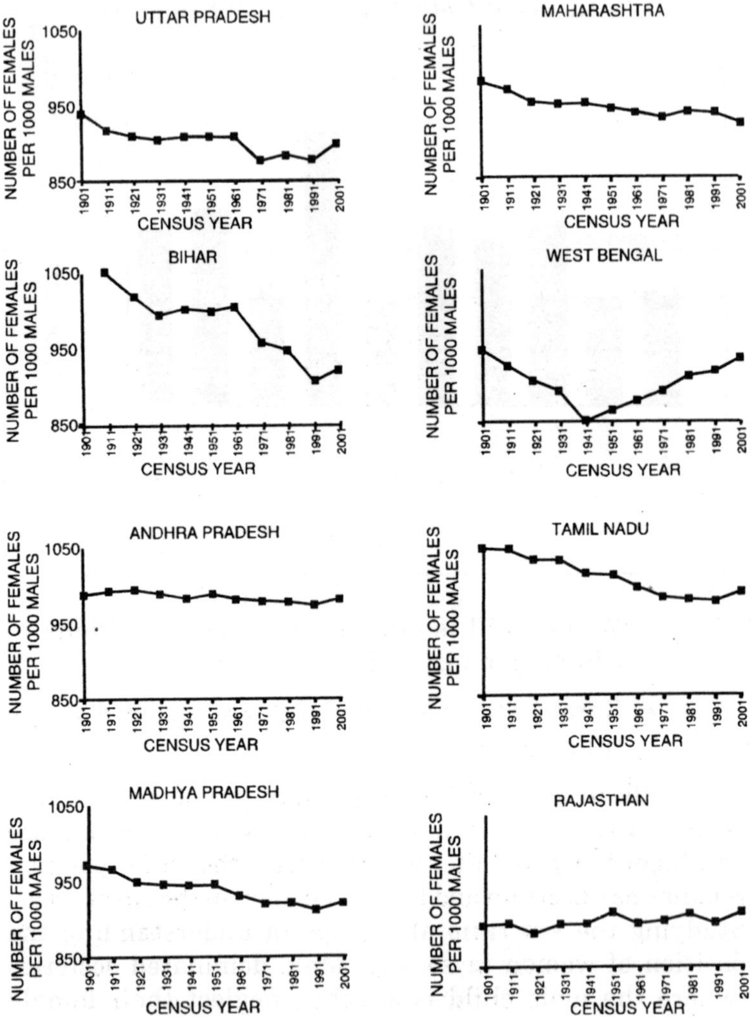

Table 3.6
Incidence of crime in India (1990-1999)

Year	*Rape*	*Kidnapping*	*Dowry Death*	*cruelty*	*molestation*	*Sexual Harassment**	*Total*
1990	1.2	1.7	crime head was not introduced				1604449
1995	1.5	1.5	0.5	3.1	2.9	0.5	1695696
1996	1.6	1.6	0.6	3.8	3.1	0.6	1709576
1997	1.6	1.6	0.6	3.8	3.2	0.6	1719820
1998	1.6	1.7	0.7	4.3	3.2	0.8	1778815
1999	1.6	1.6	0.7	4.4	3.3	0.9	1764629

Source: Crime in India, 2000.

* Ealier referred to as eve-teasing.

The diagram 3.3 shows that there is an ever increasing trend in the incidence of henious crimes such as rape and dowry deaths between 1998-2000.

In 2000, the country registered 1,28,320 cases of crime against women compared to 1,23,122 cases in 1999; 1,190,12 cases were reported in 1998. It suggests that there is a suden upsurge of 7.0 per cent in 2000 over 1999. Table 3.6 gives a brief picture of the crime situation between 1990-1999. From the table it is useful to see individual crimes where there has been a decrease in the crime as against the base year of 1990, especially in the case of dowry death, eve-teasing and molestation. However the total incidence of crime has gone up to an astronomical rate of 43.7 per cent between 1991 and 1995. Increase in trend can be noticed in the case of cruelty (29.23 per cent) and molestation, (26.74 per cent).

In 2000, the total incidences of crimes against women is 4.1 per cent over such incidences in 1999. Diagram 3.4 gives a brief idea on this.

Diagram 3.4
Incidences of Crimes Against Women in 2000

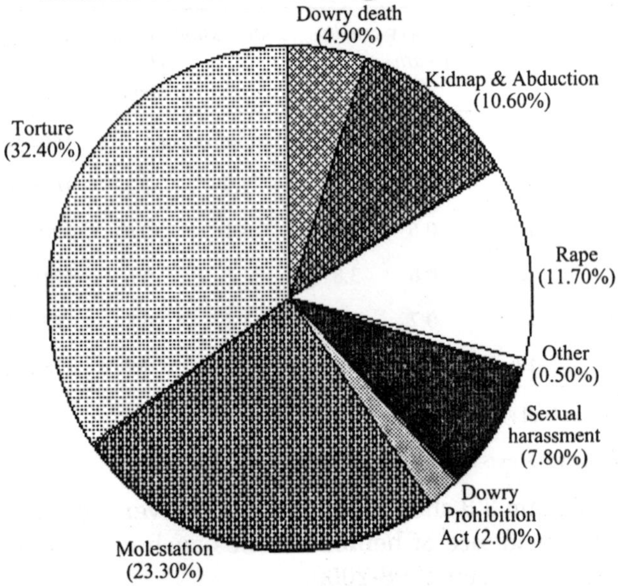

Source: Crime in India 2000.

It is evident from the data that there has been a steady increase in crimes against women. The greatest escalation has been during the period 1993-94. But the question that occurs is - whether the awareness level is increasing amongest the people or is it that crime reporting is going up with the police? These questions will be pondered on later in the research.

As in diagram 3.3. incidences of rape at the national level has been about 16,496 cases in 2000, as compared to the previous year of 15,471 (1999), showing an increase of nearly 6.6 per cent. Of these 40 per cent were in the age groups of 19-30 years followed by 4,622 (20.8 per cent) in the age group of 16-18 years. The data in crime in India also mentions that in 87.4 per cent of the cases, the offenders were known to the victims. Of these 30 per cent were neighbours to the victims.

Table 3.7
Percentage of Crime Against Women to Total Crime 1990-1996

Year	*per cent to Crime*	*Percentage Increase*
1990	4.3	
1991	4.4	8.5
1992	4.7	6.7
1993	5.2	6.2
1994	6	17.9
1995	6.27	7.6
1996	6.7	5.91
2000 (per cent increased since 1999)	6.7	4.1

Source : Compiled from Crime in India, 1996, 2000.

The law enforcement agencies have also shown a poor record of custodial management, as exhibited by two cases of custodial rape that have been reported in Orissa and Madhya Pradesh. Cases of incestual rape was reported for the first time in Crime in India, of which 93 per cent belonged to the age group of less than 30 years, while 7 per cent were over the age of 31 years.

The rest of the 15770 cases of rape of the total of 16496 cases are those of victims of rape other than incest. In this group 46 per cent of the victims belong to the age group below 30 years. The highest incidence of such cases was reported from Madhya Pradesh, Uttar Pradesh and Bihar. The incestuous rape cases is highest is Madhya Pradesh, Orissa and Tamil Nadu.

A rise in material aspirations and expectations has also led to a steady increase in dowry deaths in recent years. Unless there is a radical change in the traditional mind sets, the problem will persist. In most dowry death cases as seen in the case study on Calcutta, the mother-in law and the husbands are involved in the cases. The question is not only of material wealth but also assertion of power in the family. The motives for violence against women range from situational urge, to socio-psychological aggression as observed by Ram Ahuja (1987). In most abduction cases, the motives for kidnapping the unmarried girls or abducting the married women have been either for sexual relations, for marriage, for selling and for prostitution. The kidnapping and abduction occur as follows : with an economic motive in 12.2 per cent cases, with gratification for sex in 29.3 per cent cases with the twin object of sex and marriage in 19.5 per cent cases, and with the object of marriage in 39.0 per cent cases.[7] As regard to the cases of murder of women, the trend reflects the general characteristics of the general crime.

Table 3.8
Crime Against Women in a few Cities

Cities	*per cent Crime Against Women*
Chennai	24.0
Kanpur	5.7
Jaipur	4.8
Mumbai	5.3
New Delhi	12.6
Kolkata	3.3

Source: Crime in India 2000, MHA.

In Indian society, battered women do not leave their husbands, as they are morally, socially and financially dependent on them. Their existence is one of learned helplessness that gives an insight into the mental state of passive resignation experienced by these women.[8] Wife beating by the the spouse is not limited to any particular strata of Indian society rather it is seen everywhere leading women to remain as a suppressed class within their own domain.

State-wise Distribution of Crime Against Women

The data for the analysis of the incidence of violence and crime in the states is relatively limited in terms of crime classification as compared to the all India statistics. Table 3.8 gives a state-wise over view of crime against women in 2000.

Clearly from the table it is evident that the states such as Madhya Pradesh, Maharashtra, Uttar Pradesh, are the three most infamous states in the country regarding crime against women. The maximum incidence of crime against women is concentrated in north-central part of India. Ashok K. Datta and others (1979) tried to identify if there was a north-central sub-culture of violence. Because it represents a part of the general Indian culture, the north-central Indian region shares an already existing complexity of norms, values, attitudes, and materials traits with the balance of the country. However, due to the course of historical evolution, the region has developed a sub-culture including a patent theme current in the cluster of values that make up the life-style and socialization process. In other words, violence is more a part of social life in north-central india than in the remaining parts of the country.[9] Table 3.9 gives a detailed picture of the intensity of crime in the six states, which are more prone to crimes against women.

Table 3.9
Maximam Percentage of Crime Against Women in Five Years

Year	*M.P.*	*U.P.*	*Maharashtra*	*A.P.*	*Rajasthan*	*West Bengal*
1991	17.8	15.4	15	7.8	7.7	5.1
1992	15.7	16.3	15.1	8.1	9	4.9
1993	13.6	16.7	16.6	9.9	8.5	5.9
1994	13.7	16.1	13.7	10.4	7.5	6
1995	14.4	11.2	15.3	8.5	8.8	6
Average	15.04	15.14	15.14	8.94	8.3	5.58
2000	12.7	13.4	9.3	10.1	9.2	5.0

Source: Crime in India 1993, 1994, 1995.

Data has been shown for only 6 states showing maximum incidence of crime over a couple of years. It is evident from the table that Uttar Pradesh has the largest number of cases of crime against women followed by Madhya Pradesh and Maharashtra. However, till 1991 Madhya Pradesh used to be the center for crimes. The focal point has shifted northward. In Uttar Pradesh most of the crime is concentrated near the urban undustrial areas near Delhi (Mukerjee 1997). From 1995 on wards there is a decrease in the overall crimes against women. Diagram 3.2 Uttar Pradesh, Rajasthan, West Bengal shows a very low sex ratio and also high atrocities against women. The above mentioned six states have a very traditional society and so the women occupy a low status in society. In 1994, under the different crime heads it is seen that again the six states, which were projected in table 3.9, have the maximum number of crimes.

The table also helps in reiterating that there does exist a north central area of violence. Madhya Pradesh reached record crime rate, although Uttar Pradesh and Maharashtra have the highest incidence of crime in the country. Maharashtra, Rajasthan Andhra Pradesh, West Bengal do not have significant rank to all India total, but the first three states have a high crime rate. Although in 1994 Maharashtra had the third highest average incidence of crime in four years in 1994, in 1995 the incidence is as high as Uttar Pradesh. This is due to the fact that the number of cases for sexual harassment and torture has gone up. This may be due to the awareness level amongst the people to register a case or due to the high stress level due to urbanisation in the state, which has led to higher crime rate. In the year 1994 "crime in India", have come out with four new tables on crime against women namely, importation of girls upto 21 years, Sati Prevention Act, Immoral Traffic (Prevention Act, Indecent Represen-

Table 3.10
Various Crimes Committed In the States in 1995

Crime	*More than 10 per cent*		*Between 5 per cent to 10 per cent*	
Rape	Madhya Pradesh	22.7	Maharashtra	9.9
	Uttar Pradesh	13.1	Rajasthan	7.5
			Andhra Pradesh	6.2
			Bihar	9.5
			West Bengal	5.7
Kidnapping & Abduction	Uttar Pradesh	13.1	Gujarat	6.9
	Rajasthan	7.5	Madhya Pradesh	7.3
			Maharashtra	5.6
			Assam	8.0
Dowry	Uttar Pradesh	36.3	Maharashtra	9.2
			Andhra Pradesh	7.1
			Madhya Pradesh	8.2
			Bihar	7.5
			Rajasthan	7.2
Torture	Maharashtra	28.1	Andhra Pradesh	9.1
	Uttar Pradesh	10.2	Madhya Pradesh	8.2
	West Bengal	10.7	Gujarat	6.2
	Rajasthan	10.3		
Molestation	Madhya Pradesh	25.8	Uttar Pradesh	9.2
	Maharashtra	12.2	Andhra Pradesh	9.4
			Rajasthan	7.4
			Orissa	5.1
Sexual Harassment	Andhra Pradesh	16.2		
	Tamil Nadu	22.4	Haryana	6.2
	Madhya Pradesh	16.1		
	Maharashtra	17.0		

Source: Crime in India 1995.

tation of Women (Prohibition) Act. This has broadened the arms of the law and various complicated cases can be depthly dealt with. However, the incidence of crime may not be the correct indicator of the level of crime, as the states have varying density of population. The rate of crime (incidence per lakh of population) is considered as a balanced indicator to assess the level of crime universally.

Crime in Metropolises

The rising crime rate in developed countries is not related to the socio-cultural perspectives, but more so to the level of industrilization and urbanization. Crime is mostly concentrated in the urban areas of the country and also depends on the size of the cities. Violent crimes are associated with large cities. Population specific rates of violent crimes exhibit considerable variation in their relationship to metropolitan population size. American suicide rates have shown to increase with the size of the city. In England and Wales higher levels of crime were committed in the large and medium sized cities and town.[10]

It is believed that the urban way of life is characterized by intensive conflicts of women and values, rapid social change, increased mobility of population, emhasis on material goods and individualism. Heterogeneity is a striking characteristic of large cities and naturally brings exposure to a great diversity of women and values. As a result of large population and congestion, this often leads to breakdown of law and order.[11] From table 3.7, it is possible to understand the crime scenario in the metropolises in India. However, data on crime is published on rape cases only with a detailed break -up of the age of the victims.

From the above table it is evident that there is no definite north-south divide for rape cases. Both in 1994 and 1995 data we find that Delhi has the highest number of cases. From the table it is also evident that there is no geographical north-south division of crime. The larger the city, the bigger is the crime statistics. The all India average for Metroplitan cities is 42.6 cases in 1994 and in 1995 it is 45.07. Cities such as Delhi and Bombay (Mumbai) have extremely alarming incidences of rape cases. This is not only due to the fact that a large number of cases are reported inspite of the inhibitions that women have while reporting such cases.

Table 3.11
Incidence of Rape Cases 1994-1995

North	*1994*	*1995*	*South India*	*1994*	*1995*
Calcutta	36	54	Bombay	150	210
Delhi	252	305	Madras	14	11
Ahmedabad	20	3	Hyderabad	49	41
Kanpur	31	44	Bangalore	61	42
Lucknow	33	29	Pune	52	66
Surat	10	16	Nagpur	46	56
Jaipur	22	22	Kochi	7	7
Vadodara	13	7	Coimbatore	1	1
Patana	25	26	Indore	29	25
Varanasi	9	4	Madurai	4	7
Ludhiana	11	11	Bhopal	62	62
Average	42	43.41	Average	43.2	48

Source: Compiled From Crime in India 1995.

Besides all the forces of vice in a metropolis are applicable in this area. In general there has been little fluctuation of crime in the cities over 1993-1994 (as reported in Crime in India). There has been escalation in the 1995 data.

Table 3.12 shows the change in percentage in rape cases in 1994-1995. It is evident from the table that although Delhi and then followed by Bombay had the highest rape figures in 1995, however in the case of the greatest escalation of cases it is Madurai, Surat and Calcutta. On the other hand the number of cases have gone down significantly in Ahmedabad, Vododara and Varanasi. Delhi has the highest sexual crimes as seen in the data on rape cases. In 1994 it has dropped slightly to 252 cases but in 1995 it has increased to 305 cases.

One of the reasons for crime in Delhi that the experts feel is the lack of a suitable value system in the society. The high rate of murders is a reflection of the stress and strain, which the social structure is constantly subjected to . . . . This society is the best example of a heterogeneous society with no roots and unified culture or values. Residents of Delhi live with a very sepcified and well-defined reason, achieving which is a must for the individual. The direct off shoot of which is that an individual is running with this mind set and any obstacle encountered on the way is met with violence and ferocity.[12]

Table 3.12
Percentage Change in Rape Cases 1994-95

Decrease		*Increase*	
Ahmedabad	-85	Bombay	40
Bangalore	-31.14	Calcutta	50
Bhopal	0	Delhi	21.03
Coimbatore	0	Kanpur	41.93
Hyderabad	-16.32	Madurai	75
Indore	-13.79	Nagpur	21.73
Jaipur	0	Patna	4
Kochi	0	Pune	26.92
Lucknow	-12.12	Surat	-60
Ludhiana	0		
Madras	-21.42		
Vadodara	-46.15		
Varanasi	-55.55		

Source: Crime in India 1995.

The common hypothesis to the cause of crime which was held in the nineteenth century, were namely, poverty, lack of education and population density, which can still be used to explain crime in general as well as crime against women. V. Veeraghavans study (1994) on Delhi gave a general overview that crime is mostly concentrated in the middle and low middle class colonies. Most victims and offenders came from lower level of occupation or unskilled workers like mechanics, technicians, drivers, taxi and scooter rickshaw drivers, and vendors, The study also indicates that higher the educational level of the women, the lesser were the chances of rape. In other words, in most circumstances in India, educational qualifications are directly proportional to the financial condition of the person.

In conclusion we can emphasize that crime in India is escalating at an alarming rate, especially those crimes which were unheard of in traditional Indian society. It may be also due to the fact that the mention of certain types of crime is considered taboo. Today, the growth rate of crime has far outstripped the rate of population growth. The crime rate in 1994 was 11.0 per cent compared to 11.6 per cent in 1995.

Both population and crime are positively correlated, i.e., if there is increase in population, there is a similar escalation in the crime graph. This is especially true in the urban densely population areas. Where there is over crowding and congestion, there is resource constraint and the under privileged find a cheak living option. Economic and societal stress leads to increase in crime against women. Death and dowry related offences have increased in the last couple of years due to the social pressure of acquiring consumer items that have flooded the market. In the case of rape and cruelty towards women in section 498 (a) there has been 4.29 per cent and 26.67 per cent increase respectively over 1991-1994. Within a period of four years there has been a 120.86 per cent increase in crime. Dowry death cases and eve-teasing has decreased in 1995 as compared to the other years.

The most crime prone states are those of north-central India, Uttar Pradesh, Madhya Pradesh, Bihar, Rajasthan, Andhra Pradesh, Maharashtra and West Bengal. However, in most north-Indian states there is under-reporting of cirme, as FIR's are not lodged and women are dissuaded from reporting the cases. The sex ratio of these states especially Uttar Pradesh, Rajasthan and West Bengal is below the national average. In case of the above-mentioned states, the level of urbanization and crime against women has a strong correlation, i.e., denser the population there is an increase in crime.

The same is applicable in the case of the metropolises in the country. Delhi has an extremely cosmopolitan culture with a very large migrant population from the neighbouring states of Uttar Pradesh, Harayana, Rajasthan, Punjab and Bihar etc. There is unemployment, lack of proper facilities, large number of labor force and above all a lack of identity. This anonymity leads to an erosion of the value system in society and hence the large number of crime.

However very sadly, often statistics distort the crime scenario. Mere use of statistics to illustrate the city's crime situation often projects a distorted picture. Some police officers feel, this is the main reason for resorting to burking which means non-registration of crime incidents. This is done to induce a sense of security among the citizens, as the political and administrative bosses and also the media evaluates the police performance through statistics. Often burking is resorted to ward off both internal as well as external pressures. Hence, although often an efficient police force is projected, the victims are refused justice. Unprecedented population growth, urbanization and a burgeoning slum population defeat the efforts of the police force which does not increase with the corresponding increase in population. A controlled crime statistics has often led to a decline in crime.[9] According to researchers, it is difficult to manipulate rape and murder cases. However, crime against women is on the rise all over India due to the complex socio-cultural and economic matrix.

Rapid urbanization along with growth of population and lack of space and education has led to various social evils. Greed, feudal mind sets, economic benefit, a need to dominate along with overall degeneration of other social and moral values in society, has led to the recent situation of increasing crime against women in India. Over all development, i.e. rural as well as urban development should take place side by side. Exodus of unemployed youth should be checked from the villages to the city. In most metropolises, the migrants do not bring families. This further leads to an imblance in the family structure. The women in India even amongst the educated working women are unaware of their rights and laws to protect them (as will be seen in the case study on Calcutta). There should be more education and improvement of women and this is possible through joint effort between the government and NGO's. The attitude of the police, society and women themselves should change. Women should not be considered a burden. Independence and self- respect should be encouraged which will check crime against women to a certain extent.

While discussing the statistical data of crime against women, it is important to also understand why such crimes take place as well. Rape which is increasing by leaps and bounds, according to Rekha Pandey (1987), Crime of rape varies cross-culturally. The rate of rape in one of the most affluent societies of the world today, the USA has been rising sharply since Uniform Crime Report statistics were reported first in 1993. It is projected that in America one rape occurs every minute. And all this is happening despite the fact that, in recent years, the women's liberation movement has contributed much towards the reduction of the incidence of rape and the alienation of the circumstances faced by those who survive the rape ordeal. It may be noted that this alarming increase in rape is no more than a third of the rapes (extra marital rapes are not reported).

In the next part of the chapter the Canadian crime situation and the crimes against women are studied to help in understanding that heinous offences are not limited to a particular society but are found all over the world.

Canada As An Urban Nation

Unlike India, Canada has a nation of urban people. More than 75 per cent of the country's population lives in cities. That is one of the highest percentages of urbanization in the world. More than one in four Canadians (30 per cent) live in the metropolitan areas with populations of over a million.[13] Canadian cities like elsewhere have come under the vortex of local and international forces, which in turn has led to their tremendous growth. As observed earlier that urbanization leads to social disorder of some sort. Hence often researchers studying the quality of life in the various cities tend to use crimes of violence as an indicator of this social disorder. As in a developing country such as India, Canada too has some traditional notions about women, such as some women need to be raped or they deserve rape; at other instances, a wife should be beaten to put her in her place to execute her wifely duties and so on. So as Torrance (1986) put it, violence against women is both of public and private nature. Violence against women is more due to the personal characteristics of the offender, sometimes even the causes of group violence are believed to be due to these characteristics.

On December 6, 1989, fourteen women were murdered in Montreal. The Montreal massacre galvanized the people and today the sixth of December is mourned country wide as the day of remembrance and action on violence against women. The various types of crime in Canada is today recorded by the Canadian Uniform Crime Report (UCR) system. This includes data since 1982; the newly created Center for Justice Statistics took over these duties. It now provides sufficient "uniform" national crime data to make possible meaningful comparisons of Canadian police jurisdictions. The demographic, social and economic data to measure the several independent variables were obtained from various census materials published by Statistics Canada (1976).

Three components of urbanization are mostly taken into consideration by Statistics Canada: population size, density and heterogeneity. Population size refers to the total number of individuals living in a community. Density was operationally defined as the population per square mile of land. Heterogeneity was defined in terms of ethnic composition.

The Canadian Census also differentiates ethnic identity according to mother tongue, the proportion of minority mother tongue (either non- English) or non - French, (depending on the location of the community) was the indicator chosen for population heterogeneity.

Absolute deprivation or poverty was indicated separately for the family and non-family populations using the low-income levels established by Statistics Canada. The unemployment rate was also included as an indicator of absolute deprivation.[14]

Hartnagel and Lee (1990) developed a theory to explain the cause and effect relationship of violent crimes based on urbanization. They found that as the opportunity of crime grew so did the rate of urban violence. They also found that with the increase in the size of population, violent crimes also increased. This has been also dealt extensively in the previous chapters. However, Hartnagel and Lee's theory was unable to verify the fact whether a change in the composition of population lead to an increase in crime. They also found in theory study that the large sized cities have higher crime rates. According to the Canadian Criminal Code, some of the parameters that may be used to identify crimes against women are:

Homicide

- Murder first and second degree
- Manslaughter

Attempted murder

- Assault level 1
- Assault with weapon or causing bodily harm level 2
- aggravated assault level 3
- Unlawfully causing bodily harm

Abduction

- Abduction of person under 14
- Abduction of person under 16

Sexual Offences

- aggravated sexual assault
- sexual assault with weapon
- sexual assault
- other sexual offences

Other crimes

- Kidnapping

Although both women and men are equally likely to be victims of crime; the 23 per cent of the women who are victims (as stated by Statistics Canada) are victims of personal crimes such as rape, sexual assault etc. committed by an acquaintance. In a large number of cases the common - law partner, husband or boyfriend, commits the violence. Whereas men who are victims are more victims of crime committed by strangers. Women made up almost two-thirds (59 per cent) of all homicide victims killed in a domestic relationship, while they represented only 22 per cent of those killed by an acquaintance and just 12 per cent of those killed by a stranger.[12] The Victimization Survey and General Social Survey in Canada have both thrown light on the situation of violence against women.

Trends at the National Level

Crime Statistics (Violent Crimes in General)

- **90 per cent of violent attacks** happen in situations where the victime knew the perpetrator well.
- **82 per cent of society** will be the victims of a violent crime during their lifetimes.

- An average of **80 million** crimes of violence are reported each year.
- Over **16,000 murders** occur on average each year.
- **3 out of 4 women** will be victims of at least one violent crime during their lifetime.

Rape/Sexual Assualt

- Every hour **16 women** confront rapists.
- A women is raped every **4.5 minutes**.
- **42 per cent of rape victims** tell no one.
- Only **5 per cent of all sexual assaults** are reported to the law enforcement agencies.
- **58 per cent of sexual assaults** are not reported by the victims to either law enforcement or crisis centres.
- **78 per cent of sexual assaults** are committed by someone the victim knows.
- **42 per cent of sexual assaults** occur inside the victim's home.
- **3 out of 7 women** who are sexually assaulted, are assaulted by multiple assailants.
- **22 per cent of sexual predators** assault an average of **7 victims** before they are caught and convicted.
- Only **2 per cent of all sexual assaults** results in the assailant being convicted and imprisoned.
- The United States has a rape rate **13 times higher** than Great Britain (UK), nearly **4 times higher** than Germany, and more than **20 times higher** than Japan.

In violent assaults and battering it is seen that:

- A women is beaten by her spouse every **9 seconds**.
- **3 to 4 million women** are battered each year.

- More than **1 million women** seek medical assistace for injuries caused by battering each year.
- Females are approximately **75 per cent** of the victims of intimate murders and about **85 per cent** of the victims of non-lethal intimate violence.
- Women age **16-24** experience the highest per capita rate of intimate violence.

As common as they are disturbing, sexual assaults against women are on the rise and they remain the most under-reported cases in the criminal justice system.

Source: Statistics complied by the U.S. Department of Criminal Justice.

To understand the situation of women in Canada it is also important to study the overall crime scenario. Definitely crimes against women are on the rise and so also their reporting. Presently, Canada's crime rate for 1999 has hit the lowest level in 20 years, falling for the eighth year in row according to Statistics Canada. The overall national decrease was five percent, eith Quebec, Ontario and British Columbia leading the way. The crime also droped in the largest metropolitian areas of Canada.

The crime rate bucked the national trend and showed an increase in all four Atlantic provinces. Even with the increase, Newfoundland still had the lowst cirme rate in the country in 1999, and the crime rates in Prince Edward Island and New Brunswick were below the national average.

Saskatchewan's crime rate in 1999 was the highest of the provinces's, with 12,1555 "criminal incidents" reported for every 100,000 in population, compared to the national average of 7,733. All three territories-the Northwest Territories, the Yukon and Nunavut-had higher crime rates than any of the provinces.

The statistics also show that youth related crime in Canada dropped 7.2 per cent in 1999. That is 21 per cent lower than ten year ago.

Statistics Canada bases its analysis on the annual Juristat statistics from the Canadian Centre for Justice Statistics which receives polices data from the Uniform Crime Reporting Survey.

As in previous years, the highest provincial crime rates were in Saskatchewan, followed by Brities Columbia and Manitoba. The three territories continued to report crime rates much higher than those of the provinces. The lowest rates were again in Nefoundland and Labrador adn Quebec.

Police reported about 309,000 violent crimes in 2001, up 7,000 from 2000. This nudged the violent crime rate up 1 per cent, the second consecutive increase after seven years of decline from 1993 ot 1999. Prior to 1993, the violent crime rate had risen each year since 1977. The 2001 violent crime rate was 6 per cent ower than a decade ago, but 52 per cent higher than 20 years ago.

Minor assaults account for almost two-thirds of all violent crimes each year. In 2001, the rate of minor assaults advanced 1 per cent and was the key factor in the rise in the total violent crimes. The more serious categories of assault-assaults with a weapon and aggravated assault-increased 5 per cent, mainly because of a 7 per cent increase in Quebec and a 14 per cent jump in Saskatchewan.

The overall rate of sexual assaults rose slightly (+0.7 per cent), primarily because of an 8 per cent increase in Quebec. However, still reported the lowest rate among the provinces. The slight increase at the national level was the first increase in sexual assault since 1993. The 2001 sexual assault rate 27 per cent lower than in 1991.

The more serious categories of sexual assault declined. The rate of sexual assaults with a weapon declined 17 per cent and aggravated sexual assaults dropped 9 per cent.

The rate of criminal harassment, commonly known as stalking, fell 5 per cent according to data from a group of 95 police services representing 42 per cent of the national volume of crime. However, this rate had increased 45 per cent from 1996 to 2000.

Six provinces and all three territories reported increases in violent crime in 2001. The largest provinicial increases were in Saskatchewan (+8 per cent), Nova WScotia (+6 per cent) and New Brunswick (+5 per cent). The largest declines were in British Columbia (-3 per cent) and Manitoba (-2 per cent).

Among the provinces, Saskatchewan and Manitoba reported the highest violent crime rates and Quebec and Prince Edward Island continued to report the lowest.

Table 3.13
Criminal Code and Other Federal Statute Incidents Reported to Police

	2001 Number	*2001 Rate*	*2000-2001 per cent change in rate*
Homicide	554	1.8	0.4
Attempted murder	721	2.3	-6.9
Assaults (levels 1, 2, 3)	239,163	769.5	1.3
Other assaults	13,091	42.1	6.5
Sexual assaults (levels 1, 2, 3)	24,419	78.6	0.7
Other sexual offences	3,026	9.7	-3.8
Abduction	713	2.3	-5.9
Robbery	27,414	88.2	0.4
Violent crime total	**309,101**	**994.5**	**1.3**
Break and enter	282,512	908.9	-4.7
Motor vehicle theft	170,213	547.6	5.1
Theft over $5,000	21,146	68.0	2.0
Theft $5,000 and under	665,961	2,142.6	-0.6
Possession of stolen goods	29,565	95.1	2.6
Fraud	88,332	284.2	1.9
Property crime total	**1,257,729**	**4,046.5**	**-0.6**
Mischief	338,425	1,088.8	2.7
Counterfeiting currency	37,771	121.5	4.0
Bail violation	91,249	293.6	15.7
Disturbing the peace	88,729	285.5	9.7

Offensive weapons	17,456	56.2	12.8
Prostitution	5,103	16.4	0.0
Arson	14,513	46.7	4.6
Other	247,945	797.7	0.7
Other Criminal Code total	**841,191**	**2,706.4**	**4.3**
Total Criminal Code (Excluding traffic)	**2,408,021**	**7,747.3**	**1.3**
Impaired driving	90,454	291.0	6.5
Other Criminal Code Traffic	35,844	115.3	6.9
Total Criminal Code	**2,534,319**	**8,153.7**	**1.6**
Cannabis	70,624	227.2	5.5
Cocaine	12,233	39.4	-5.6
Heroin	965	3.1	-22.1
Other drugs	8,098	26.1	3.3
Drugs total	**91,920**	**295.7**	**3.3**
Other federal statutes	**38,257**	**123.1**	**9.4**
Total federal statutes	**2,664,496**	**8,572.5**	**1.7**

1. **Rates are calculated on the basis of 100,000 population.**

Table 3.14
Crime Rates by Province and Terirtory

	Violent Crime		*Poverty Crime*		*Total Criminal Code Offences*	
	2001 rate	*2000 to 2001 % change in rate*	*2001 rate*	*2000 to 2001 % change in rate*	*2001 rate*	*2000 to 2001 % change in rate*
Canada	994	1.3	4,047	-0.6	7,747	1.3
Newsfoundland and Labrador	892	-1.4	2,284	-5.6	5,635	-1.8
Prince Edward Island	746	2.0	2,950	-2.2	6,773	0.0
Nova Scotia	1,046	5.8	3,449	-3.6	7,637	1.0
New Brunswick	988	4.8	2,827	-3.4	6,479	-1.1
Quebec	719	0.3	3,510	-3.8	5,869	-2.6
Ontario	903	1.8	3,400	0.7	6,509	1.6
Manitoba	1,620	-1.5	5,136	3.1	11,365	5.6
Saskatchewan	1,802	8.0	5,862	-0.3	13,458	5.4

Alberta	1,099	3.8	4,405	-1.8	9,050	3.9
British Colombia	1,217	-2.8	6,451	1.2	11,430	1.3
Yukon	3,751	12.4	7,218	-11.8	24,865	5.1
Northwest Territories	4,922	1.5	5,184	-11.5	30,149	6.9
Nunavut	6,573	8.7	5,501	12.0	24,958	18.8

- Total Criminal Code offences also include other Criminal Code offences (excluding traffic) not shown in this table.
- Rates are based on criminal incidents per 100,000 population.
- Ontario Provincial Police data for 2001were not a available due to implementation of a new records management system. As such, 2000 data

Table 3.15
Crime rates by census metropolitan area

	Violent Crime		*Poverty Crime*		*Total Criminal Code Offences*	
	2001 rate	*2000 to 2001 % change in rate*	*2001 rate*	*2000 to 2001 % change in rate*	*2001 rate*	*2000 to 2001 % change in rate*
Regina	1,614	0.0	9.661	14.0	16,387	10.1
Saskatoon	1,663	11.2	6,616	-4.0	13,360	2.9
Vancouver	1,053	-4.5	7,347	1.4	11,314	1.2
Winnipeg	1,309	-3.3	5,967	4.7	10,947	5.6
VIctoria	1,132	1.1	5,382	-3.0	9,996	-5.7
Halifax	1,266	12.4	5,091	-2.1	9,354	6.1
Edmonton	969	2.8	4,811	3.2	9,032	7.9
Thunder Bay	1,390	0.0	3,916	-8.8	8,602	-3.7
London	761	-9.0	4,796	-9.5	7,894	-9.3
Sudbury	1,163	20.1	3,935	6.2	7,535	11.8
Windsor	783	4.5	3,936	3.6	7,374	4.9
Calgary	871	-1.5	4,380	-3.5	7,137	-0.3
Hmilton	1,015	0.8	3.823	7.3	7,102	8.3
Montreal	878	-4.8	4,142	-6.0	6,830	-5.7
St. Catharines-Niagara	664	6.9	3,861	4.5	6,826	4.5

Saint John	1,146	8.0	3,107	1.7	6,612	3.8
Sherbrooke	461	6.0	4,293	9.8	6,541	12.7
St. John's	885	4.5	3,433	-10.0	6,406	-4.8
Hull[2]	910	17.7	3,320	-10.1	6,185	-3.8
Ottawa[3]	754	10.0	3,384	2.4	5,946	5.4
Kitchener	633	-8.3	3,535	-2.3	5,709	-3.7
Toronto	876	1.1	2,932	0.0	5,343	1.3
Trois-Rivieres	492	7.8	2,982	-9.2	5,094	-2.3
Chicoutimi-Jonquiere	517	-8.0	2,941	-6.1	4,986	-2.1
Quebec	532	3.6	3,084	-1.3	4,986	-2.3

- Rates are calculated per 100,000 population.
- Hull refers to the Quebec part of the Ottawa-Hull cencus Metropolitan Area.
- Ottawa refers to the ontario part of the Ottawa-Hull Census Metropoitan Area.

Table 3.16
Crime by offence type

(rate per 100,000 population)

	1998	*1999*	*2000*	*2001*	*2002*
All incidents	**8,956.0**	**8,500.9**	**8,404.7**	**8,429.5**	**8,386.6**
Criminal Code Offenences (excluding traffic offences	8,136.5	7,725.0	7,641.1	7,633.5	7,589.8
Crimies of violence	979.1	954.9	981.1	981.0	965.5
Homicide	1.8	1.8	1.8	1.8	1.9
Attempted murder	2.5	2.3	2.5	2.3	2.2
Assaults (levels 1 to 3)[1]	740.3	725.5	759.1	761.7	748.9
Sexual assault	84.5	78.2	78.0	77.3	77.5
Other sexual offences	11.4	10.2	10.1	8.6	8.7
Robbery	95.8	94.2	87.8	87.7	85.0
Other crimes of violenec[2]	42.1	41.7	41.8	41.5	41.3
Property crimes	4,555.3	4.260.9	4,067.4	3,992.0	3,959.8

Breaking and entering	1,159.6	1,042.5	952.7	898.3	875.1
Motor vehicle theft	548.5	529.0	520.7	541.9	514.1
Theft over $5,000	78.0	73.7	69.4	67.0	63.3
Theft $5,000 and under	2,359.2	2,223.5	2,153.4	2,120.1	2,128.3
Possession of stolen goods	96.4	96.1	92.7	86.7	88.6
Frauds	313.5	296.2	278.6	278.0	290.4
Other Criminal Code offences	2,602.1	2,509.1	2,592.6	2,660.5	2,664.4
Crimnal Code offences (traffic offenes)	466.7	385.6	365.2	386.5	374.5
Impaired driving	289.8	281.9	257.3	265.9	257.2
Other traffic offences[3]	123.5	120.0	119.4	117.6	117.3
Federal statutes	352.9	390.3	398.4	409.5	422.3
Drugs	234.5	262.7	286.1	287.4	294.7
Other federal statutes	118.4	127.6	112.3	122.2	127.6

1. "Assault level 1" is the first level of assault. It constitutes the intentional application of force without consent, attempt or threat to apply force to another person, and openly wearing a weapon (or an imitation) and accosting or impeding another person. "Assault with weapon or causing bodily harm" is the second level of assault. It constitutes assault with a weapon, threats to us e a weapon (or a an imitation), or assault causing bodily harm. " Aggravated assault level 3" is the third level of assault. It applies to anyone who wounds, maims, disfigures or endangers the life of complainant.

2. Includes unlawfully causing bodily harm, discharging firearms with intent, abductions, assaults against police officers, assaults against other peace or public officers and other assaults.

3. Includes dangerous operation of motor vehicle, boat, vessel or aircraft, dangerous operation of motor vehicle, boat, vessel or aircraft causing bodily harm or death, driving motor vehicle while prohibited and failure to stop or remain.

Source: Statistics Canada, CANSIM tables.

Table 3.16
Criminal Offences in Provinces and Territories

(rate per 100,000 population)

	Canada	*Newfoundland and Labrador*	*Prince Edward Island*	*Nova Scotia*	*New Brunswick*
All incidents	**8,386.6**	**6,384.4**	**8,484.6**	**8,320.7**	**7,514.2**
Criminal Code Offenences (excluding traffic offences	7,589.8	5,893.7	7,628.3	7,609.3	6,608.2
Crimies of violence	965.5	893.7	864.8	1,098.7	974.4
Homicide	1.9	0.4	0.7	1.0	1.2
Attempted murder	2.2	0.6	0.4	2.9	0.5
Assaults (levels 1 to 3)[1]	748.9	746.1	705.4	902.6	781.6
Sexual assault	77.5	103.8	105.1	94.4	98.3
Other sexual offences	8.7	6.0	10.7	5.9	14.1
Robbery	85.0	15.6	13.6	59.0	30.5
Other crimes of violence[2]	41.3	21.3	27.9	48.1	33.0
Property crimes	3,959.8	2,422.0	3,204.1	3,322.0	2,812.4
Breaking and entering	875.1	650.9	690.4	696.6	635.0
Motor vehicle theft	514.1	112.7	174.4	279.3	208.3
Theft over $5,000	63.3	29.9	47.9	27.9	42.0
Theft $5,000 and under	2,128.3	1,393.5	1,946.9	2,035.7	1,557.1
Possession of stolen goods	88.6	27.8	36.5	27.5	57.5
Frauds	290.4	207.1	308.1	254.9	312.4
Other Criminal Code offences	2,664.4	2,516.4	3,559.4	3,188.6	2,821.4
Crimnal Code offences (traffic offenes)	374.5	251.1	465.3	299.8	358.3
Impaired driving	257.2	173.6	396.7	260.2	280.6
Other traffic offences[3]	117.3	77.5	68.6	77.4	39.6

Federal statutes	422.3	301.2	391.0	411.6	547.7
Drugs	294.7	169.3	242.3	266.2	343.1
Other federal statutes	127.6	131.9	148.7	145.4	204.6

1. "Assault level 1" is the first level of assault. It constitutes the intentional application of force without consent, attempt or threat to apply force to another person, and openly wearing a weapon (or an imitation) and accosting or impeding another person. "Assault with weapon or causing bodily harm" is the second level of assault. It constitutes assault with a weapon, threats to use a weapon (or a an imitation), or assault causing bodily harm. "Aggravated assault level 3" is the third level of assault. It applies to anyone who wounds, maims, disfigures or endangers the life of complainant.
2. Includes unlawfully causing bodily harm, discharging firearms with intent, abductions, assaults against police officers, assaults against other peace or public officers and other assaults.
3. Includes dangerous operation of motor vehicle, boat, vessel or aircraft, dangerous operation of motor vehicle, boat, vessel or aircraft causing bodily harm or death, driving motor vehicle while prohibited and failure to stop or remain.

Source: Statistics Canada, CANSIM, tables

As noted above that urbanization, more specifically density of population and crime seems to have gone hand in hand. Although the population growth has not been as rapid as in the developing countries, since 1986 onwards the rate of population in Canada has increased rapidly. Diagram 3.5 gives us an idea of the growth in population and violent crime, since 1962.

Diagram 3.5

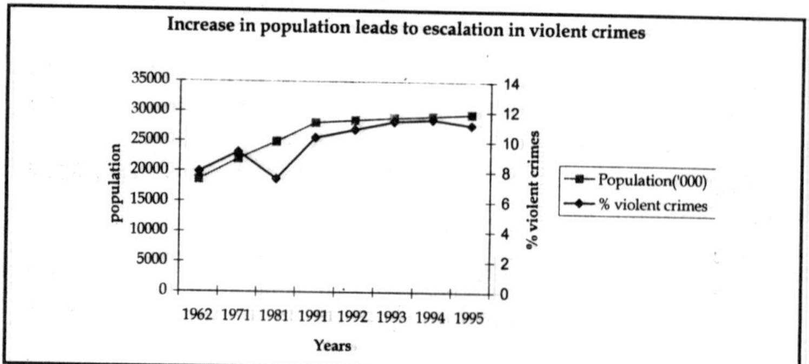

Source: Compiled by Author.

Infact since 1994, there seems to be a slight downward movement of both violent crimes as well as population.

Around 1986, the growth in population was a natural growth of 76.8 per cent of national growth, by 1991 it accounted for 59.2 per cent and in 1993 immigration actually equalled the contribution of natural increase. As rates of natural increase have stabilized, and become more uniform across the country, internal migration and foreign immigration now hold the key to explaining differential urban and regional growth (Bourne 1995). As both skilled and highly qualified technical workers have flooded the Canadian economy, ever since 1981, there has been an employment slump (since late 1980's) which have led to unemployment, under employment and lay - off. The pressure of immigrants, housing crisis in the employment market, crime especially violent crimes have also escalated in the developed countries as well.

Diagram 3.6

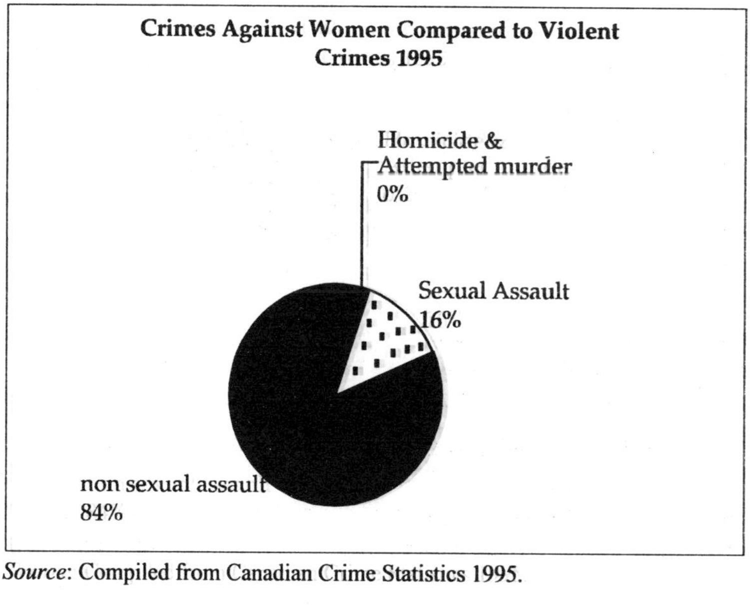

Source: Compiled from Canadian Crime Statistics 1995.

When the question of gender comes into the picture, the

total number of offences committed against women in 1995 was 21.35 per cent of total violent crimes; this involved personal crimes only. However, crimes against women are 2.37 per cent of total crimes recorded in Canada. From the Diagram 3.6 it is possible to see the different types of crimes committed against women in Canada.

From the data records published by Canadian Crime Statistics, it is also evident that the largest share of crimes committed against women is by people whom the victim knew and trusted. The culprits range from spouse, ex- spouse, parents and acquaintances.

Diagram 3.7

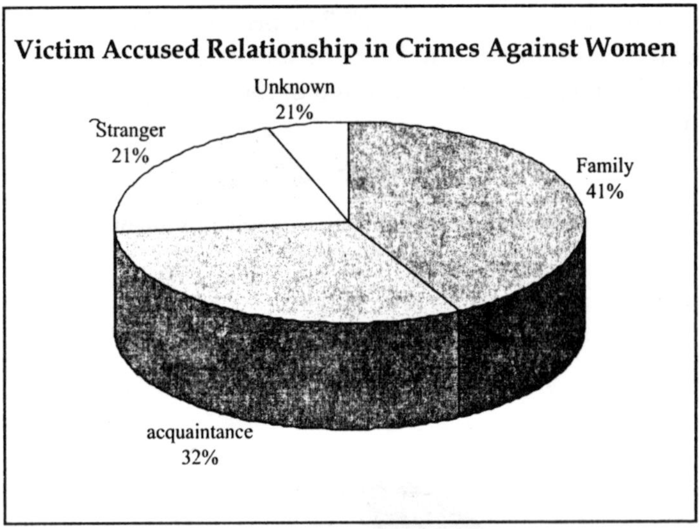

Source: Compiled from Canadian Crime Statistics, 1995.

The above figure infact aptly proves the relationship between the accused and the victim. The myth that strangers only assault women in dark alleys is only 21 per cent as compared to the actual perpetrators who attack the victim at home. These perpetrators are known to the victim in 73 per cent of the cases. The VAW survey by the U.S. Department of Criminal Justice placed this figure at 90 per cent as mentioned earlier in the chapter.

The largest section of women according to the official reports who are victimized are women between the age group of 20 to 24 years (15.2 per cent); followed by youth population between 12 to 17 years (13.8 per cent) and 25 to 29 years age group 13.4 per cent. This makes it evident that the younger women are most vulnerable as this group is also the most mobile.From table 3.13 to 3.16 it is evident that the crime rate is moving uphill, this may not be only due to the fact that the incidences are increasing but definitely younger women are now more bold to report the cases and get justice for themselves. This was less often the case almost two decads ago.

Table 3.17
Increase Of Crime Rates in Canada 1987 - 1991

Crimes	1997	1998	1989	1990	1991
Sexual	87	96	102	105	112
Assault	661	687	724	779	839

Source: Canadian Crime Statistics

There has been an astronomical increase in sexual assaults on women. Today the average Canadian woman is more mobile than women two decades ago. The interesting feature about Canada is that the society is multicultural with a distinct ethnic diversity. There is ethnic segregation to the extent that it is evident even in the residential patterns. Occupational, educational and income composition of the ethnic groups differ. This further leads to a checkered pattern in society, which may at some stage create an imbalance. Balakrishnan and Selvanathan (1990) felt that the Canadian ethnic composition has a "selective background." In other words the immigrants from the various countries live amongst their own occupational types as seen in the case of immigrants from Guyana, India, China etc.

Diagram 3.8 shows the ethnic composition of the population in 1991.

Diagram 3.8

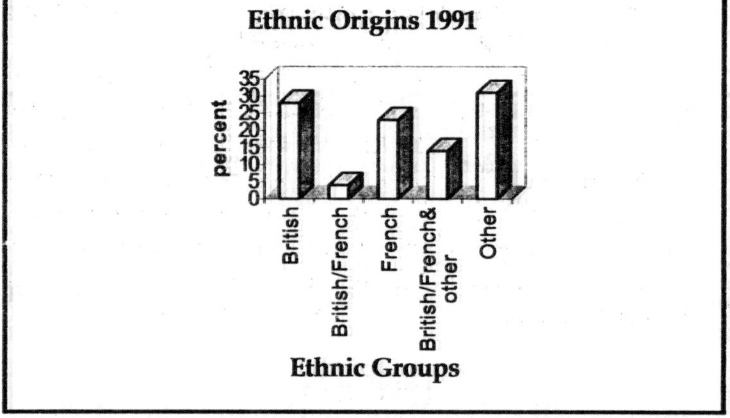

Source: Compiled by Author.

In recent years, the percentage of the "others" such as immigrants from Asian and Latin American countries are on the rise. In other words the traditional immigration pattern is changing for people to emigrate from the non-traditional areas. The shift has been from Western Europe to Southern and Eastern European in the 1950's and 1960's and in the last two decades from European to Third World origins.[16] The immigrant population leads to rapid rise in the total number in the population. Through research and data which will be examined later it is seen that the immigrant women are the most prone to violence due to their lower educational background, language barriers and lower economic status coupled with the fact that they come from traditional societies where the status of women is held in low esteem. According to recent Canadian Victimization survey, racial and ethnic minority women as well as Aboriginal and disabled women also experience high rates of violence. For most immigrant women and refugees, isolation and abuse is compounded by language and cultural barriers, by racism, and by the fact that great distances separate many immigrant and refugee women from their families.

According to Statistics Canada reports, six - in - ten Canadian women who walk alone in their own area after dark feel unsafe. Because of this perception of violence, women restrict their movement, working hours and often job types. Gill Valentine (1992) wrote that women developed mental maps of places where physical danger may occur. This perception of fear is mostly from strangers in a dark alley. She also said in her research that women are assaulted more at home by people whom she trusts than strangers. Women's fear of male violence does not therefore just take place in space but is tied up with the way public space is used, occupied and controlled by different groups at different times. There is a vicious circle in operation. The majority of women still adopt a traditional gender role, and as a consequence are pressurized into a temporally segregated use of space.[17] In 1993, Statistics Canada conducted the Violence Against Women Survey, where 12300 women aged 18 and over were randomly interviewed on telephone and asked about their perception of personal safety and whether they had been victims of physical and sexual violence. In the General Social Survey also conducted by Statistics Canada (1993) it was found that several women preferred not to report a case to the police as they feared further trauma in the hands of the police, revenge by the male attacker, and further harassment and humiliation. Infact research has shown that violence does not stop in case of pregnancy as well.

Two major surveys namely, the General Social Survey (GSS) and the Violence Against Women (VAW) Survey has thrown some light on the condition of violence in Canada. The GSS was initiated by Statistics Canada in 1988, 1993 to understand the socio - economic situation of the country. A part of the research was based on criminal victimization. The target population were all persons 15 years and over, who were interviewed by telephone.

The 1993 national survey on violence against women provided a reliable estimate on the extent of male violence against women in Canada. The survey was a random sample survey. The questionnaire was quite exhaustive seeking information on levels of fear about violence, about sexual harassment, about violence and threats of violence by strangers and dates, and about violence and emotional abuse by both current and previous spouses and partners. Data on the respondent's marital history were gathered, and there were classified questions designed to elicit information about the socio demographic characteristics of the respondents.[18] Victimization surveys are based on the idea of going straight to the people to ask them to indicate whether they have been victims of criminal acts which the Criminal Code defines as criminal, to describe the nature and consequences of their victimization experiences; to describe the criminal justice response; to indicate whether victims or others brought the incidents to official attention, and, if not; to indicate their perceptions and attitudes about crime and criminal justice in Canada.[19]

According to the GSS, only 30 per cent of assault cases are reported to the police. The cases go unreported as the victims prefer to deal with their problems in a different way, and the incidents are sometimes too personal to be reported to the police or sometimes, they consider the incident to be too minor to report. From the GSS in 1988 it was discovered that there were 68 victimizations per 1000 population. By 1993 survey report, there were 67-assault victimizations per 1000 population (Statistics Canada 1993). The results of the survey suggested that one - half of women have experienced violence. This is mostly in the hands of a male partner. The VAW survey found the following as given in table 3.18.

Table 3.18
The VAW Survey

Violence:	25 per cent of the women have experienced both physical and sexual violence at the hands of a marital partner or common - law partner. 45 per cent of all women experienced violence by men known to them.

Children:	Witness the violence against their mothers in four marriages where violence was reported.
Highest:	Violence cases were reported in British Columbia (59 per cent)
	Women living in large urban centers reported higher rates of violence (54 per cent) than did women living outside large urban areas (46 per cent).
	Women between the age group of 18 to 24 years are victimized the most.
Type:	Most violence is in the form of pushing, grabbing, and shoving (26 per cent) followed by threats (19 per cent)
Men:	Who have witnessed violence against their mother has a tendency of being violent towards their spouse.
Alcohol:	is a prominent factor in women's experiences of violence.40 per cent of violent incidents show that the perpetrator was indulging in drinking.
Effects:	18 per cent of the victims have physical injury. 46 per cent of the victims experience injury other than sexual or physical.
Weapon:	6 per cent of violent incidents by men other than spouses involved a weapon or something that was used as a weapon; 1 per cent involved guns; 3 per cent involved knives; 2 per cent involved blunt instruments; 44 per cent of the violent spouses used weapons.
Reporting:	14 per cent of the total incidents reported to the police.
Social Services:	Only 9 per cent of the victims used social services.
Perceptions:	Six out of ten women were fearful in their own areas.

Source: Compiled from Statistics Canada, Nov. 1993.

The VAW as well as the GSS surveys were able to bring out the facts of violence against women in Canada in the open. The Victimization Surveys were able to address a problem, which the official statistics were able to show. It became evident that a great deal of crime was not reported or even under reported. The surveys were able to instill hope amongst the women, as victims realized that there were others who had experienced the same problem as them. This helped several organisations and the civil society to help victims to speak about their trauma and creating further awareness in the process.

Crime Against Women Province - Wise

As there is a spatial difference in crime between Developed and Developing countries, there is also difference in levels of crime in the different provinces. The crime rates are dependent on the population in a province. For example even if there is average crime, a small province may seem to have a very high crime rate. Table 3.19 gives a holistic picture of the crime scenario in the different provinces in Canada.

Table 3.19
Crime Rate and Population in the Province 1994

Povince	*violent crime rate ('00000)*	*per cent of population*
Alberta	1050	9.55
British Columbia	1464	12.89
Manitoba	1600	3.97
New Brunswick	935	2.66
New Foundland	1102	2.04
Nova Scotia	1088	3.29
Ontario	994	38.43
Prince Edward Island	765	0.47
Quebec	730	25.6
Saskatchewan	1208	3.57
North West Territories	5543	0.22
Yukon Territory	2714	0.1

Source: Compiled from Canadian Crime Statistics, 1994.

From table 3.19 it is evident that the highest and most violent crimes take place in the North West Territories, followed by Yukon and Manitoba. This is a classic example of where Statistics can misguide and paint a false picture. From the column of percentages of population it becomes evident that NorthWest Territories, Yukon and Manitoba has one of the lowest population in the country. In this case the crime rate is high in North West Territories inspite of the low population. As far as the actual numbers of crime is concerned crimes against women namely data on sexual assault gives an insight into the situation of violence against women. Diagram 3.9 shows the offences of sexual assault in the different provinces in Canada.

Diagram 3.9

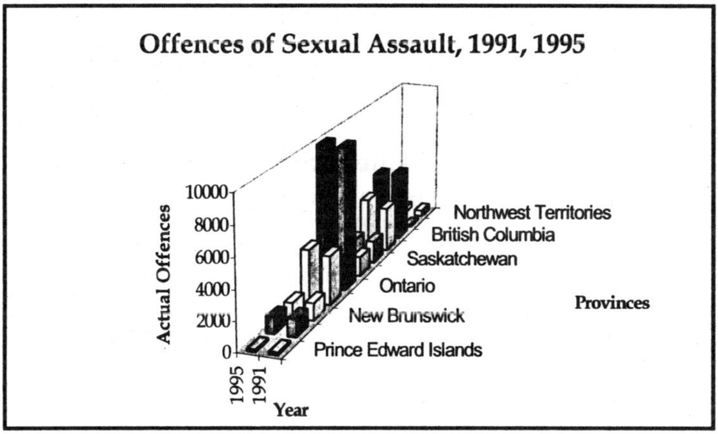

Source: Compiled From Juristat, 1994, 1995.

Hence from the diagram it becomes evident that Ontario followed by British Columbia and Alberta have the highest number of sexual assault cases. It is important to note that Ontario also has the highest population and also has the largest number of industries, hence, there is a large population which promotes crime. One commendable feature is that actual offences have gone down in 1995 since 1991.

Crime in Cities

Urban areas have the largest populations as well as the maximum vices. Cities are a nerve center for a multitude of social and economic problems. People who migrate to the cities from rural areas come with ambitions to be successful in life and often in the process are detached from their families and get assimilated in the various urban ways of life, which involves anonymity. As developed by Wirth (1938) urbanization the increased size, density and heterogeneity of a population leads to the weakening of interpersonal ties, primary social relations and normative consensus, with the ultimate consequences of individual alienation, and an increased prevalence of deviant behaviors (Fisher 1975). The youth in an urban area are usually less assimilated in society, and hence they face further anonymity. Table 3.20 shows violent crimes for major census metropolitan areas in 1995.

Table 3.20
Crime Rate For Major Census Metropolitan Areas (1995)

City	*Violent crime*	*Sexual assault*
Vancouver	1300	87
Winnipeg	1200	62
Ottawa	1000	90
Toronto	900	63
Montreal	850	46
Quebec	580	40

Source: Juristat, 1995.

Vancouver has the most violent crimes (in British Columbia) while Ontario has the highest number of sexual offences; Toronto has a much lower rate of violent incidences. However, it is for the case of all violent incidents and not gender specific. From data published by Statistics Canada it is also evident that Ontario has the highest adult population above the age of 18 years. Using a correlation the rate of violent crime and population has a relation which is evident in Diagram 3.10.

Diagram 3.10

Correlation between Population and Sexual Assault in Cities 1995

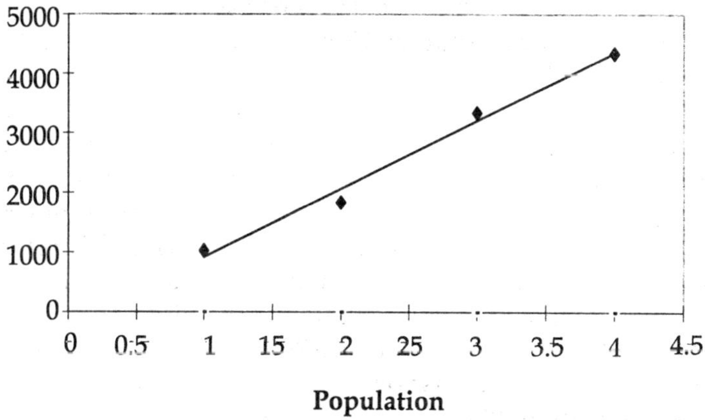

Source: Compiled By Author.

A strong positive correlation is evident hence, in the urban areas in Canada due to increase in the population, urban pressures, result in urban crisis and indirectly lead to increase in cases of sexual assault. In the next chapter it will become more evident whether crime reporting has increased or actual incidences increased.

Canada is a multicultural, multiracial country, which has experienced rapid urbanization. However, along with rapid rise of population growth, there has been an increase in vices in society. It is important to note that the definition of urbanization in Canada is different to the urbanization in India. In the Indian context, urbanization is escalation of population, an exodus from rural to urban areas. However, urbanization in Canada is not related to population growth but is based on civic amenities, infrastructural facilities which make a place urban.

Women have a high rate of victimization, as the number of reporting is very high due to awareness amongst women and level of literacy. In the recent past, the two victimization surveys have further been able to inculcate hope and better awareness amongst women, although the figures are rather alarming. However as the virus of violence against women has been identified, Canadian society has been able to take steps to combat such offences in a more decisive manner which will be studied in the chapter on Toronto.It is heartening to see that in 1995, figures, crime rates have declined in Canada in the case of violent crimes by (-4 per cent) according to Statistics Canada. The present study involves a comparative study between a city in a Developed country and a city in a Developing country. The socio – economic environment in both the situations is entirely different. Hence the case studies on Calcutta and Toronto is diverse. Canada on the one hand has a low population density of 7.38 persons per square kilometer, while India has a population density of 316 (in 2000) persons per square kilometers. Hence the two cases are showing extreme featues of urbanisation. The Canadian society is more literate; 43 per cent of the people have a university degree, while in India the total literacy is 52.21 per cent. Due to this the status of women is also different.

On the other hand we can also say that the crime scenario has certain similarities in both countries in terms of the positive correlation between population and crime and in the ever spiralling graph of crimes against women. The next chapter gives a detail of the crime situation in a Developing country with a case study of Calcutta city.

References

1. D.J. Evans and D.T. Herbert, *the Geography of Crime (Routlege : London, 1989), p. 27.*
2. W.Walter Menninger, *Crime in Urban Society (Combridge, 1970)*
3. Ronald H. Beattie, *The Sources of Criminal Statistics*, The Annuls of the American Academy of Political and Social Science, Philadelphia, 1941 Sept, Vol. 217, p. 20.
4. S. Venugopala Rao, *Facets of Crime in india*, Bombay, Allied Publishers, 1967, p. 4.

5. R. Ghadially ed. *Women in Indian Society: A Reader*, New Delhi, 1988, p. 156.
6. A. Sivamurthy, *Indian Journal of Criminology*, Vol. 4, No. 1, Jan 1986, p. 17.
7. *Ibid.*
8. Rehha Pandey, *Indian Journal of Society Work*, Vol. 48, 1987, p, 103.
9. A. Sivamurthy, *Indian Journal of Criminology*, Vol 1.4, No. 1, Jan, 1986, p. 17.
10. Alan F.J. Artibise, *Daedalus: Journal of the American Academy of Arts and Sciences* (1988) fall, Vol. 117 No.4, p. 237.
11. Timothy F. Hartnagel and G.Won Lee, *Crime in Canadian Society*, (1990), p. 176.
12. *Women in Canada:A Statistical Report*, Third Edition, Statistics Canada,1995, p. 10.
13. T.R. Balakrishnan and K. Selvanthan, *Ethnic Residential Segregation in Metropolitan Canada*, 1990 p. 1.
14. Gill Valentine, *Area* 24(1), p. 383, 1992.
15. Bob Granger, *Crime Counts*, Toronto, 1996 p. 36.
16. T.R. Balekrishnan and K. Selvanthen, *Ethnic Residential Segregation in Metropolitan Canada,* 1990, p. 1.
17. R.A. Silverman, *Crime in Canadian Society*, Toronto 1991, p. 173.
18. Bob. Granger, Crime Counts, Toronto, 1996, p. 36.
19. Rick Linden, Ed., Criminology, Toronto, 1996, p. 79.

4

Crime in Kolkata City

Multitude, misery, dilapidation, violence... Kolkata, an urban monster, a city of hell... We have heard too much about these clichés broadcast by the international media moved by the lame beggars outside five - star hotels, by the scenes in the streets, by the tragedies of recent history.[1] Kolkata has been labeled as the greatest urban disaster of all times. The city is a typical example of a primate city. Apart from size, Kolkata is indeed Bengal in a cultural and economic sense. It is most unlikely that Kolkata's present preeminent position will be altered in the foreseeable future.[2]

The city is characterized by widespread human poverty ever increasing employment, child labor, and wide socio-economic disparities, a large immigrant population. Kolkata has become the city of refuge in the last fifty years. Due to the large migrant and refugee population (Kolkata due to its physical constraints which has prevented its lateral growth) the city has gone through an economic crisis; a crisis in housing, employment, transport, water etc. like any other city in Afro-Asia. Hence, the crisis in Kolkata is deep rooted in its physical, socio-cultural, economic, environmental and politico-administrative city structures. The city portrays a physical crisis, in the sense that very limited space is available for its areal growth.

The housing crisis is the most common as in other cities in South Asia. The fast growing slums and squatters are the manifestations of such crisis. Nearly one - third of the metropolitan population live in over crowded settlements of single storey hutments of temporary construction. About 1.8 million people in the city proper and three million people in the whole metropolis do not have adequate shelter and live in bustees (shanty settlements). They constitute more than half of the population and about 58 per cent of the total metropolitan bustee population.[3]

Given such tremendous space constraints and virtual non-availability of any scope for physical expansion there is a severe economic crisis. This complete degradation and dilapidation of the city has even eroded the traditional genteel Bengali disposition towards women as the most respected and sheltered segment of the social fabric and made them the targets of the most heinous forms of social attack.

The present study is based on primary data collected from the police stations in Kolkata over a period of seven years namely, 1991 to 1996. Some data of 1981 was taken to see the decade change in crime, which is due to the socio-economic factors prevailing in the city. In other words the study is based on the fact that change in environment leads to an increase or decrease in the crime graph. The empirical study takes care of the demographic and socio - cultural variables of spatial and temporal aspects of the city along with crime. The data on crime has been limited to the First Information Report (FIR) of 1981 and the Crime Index of (1991 - 1996) as this seemed to be the most exhaustive source of information. Besides this a content analysis was also done of the widely circulated "Statesman" for the above mentioned years. The police records for crime data are neither a model of accuracy, nor is grossly inaccurate and unusable. A total of nine parameters of crime have been used to emphasize the magnitude of crime against women in the city.

The information available in the FIR as well as the Crime Index in most cases were found to be incomplete. At several instances the name of the victim was not mentioned, nor the time of incidence or the address or age of the victim etc. While the researcher was trying to analyse, it was quite incomprehensible as to why the information was acceptable by the police management to remain incomplete. Possibly the blanks and the empty spaces helped in preparing the vortex of corruption. In the case of the data of 1981, there was non-availability of data from some police stations as the researcher was informed that the one of the floods in Kolkata had destroyed several of the police station documents.

Inspite of these constraints, each case was read with care. Hence at several instances while reading the case history of cases of suicide, several were placed under the heading of abetment to commit suicide; while cases which were booked under several sections, the highest section was used to record the case; Besides this misappropriation of Stridhan has been included in cases of section 498A (harassment or cruelty); Through this study it was evident that there is more exhaustive data of each case with the prisons on individual offenders rather than information available at the police station.

The present study involves the studying and identifying the dominant factors explaining geography of crimes against women and the emerging spatial patterns in the city. In other words the study is the socio- spatial - temporal analysis of crime against women in Kolkata. The study involves:

- Areas with higher density of population and with greater urban deprivation shows higher rate of total crimes against women in the city than low-density areas.
- The rate of total urban crime against women is more in the low-rent residential areas than in the high rent residential areas within the city.
- Higher the male population in a city, greater are the number of crimes. Also the higher the male illiteracy, higher the number of offenses; Higher male non-workers higher the incidence of crime.

- Certain types of crime are more prominent in specific areas in a city. However, the total crimes against women are more in the urban periphery or suburbs than in the city core.
- There exists a correlation between time period and the incidence of crime. The highest incidence of crimes takes place during particular season and also during certain hours during the day.

Crime in the City: The Macro Study

A research study on women in Kolkata showed:

RESEARCH ON KOLKATA

Table 4.1

In percentage

Physical Violence	Sexual Violence	Either/Or	Both	No Violence
29	15	79	35	21
83% said they sustained injuries from the violence				
		Resisting		
Do nothing 14	Avoiding husbands 17	alone 32	With help 32	
Very few retaliated with violence				
Women leave men	Men leave women	Live with husband	Violence continues	
67 83	50	50		

Source: Statesman, 9 March 1997.

This study aptly proves the gravity of the situation in Kolkata. The crime data collected from police headquarters as shown in table 4.2 is data assimilated with minor variations as mentioned earlier.

Table 4.2
Crime in Kolkata

Crime	*1981*	*1991*	*1992*	*1993*	*1994*	*1995*	*1996*
Murder	14	26	17	14	10	20	12
Molestation	92	90	116	109	163	138	138
Kidnapping	78	71	92	96	75	85	101
Rape	5	27	39	34	36	54	28
Dowry Death	0	0	7	4	9	11	7
Eve-Teasing	5	0	0	0	0	0	1
Cruelty	1	51	133	131	137	111	108
Attempt to murder	0	0	15	0	11	11	9
Abetment to suicide	0	64	27	27	30	28	25
Total	**195**	**329**	**446**	**415**	**471**	**458**	**429**

Source: Compiled by Author from Police Records, Kolkata.

From the above data it is evident that there has been a steady increase in the crime since 1981. The increase between 1991 and 1992 has been phenomenal over 35.56 per cent. However, the 1992 and 1993 data has shown a downward trend. The decrease has been by - 6.95 per cent. After 1993, 1994 has shown the highest ever crimes of 471 incidents and then a decrease. Infact 1996 data shows a negative trend of - 3.81 per cent over five years. Diagram 4.1 shows that with escalation of crime there is equal increase in the population.

Diagram 4.1
Uniformity of Population and Crime in the Police Stations in Kolkata 1996

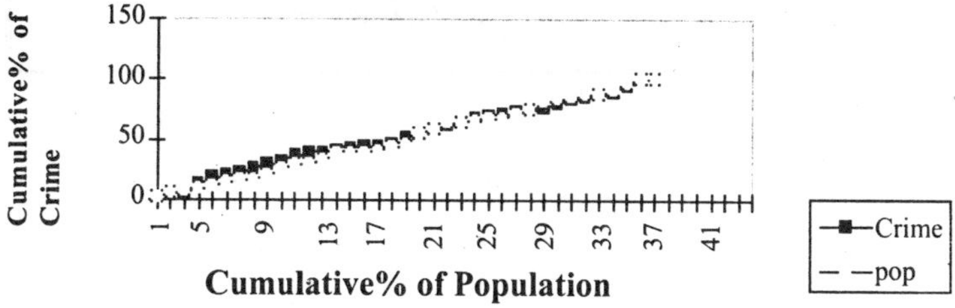

Source: Compiled By Author.

Map 4.1
Distribution of Incidence of Crime in Kolkata 1991

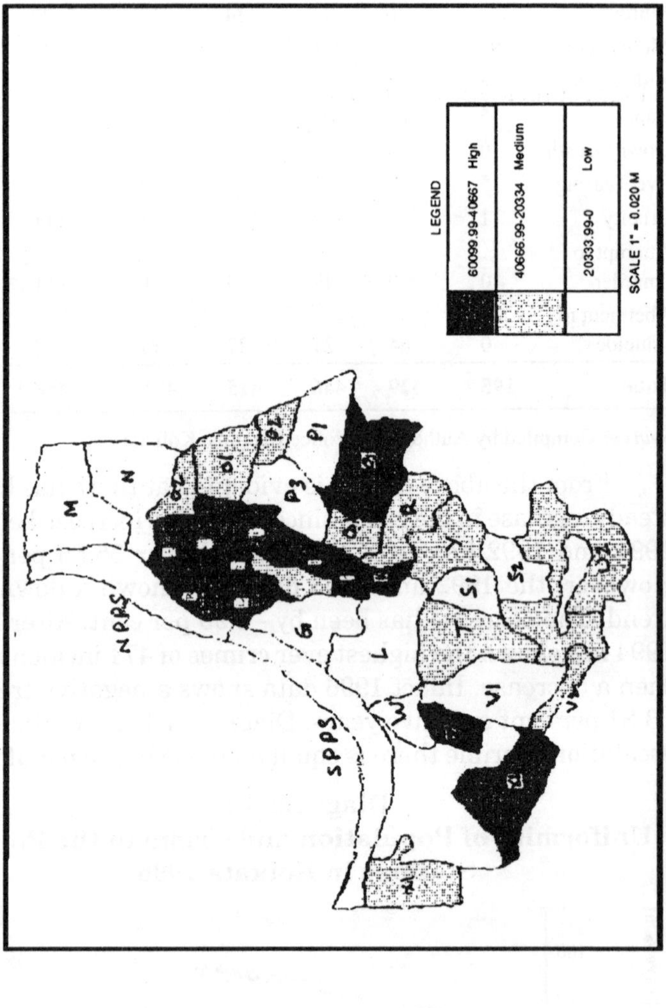

Source: Compiled by Author From Police Records, Kolkata.

The eight parameters of crime were taken as it was felt that in the Indian Penal Code, these crimes most aptly expressed the gravity, of the situation of crimes against women. While talking about the background of the city of Kolkata, it is necessary to talk about the administrative structure as well. The city has five police districts for convenience in police administration with a total of 36 police stations (in 1996). Some of these police stations were formed way back in the late nineteenth century. In 1981 there were 34 police stations. In 1987, Tangra was formed and in 1994, Garden Reach police station was sub-divided to form Taratola. From the Census records of 1981 and 1991 it is evident that the Eastern Suburban Division has the largest area of 22.3 sq. kms. and the north - central part of the city is densely populated, especially areas of Shyampukur (Sec. A), Jorabagan (Sec. B), Burtolla (Sec. C), Burrabazar (Sec. D), Jorasanko (Sec. E), Amherst Street (Sec. F), Muchipara (Sec. I), Taltolla (Sec. J). Amongst the core areas of the city are Taltolla (Sec. J) and Muchipara (Sec. I) and parts of Hare Street (Sec. G) and Park Street (Sec. K). This region also forms the main CBD in Kolkata. Three of the peripheral areas with high population density are Ekbalpur (Sec. Z), Taratolla (Sec. X2) and Tangra (Sec. Q2). Earlier (i.e. before 1987) Tangra was a part of Entally.

As mentioned earlier, the large population density is in the CBD area. The main old CBD area was Muchipara (Sec.I). There are shops belonging to goldsmiths, the Kole and the Baithak Khana Market. The newer and a small part of the contemporary cosmopolitan area is Taltolla, with the now dilapidated (older) Hogg Market, the New Market area with its cinema halls and the older colonial buildings. Parts of Hare Street (Sec. G) has the office area, the secretariat and police Headquarters etc. and so also the Park street area (Sec. K).

While still talking about crime, it is imperative to study the map of Kolkata. The bustees and the squatter settlements of Kolkata are in the Eastern Suburban Division, with another concentrated in the North Division in the police stations of Cossipore (Sec. M) and Chitpur (Sec. N). Besides this there are also areas in Watgunge (Sec W) and the South Port (Sec. SPPS) area where there are bustees.

The area of the Eastern Suburban Division is an outer industrial belt. The bustees are characterized by tight clustering of tiny huts normally made up of walls of bamboo frames with mud plastered on them having roofs of corrugated tin or other cheap material like the tiles. The basic amenities of drainage, sewerage, water supply, electricity etc. are lacking, making these slums highly unhygienic places to live in. Such bustees have been the breeding ground of anti - social elements and the foci of many endemic and epidemic diseases.[4]

The demographic trend of Kolkata is that the city is made up of a large number of immigrants. In 1960 - 61 the total number was 87790 and in 1970 - 71 it was 15140 (Racine, 1986). Hence, there has been a constant influx of population, but no physical growth of the city. The maps of 1991 and 1996 shows that the concentration of crime has been moving. At first glance it is obvious that in the Eastern Suburban area, there is a high incidence of crime. However, in all the three different years, the focus has changed. In 1981, Q1 i.e. the Entally area had the highest incidence of crime, followed by Burtolla (Sec.C) and Beliaghata (Sec. P1). However, in 1991, the scenario has changed to the Beniapukur area (Sec. R), with the highest incidence of crime. This area is followed by Lake (Sec.V2), Taltolla (Sec. J), Shyampukur (Sec. A), Ekbalpur (Sec. Z). In this year we find that in 1981 Entally had the largest incidence of crime. However, this area was subdivided into two areas (Sec Q1 and Sec. Q2) in 1987. However, in 1996, the Eastern Suburban Division has more incidences of crimes (as seen in Appendix 1). The highest incidence is in Beliaghata (Sec. P1) followed by Watgunge (Sec W), and Narkeldanga (Sec. P3) and Beniapukur (Sec. R).

Hence it is evident that areas like the Eastern Suburban Division which although, has an average to low density population, has pockets of very high density especially in the form of bustees as seen in the maps. The population density mentions that Sec, Z (namely Ekbalpur) has an average crime with a high density of population; same is the case with Taltolla (Sec. J) which has average to high crime as seen in table 4.3. Burtolla (Sec.C) also has a relatively high incidence of crime. Hence, we find that where there is high density of population there is high to more than average incidence of crime.

While studying the table on crime in different administrative divisions in 1981, 1991,1996 it becomes evident that in recent years, the Eastern Suburban Division is showing a high incidence of crime. The highest incidence of crime since 1991 has been in 1993. Ever since 1993 we find that crime in this Eastern Suburban Division has gone down. It is important to note that the area under the Eastern Suburban Division is maximum of 22.3 kms, as against North Division which is 8.11 kms, Central Division of 11.31 kms, South Division of 18.5 kms and the Port Division of 15.25 kms.

In 1996, we can see under the different heads of crime reported in the different areas of the city. Different types of crime are area specific i.e. they are not uniformly committed throughout the city. In this section we notice that the highest incidences of all cases are seen in Beliaghata or P1, followed by Watgunge (Sec.W) and Narkeldanga (Sec. P3) and Beniapukur (Sec. R). Out of these four areas, Sec P1, P3 and R belong to the Eastern Suburban Division.

Watgunge is a mixed area with smuggled goods market better known as the Fancy Market; A red light area in Munshigunge etc. and a large bustee area. The Beliaghata or Sec P1 area has large slums like Chawalputti, Mia Bagan bustee, small-scale industries and two large markets the Sarkar Bazar and the Rashmoni Bazaar Market. In case of

Table 4.3
Crime in Different Administrative Divisions, 1981, 1991-1996

Administrative Division	*P.S.Code*	*Area (Kms)*	*1981*	*1991*	*1992*	*1993*	*1994*	*1995*	*1996*
North Division		**8.11**	**45**	**56**	**79**	**65**	**109**	**87**	**76**
Shyampukur	A	1.5	9	15	16	4	15	7	8
Jorabagan	B	1.5	1	8	9	9	12	9	7
Burtolla	C	1.03	16	9	15	16	33	27	16
Amherst St.	F	1.5	N.A.	8	12	11	18	9	14
Cossipore	M	1.08	10	9	17	15	18	21	18
Chitpur	N	1.5	9	7	10	10	13	14	13
Central Division									
Burrabazar	D	1	4	10	3	3	8	10	11
Jorasanko	E	2.4	N.A.	11	16	15	18	11	22
Hare St.	G	2.56	4	9	5	4	6	4	4
Bowbazar	H	1.25	3	9	8	7	10	15	7
Muchipara	I	2.5	8	10	10	10	11	5	3
Taltolla	J	1.6	N.A.	17	26	20	29	16	14
South Division		**18.5**	**48**	**91**	**121**	**91**	**95**	**114**	**95**
Park St.	K	1.75	4	10	3	3	8	10	11
Hastings	L	2.5	5	2	2	3	1	6	3
Ballygunge	S1	2.5	11	4	3	1	6	6	2
Gariahat	S2	1.25	N.A.	4	14	8	4	10	8

Bhowanipur	T	1.5	7	13	28	16	23	27	12
Tollygunge	U1	1.75	N.A.	9	12	8	13	22	14
Lake	U2	2	5	19	18	8	8	6	12
Alipur	V1	1.5	5	8	6	6	7	3	10
New Alipur	V2	1.75	6	11	9	12	10	9	6
Karaya	Y	2	9	11	13	20	11	14	17
Eastern Suburban Division22.3		**62**	**69**	**109**	**145**	**122**	**139**	**131**	
Manicktola	O1	2	4	9	14	18	18	16	18
Ultadanga	O2	2	5	7	11	9	10	10	19
Beliaghata	P1	2	14	6	11	14	12	13	26
Phulbagan	P2	1.25	N.A.	6	8	13	10	15	9
Narkeldanga	P3	2.55	8	5	13	23	25	44	22
Entally	Q1	3.25	20	9	12	25	20	8	7
Tangra	Q2	2.75	11	7	9	18	16	22	8
Beniapukur	R	6.5	N.A.	20	31	25	11	11	22
Port Division		**15.25**	**21**	**47**	**69**	**55**	**63**	**57**	**66**
Watgunge	W	1.5	4	11	8	15	20	18	24
Garden Reach	X1	2.5	9	12	17	14	1	5	7
Ekbalpur	Z	2.75	5	16	31	19	27	23	13
South Port	SPPS	5	2	6	10	6	13	7	16
North Port	NPPS	2	1	2	3	1	1	1	3
Taratola	X2	1.5					1	3	3
Total		**72.37**	**195**	**329**	**446**	**415**	**471**	**458**	**429**

Source: Police Headquarters, Kolkata.

Table 4.4
Crime in Different Administrative Divisions, 1996

Administrative Division	*302*	*376*	*363-366*	*498A*	*306*	*354*	*294, 509*	*304B*	*307*	*Total*
Administrative Division										
Shyampukur			3		2	2		1		8
Jorabagan	1		4	1		1				7
Burtolla		1	4	5		6				16
Amherst St.	1		6	2	1	3		1		14
Cossipore			7	4	2	5				18
Chitpur			2	2	6	2		1		13
Central Division										
Burrabazar			2	4		3			2	11
Jorasanko	2	5	6	5	1	3				22
Hare St.		1	1			2				4
Bowbazar			2	2		2		1		7
Muchipara		1				2				3
Taltolla	1		2	4		7				13
South Division										
Park St.			3	2		6				11
Hastings		1	2							3
Ballygunge						2				2
Gariahat	1	2		5						8

Bhowanipur			2	2	1	6		1		12
Tollygunge			2	9		2		1		14
Lake	1		2	3		6				12
Alipur		1	6			3				10
New Alipur				4		2				6
Karaya			5	4	1	6			1	17
Eastern Suburban Division										
Manicktola		1	3	4	2	8				18
Ultadanga		3	3	4	1	7	1			19
Beliaghata		1	4	9	3	7			2	26
Phulbagan			1	3		3		1	1	9
Narkeldanga		1	5	7	1	8				22
Entally	1		4	1					1	7
Tangra		2	1	4	1					8
Beniapukur	1	3	5	6		7				22
Port Division										
Watgunge		1	7	6		10				24
Garden Reach	2		3			1			1	7
Ekbalpur		2	1	4	1	4			1	13
South Port	1	1	2	2	1	9				16
North Port		1	1			1				3
Taltolla				1		3				4
Total	**12**	**28**	**101**	**108**	**25**	**138**	**1**	**7**	**9**	**429**

Source: Police Headquarters, Kolkata.

the Beniapukur area (Sec R), this is a mixed religious - cultural area, better known as Park Circus with a large Muslim, Christian and Hindu population. There is a rail line passing this area and small-scale industries in the form of leather tanneries. Crime is high in this area, as there are a large number of women's institutions such as Lady Brabourne College, National Medical College and working women's hostel. The Narkeldanga area or (Sec P3) also has a mixed ethnic population. This is also part of the older residential area of Kolkata. The area is congested due to the Sealdah station and the various railway quarters. While taking the individual crimes, murder is highest in the Jorasanko area. However, till date the incidence of murder has been relatively low.

As for the case of rape, the largest number of such cases is also in the Jorasanko area. This area has old Bania houses in Ahiritola and Sova Bazaar. There are small shops for woodwork etc. and commercial area along with a dairy market. However adjoining this area are some red light areas of Burtolla (the Sonagachi) which is the road opposite to Jorabagan. The red-light area is also known as Rambagan. Hence, several girls were recovered from brothels and some were also kidnapped and raped.

In kidnapping, the highest number of offenses were in Cossipore (Sec M) an outer industrial belt with a gun and shell factory, mixed ethnic population and large bustee areas; followed by Amherst Street (Sec F). This area is also known as the College area with the Presidency College, Kolkata University, Sanskrit College, Hindu School, City College etc. just to name a few. Besides this, is a mixed ethnic residential area as well with Hindu and Muslim population. Jorasanko (Sec E) again has a high incidence of kidnapping possibly in the red light area. Another notorious area is Watgung (Sec W) and Alipur (Sec V1). Watgunge as already mentioned has a large slum population and is a mixed area with the Munshigunge red-light area and the docks nearby. Hence this is not an ideal residential area. Docks have always been

Map 4.2
Distribution of Incidence of Crime in Kolkata 1996

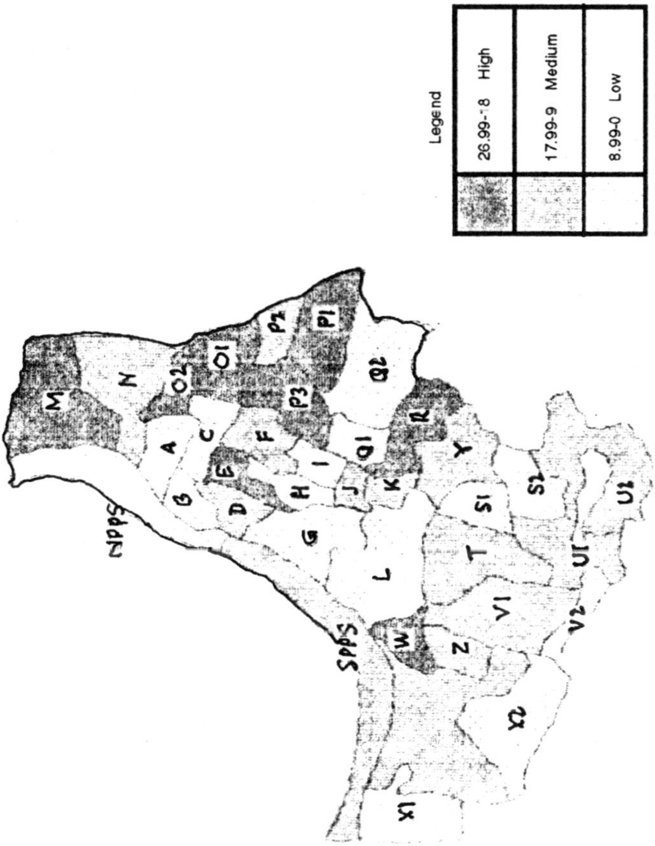

Source: Compiled by Author from Police Records

known as the breeding ground of anti-social activity. Alipur has a very low-density population with large open expanses with hospitals such as Command Hospital, Birla Heart Research Center, Kolkata Hospital etc. This particular area goes against the objective theory of high population density and high incidence of crime.

Cruelty is uniformly found in all police stations, like kidnapping. The highest incidence of harassment cases is in Beliaghata (Sec P1) and Tollygunge (Sec V1). Followed by Narkeldanga (Sec P3), Beniapukur (Sec R) and Watgunge (Sec W). Tollygunge (SecU1) like all the other areas has large slums with a large refugee population and the Lokarmaat red-light area. Hence we see that cruelty or cases of harassment reporting are more in the low class residential areas. Medium incidence of reporting of crimes of harassment is in Burtolla, Jorasanko and Gariahat area.

Abetment to commit suicide also comes under cruelty to a certain extent as because of excessive torture the victims try to find an easy solution for themselves. The largest number of such cases is in the Chitpur (outer industrial area) as discussed earlier followed by Beliaghata. However, the largest number of such incidents is in the North Division and in the case of cruelty, it is the Eastern Suburban Division.

Molestation is again uniformly reported in all parts of the city. The largest incidence is in South Port area, Watgunge, Maniktolla and Ultadanga, Beliaghata, Beniapukur, Taltolla. Again the reporting is mostly from industrial areas where there are workshops and small factories as in the Eastern Suburban subdivision and the Cossipore area.

Eve- teasing cases have not been registered inspite of sections under the Indian Penal Code. Gestures and songs and words of sexual connotation are not registered as the police often feel that they can register as the crimes are of non serious nature. However, while researching the description of one case in the Crime Index was definitely one

Table 4.5
Relative Speciality Crime in Kolkata 1996

Section IPC	Crime	363-366	498A	376	per cent Crime	percentage 363-366	498A	376	Location Quotient Kidnap	Cruelty	Rape
P.S.											
Alipur	10	6	0	3	2.331	0.6	0	0.3	2.6087	0	0.9375
Amherst St.	14	6	2	3	3.2634	0.42857	0.143	0.214	1.86335	0.5714	0.6696
Ballygunge	2	0	0	2	0.4662	0	0	1	0	0	3.125
Beliaghata	26	4	9	7	6.0606	0.15385	0.346	0.269	0.6689	1.3846	0.8413
Beniapukur	22	5	6	7	5.1282	0.22727	0.273	0.318	0.98814	1.0909	0.9943
Bhowanipur	12	2	2	6	2.7972	0.16667	0.167	0.5	0.72464	0.6667	1.5625
Bowbazar	7	2	2	2	1.6317	0.28571	0.286	0.286	1.24224	1.1429	0.8929
Burrabazar	11	2	4	3	2.5641	0.18182	0.364	0.273	0.79051	1.4545	0.8523
Burtolla	16	4	5	6	3.7296	0.25	0.313	0.375	1.08696	1.25	1.1719
Chitpur	13	2	2	2	3.0303	0.15385	0.154	0.154	0.6689	0.6154	0.4808
Cossipore	18	7	4	5	4.1958	0.38889	0.222	0.278	1.69082	0.8889	0.8681
Ekbalpur	13	1	4	4	3.0303	0.07692	0.308	0.308	0.33445	1.2308	0.9615
Entally	7	4	1	0	1.6317	0.57143	0.143	0	2.48447	0.5714	0
Garden Reach	7	3	0	1	1.6317	0.42857	0	0.143	1.86335	0	0.4464
Gariahat	8	0	5	0	1.8648	0	0.625	0	0	2.5	0
Hare St.	4	1	0	2	0.9324	0.25	0	0.5	1.08696	0	1.5625

Hastings	3	2	0	0	0.6993	0.66667	0	0	2.89855	0	0
Jorabagan	7	4	1	1	1.6317	0.57143	0.143	0.143	2.48447	0.5714	0.4464
Jorasanko	22	6	5	3	5.1282	0.27273	0.227	0.136	1.18577	0.9091	0.4261
Karaya	17	5	4	6	3.9627	0.29412	0.235	0.353	1.27877	0.9412	1.1029
Lake	12	2	3	6	2.7972	0.16667	0.25	0.5	0.72464	1	1.5625
Manicktola	18	3	4	8	4.1958	0.16667	0.222	0.444	0.72464	0.8889	1.3889
Muchipara	3	0	0	2	0.6993	0	0	0.667	0	0	2.0833
Narkeldanga	22	5	7	8	5.1282	0.22727	0.318	0.364	0.98814	1.2727	1.1364
New Alipur	6	0	4	2	1.3986	0	0.667	0.333	0	2.6667	1.0417
North Port	3	1	0	1	0.6993	0.33333	0	0.333	1.44928	0	1.0417
Park St.	11	3	2	6	2.5641	0.27273	0.182	0.545	1.18577	0.7273	1.7045
Phulbagan	9	1	3	3	2.0979	0.11111	0.333	0.333	0.48309	1.3333	1.0417
Shyampukur	8	3	0	2	1.8648	0.375	0	0.25	1.63043	0	0.7813
South Port	16	2	2	9	3.7296	0.125	0.125	0.563	0.54348	0.5	1.7578
Taltola	13	2	4	7	3.0303	0.15385	0.308	0.538	0.6689	1.2308	1.6827
Taratola	4	0	1	3	0.9324	0	0.25	0.57	0	1	2.3438
Tangra	8	1	4	0	1.8648	0.125	0.5	0	0.54348	2	0
Tollygunge	14	2	9	2	3.2634	0.14286	0.643	0.143	0.62112	2.5714	0.4464
Ultadanga	19	3	4	7	4.4289	0.15789	0.211	0.368	0.6865	0.8421	1.1513
Watgunge	24	7	6	10	5.5944	0.29167	0.25	0.417	1.26812	1	1.3021
Total	**429**	**91**	**108**	**138**	**100**	**0.21212**	**0.252**	**0.322**		**1.007**	**1.0052**

Source: Compiled by author.

that could have been placed under eve-teasing and not molestation. Hence, the policemen at the police stations are not aware or they are insensitive to register such cases.

Attempt to murder and dowry death cases are few and maximum concentration for the former is in the Eastern Suburban Division area.

Through the method of location quotient it will be clearer to understand a particular crime occurrence in a specific area as compared to the surrounding areas. In this case as in table showing crime specialty, it is possible to see the visual images of crime in a city. At a glance we can see that maximum concentration of kidnapping is in the Hastings area as compared to the total kidnapping and crime in the city. The index used is

$$\text{L.Q.} = \frac{\dfrac{\text{Percentage of kidnapping to total crime in a Section}}{\text{Total percentage of crime in that section}}}{\dfrac{\text{Percentage to total kidnapping in the city}}{\text{Total percentage of crime}}}$$

Hence, Entally and Jorabagan, and Alipur follow Hastings. The deductions here are more accurate while talking on a comparative scale. In case of cruelty or Sec. 498A, the largest concentration as compared to the total crime of the area of the city is New Alipur, Tollygunge, followed by Gariahat. In this case the earlier view that crime takes place in congested, low class residential area fails. However, the next three areas of Burrabazar, Beliaghata and Phulbagan aptly elaborates the previous theory that where there are slums or low cost housing and congestion, there is more crime in the form of cruelty and harassment. However, this form of crime has been fairly uniform all over the city and must be only a fraction of the actual number of incidences as women often feel hesitant to report such cases to the police. In the case of rape, the concentration is highest in Ballygunge, Taratolla and Muchipara, followed by South Port, Park Street and Taltolla.

Most of these above-mentioned areas have large slums, and red-light areas except for Ballygunge and Park Street. Ballygunge is a middle class to high-class residential area; while Park Street has mostly offices, restaurants and high residential areas. The incidence of rapes in both these areas, is average, however, it is high as compared to the other crimes in the area. The location quotient of only three crimes could be calculated due to the uniform reporting in all the police stations. Hence through the location quotient method, it is possible to study the relativity of crime in relation to the larger environment, namely, the city.

Theoretical Explanation of Crime in the City

While understanding the spatial distribution of crime it is also important to study some of the contributions in Environmental Criminology which is also known as the Chicago School. This theory is based on the observations of city life, for the various kinds of social phenomenon like crime, and deviance. One of the most noticeable patterns observed by social scientists at the University of Chicago was that the city area is inhabited predominantly by the poor, by recent immigrants, and by ethnic minorities, displayed high rates of non-conformity. Human ecology likens human communities to plant and animal communities and in the process, makes two simple observations: racial, class and other groups affect one another's daily lives; and these groups are also affected by a variety of conditions in the urban environment, including land use, property values, the location of industry, and natural boundaries such as rivers, highways, and railroad lines.

In particular, two central and interrelated concepts from the science of plant ecology were adapted and applied to the sociological analysis of city life. The first was the notion of symbiosis and the second was the idea of invasion, dominance and succession (Vold and Bernard, 1986). Symbiosis refers to a condition of mutual interdependence among organisms in an environment that is necessary for their survival.[5]

The growth process of a city takes place by invasion, dominance and succession like any species on earth. There is a forward invasion which is followed by retreat. New parts of the city of today gradually become older parts, which ultimately dilapidate and become the older part of the city. According to Chicago ecologists, land is most expensive at the core of the city. Only commerce, industry, and government can afford the high prices there. They dominate the core by erecting banks, stores, theaters, hotels, public transportation centers, and government offices. The band immediately adjacent to the central business district is the transitional zone. Located next to the ever-expanding industrial core, the transitional zone's property values are sharply eroded. Since property owners believe that buildings in this sector will eventually be torn down to make room for industrial and commercial expansion, they do not maintain the buildings. Residential areas in this zone deteriorate as higher - status residents flee to the suburbs. Their low rents make these dilapidated and run down dwellings attractive to improvised ethnic and immigrant populations.

The third zone contains relatively inexpensive two and three family dwellings inhabited by members of the working class, who had previously migrated outward from the transitional zone. In the fourth zone are the more expensive apartments and single-family dwellings occupied by the middle class. Small business and professional offices are also present in this ring. In the outer most sector are the residences of the more affluent commuter population. This outlying suburban area has more recently become the contemporary Satellite City.

Each of the five zones contains natural areas. In the transitional band, the natural areas are ghettos. In the third and fourth zones, the natural areas are communities united by ethnic or religious ties. Often physical boundaries such as railway tracks, rivers, roads separate these areas from other parts of the city.[6]

It is believed that the industrial zone with all its congestion, squatter settlements etc. is the breeding ground for crime. This is like vicious circle as shown in Diagram 4.2.

Diagram 4.2

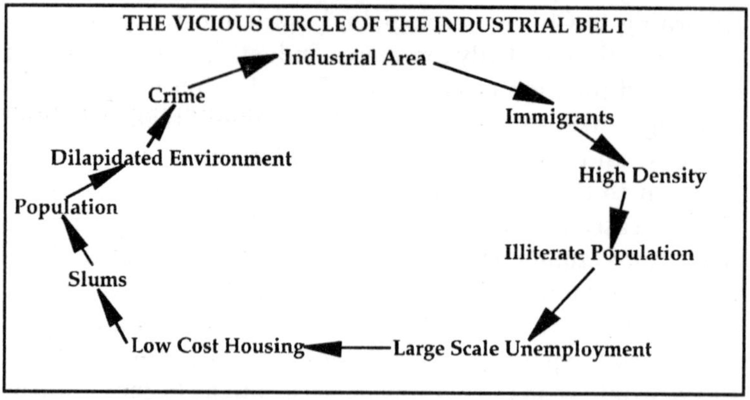

Where there is an industrial zone, there are both skilled and unskilled labors, who come as immigrants from the hinterland or from the neighboring states. Since this is an employment zone, there is high population density, which is mostly composed of industrial labour being for low cost housing. The immigrant laborers are illiterate as seen in the case study of Kolkata. There is also large-scale unemployment, and general dilapidation of the area, where there are degraded social values and violence. A diagram of the Chicago model is in the chapter on Toronto.

Land values also fell in the adjacent area of the industrial belt as the population moves to more desirable locations." Consequently, living conditions in the transitional area deteriorate, and the area fills with a heterogeneous mix of marginally employed or unemployed lower class immigrant groups. The deleterious effects of diversity, geographical mobility, and conflict are compounded in the transitional zone by poverty, substandard housing, and inadequate social services, education, and recreation.[7] Clifford Shaw and Henry McKey (in 1969) said that these conditions erode traditional social controls and encourage unconventional activity. The traditional social values erode and the youth often take to crime as criminal behavior is learned in interaction with other persons (according to Sutherland).

When we draw a socio - economic crime gradient of Kolkata, we can compare the Chicago model with Kolkata. The gradient for land use has been taken from the landuse map (A Socio Economic Gradient of Kolkata) which also helps in understanding the overall landuse of the city. If Kolkata is compared to Burgess's model of Chicago (see diagram in Chapter 5), then the eastern part of the city from the CBD would be applicable. Starting from the high rent structure in the CBD to a transitional zone of residential cum industrial area and ultimately culminates into the commuter zone or the Eldorado of Kolkata i.e. Salt Lake city further in the east (not included in the map.) Through observation it has been noticed that the Eastern Suburban Division of Kolkata has a mixed ethnic and religious population.

Hence, the human ecological approach is able to explain the geographical distribution of crime in urban areas. Places which are dilapidated and are older parts of the city have more criminal activity. Hence, the Eastern Suburban Division follows such a norm. As crime is reviewed by Calvin F Schmid, in 1960, it is found that the Central zone or CBD has different types of crime at different sub areas. According to his study on Seattle, he found that sex violations were highest in this area. In the study on Kolkata, it was found that the CBD has a very high incidence of molestation, as there is a high mobile female population. In this case the main CBD has been accepted as Sec J (or Taltolla). However, the concept that crime decreases with distance from the CBD is not acceptable in the case of crime against women as seen in the case of Kolkata viz. the Eastern Suburban Division, thus making crimes against women more in the periphery than in the core of the city.

Diagram 4.3
A Socio-Economic Gradient of Kolkata

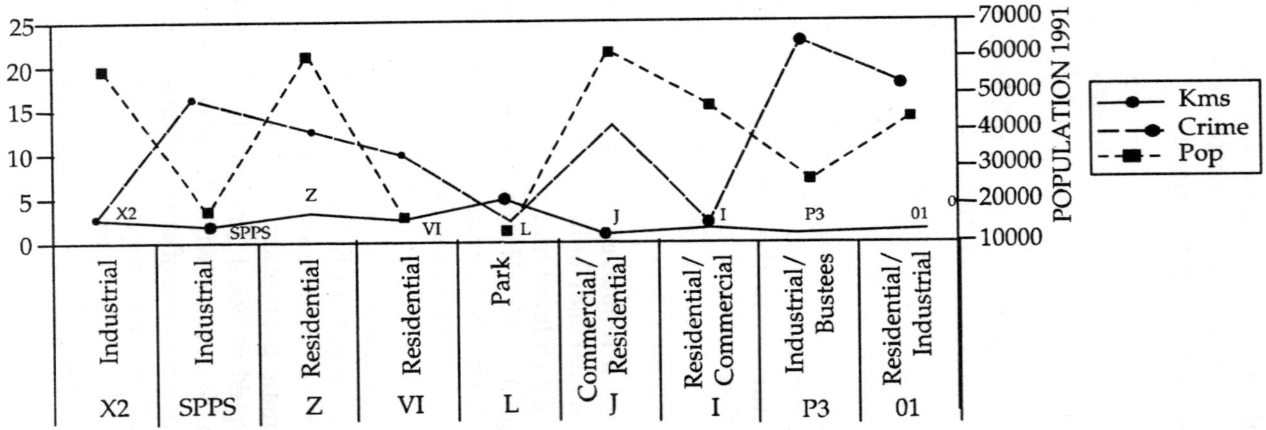

Source: Compiled by author

The Micro Study: Eastern Suburban Division

Since the Eastern Suburban Division has been highlighted as having a high incidence of crime, hence, it is important to do a brief micro study of this area.

In table 4.3 it is evident that the Eastern Suburban Division has the largest area of 22.3 kms. The data shows 1991 census along with crime incidence in 1996. The crime is highest in the Eastern Suburban Subdivision area, with a reasonably large percentage of population; a large male population; a large male population, with 26 per cent male non- workers and a low male literacy.

Table 4.6
Socio-Economic Variables and Crime Situation in the Police Districts 1991

Police Districts	*Area (Kms)*	*Crime*	*% Pop.*	*% Male Pop.*	*%Male Literacy*	*%Male Non Workers*
North Division	8.11	56	26.3	25.24	27.9	24.68
Central Division	11.31	66	8.4	9.06	9.69	24.45
South Division	18.5	91	29.1	28.61	28.93	25.8
Eastern Sub. Division	22.3	69	22.1	21.69	20.97	26
Port Division	15.25	47	14.1	15.4	13.31	31.9

Source: Compiled By Author from Police Records, Kolkata.

In table 4.6 and 4.7 we can study the police station and the socio economic variables in each sub area.

In the table we find that although Beliaghata Sec P1 has the largest percentage of area, it does not have the largest incidence of crime. However, in this respect Beniapukur (Sec R) has the largest crime and also boasts of a high total population and a male population as well. Beniapukur as mentioned before, has a mixed ethnic population of mostly, Muslims and Christians. There are large slums and small-scale industries. The other notorious areas are Manicktala and Entally. Manicktala has a very large population (in fact the largest in the area with the largest bustees. Entally on the other hand has a middle class residential area, small workshops and bustees as well.

Table 4.7
Socio-Economic Variables and Crime Situation in the Police Districts 1991

P.S.	*% Area (kms) to Total*	*%Population to Total*	*% Crime to Total*	*%Male to Total*	*%Illiteracy to Total*
Manicktala	3.12	5.01	2.73	4.91	95.11
Ultadanga	3.18	4.49	2.12	4.37	95.44
Beliaghata	5.62	1.54	1.82	1.57	98.73
Phulbagan	4.02	3.56	1.82	3.33	96.14
Narkeldanga	1.17	0.9	1.51	1.01	99.36
Entally	1.55	2.22	2.73	2.19	97.84
Tangra	0.79	1.39	2.12	1.36	98.81
Beniapukur	3.07	3.31	6.07	3.17	97.26

Source: Compiled By Author from Police Records, Kolkata.

In table 4.6 it is evident that where there is low literacy and high male population and male non- workers there is highest incidence of crime against women. As for the case of crime against women and male non-workers, the Spearman's Rank correlation has been used to see whether there is any interrelation or not.

Diagram 4.4

EASTERN SUBURBAN DIVISION
Increase in Male Non-Workers Leads to An Increase in Crime
1991

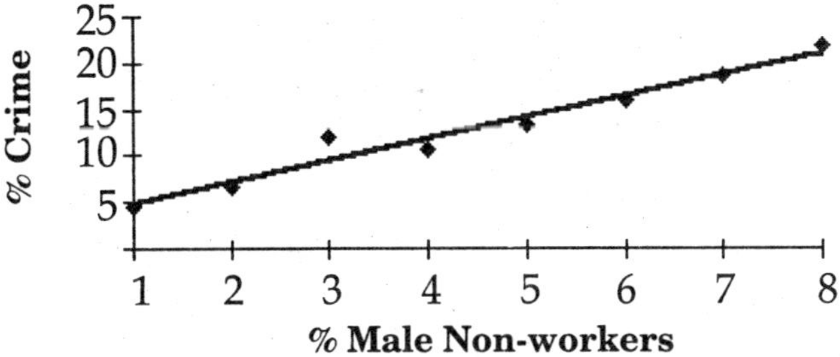

Source: Compiled By Author from Crime Records, Kolkata.

The correlation between increase in male non-workers vis –a-vis crime shows that when there is an increase in male non-workers, there is an increase in crime. "Notwithstanding through these complications, it is clearly possible to see that economic distress, particularly unemployment, may have a more pronounced effect on some segments of the population than on others..... specifically, youth and minority populations disproportionately occupy unstable, low wage jobs, and are especially vulnerable to economic downturns. At the same time these groups also exhibit high levels of criminal involvement."[8] According to research by Brantingham and Brantingham, 1984, they found that there is a stronger relationship between property offenses and unemployment than violent crimes. However, it is important to understand that where there is poverty, unemployment, a degraded environment, there is also more violence, drunkenness and frustration. In the Eastern Suburban area, in 1996 the maximum types of crime have been rape, kidnapping, cruelty and molestation. The literacy levels are very low in this area. Hence diagram 4.5 shows correlation between male illiteracy and rise in crime where we find that when there is increase in male illiteracy, there is rise in crime. In other words, although the women in this area may be working as maids and daily wage laborers, they are socially not at par with the men. Cases for merciless beatings and violence due to drunkenness are rampant in the area.

Diagram 4.5
Eastern Suburban Division
Increase in Male Illiteracy Leads to Rise in Crime
1991

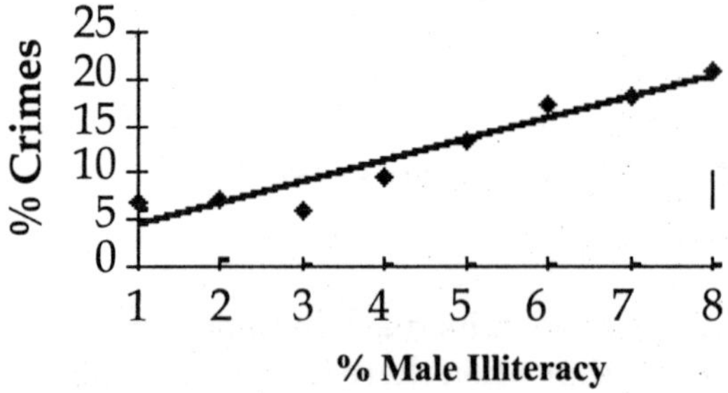

Source: Compiled By Author from Police Records, Kolkata.

Social Variables and Crime

Crime is evident not only in the spatial context but also takes place in time. Besides this there are several social factors which are evident in criminal acts. From the study of crime against women in Kolkata, it is evident from the data on 1996 as to what is the sociological aspect of violence. In other words, who committed the violence, and the type of abuse involved. From the victim-accused relationship and the type of crime involved in 1996, it is evident that the maximum case of violence is perpetrated by the joint involvement of the in-laws and spouse. Amazingly, through the study of the individual cases, it was evident that the women in the family of the groom, both mentally and physically tortured the bride. In most such cases it is cruelty and dowry death or abetment to suicide. In most cases of section 498A, the cruelty and harassment was for material goods. Hence, it is evident here that the crime against women in 62.73 per cent of the cases was by women to fulfill their economic ambitions. It is important to educate the family and the women folk as well as that a single person cannot bring economic prosperity to a family.

Table 4.8
Victim-Accused Relationships and the Type of Crime 1996

Relationship	*% violence*	*%murder/dowry death/abetment to suicide*	*cruelty*	*rape/ molestation*	*kidnap*
Parent		—	—	—	—
Spouse/ex-spouse/In-laws	16.78	5.59	11.18	—	—
In-laws/spouse	62.73	9.93	52.79	—	—
Others	13.04	4.34	—	3.72	4.96
Total	100	20.49	70.82	3.73	4.96

Source: Compiled by Author from Police Records, Kolkata.

Violence from the spouse or partner is mostly in the form of cruelty and misappropriation of stridhan. Amazingly, while studying each case it became evident that dowry related violence or misappropriation of stridhan was not limited to only the Hindu families. Both Muslim as well as Christian women reported cases related to this Hindu phenomenon. Violence from others such as acquaintances and only from in-laws is of a small category. Violence in the form of rape and kidnapping is committed by strangers. The parameter of relationship between accused and victim for only in-laws is minor. It is evident that both the partner and groom and the rest of his family routinely and knowingly torture the victims.

Table 4.9
Age of Victims Under Different Crime Heads

			Percentage		
Age Group	*Victim*	*Rape*	*Molestation*	*Kidnapping*	*Violence*
0-15	58.28	51.7	44.44	67.53	31.22
16-30	37.74	44.5	44.44	32.46	56.13
31-45	3.98	3.8	11.12	—	8.44
46-60	—	—	—	—	2.95
Above 60	—	—	—	—	1.26

Source: Compiled By Author from Police Records, Kolkata.

Table 4.9 gives the details of age wise distribution under different heads of crime and their age -wise break-up. The maximum victims are from the age groups of 0-15 years and 16-30. While the percentage of violence experienced in all cases is with the age group of 16-30 years. In the case of rape, molestation and kidnapping, the most vulnerable group is 0-15 and 16-30 years. This may be due to the fact that this group is the most mobile and vulnerable.

As this study is on the geographical aspect of crime, a time veleted details on crime study has been given in proved table 4.10. That maximum number of incidents take place between 3.00 PM and 5:59 PM. That is in the early hours of the evening and late afternoon, followed by 12:00 PM - 2.59 PM. This is also the time when the maximum number of women and children are mobile. Violence comes in the form of kidnapping, rape and cruelty. Often cruelty under Sec.498A takes place during the late afternoon or the early evening hours in the hands of the in-laws.

Besides the demographic concept of crime, early branches of Geography had also emphasized on the deterministic concept of personal and environmental forces. Criminologists such as Lombroso emphasized on the physical attributes of criminals as the cause of offences. However some early works also emphasized on the "influence of physical environment on criminal behavior. There are also studies relating to climatic variations and seasonality of crime with a frequent assertion that an increase in violent crimes takes place during the summer and on property offenses during the winter.[9]

In the nineteenth century, M.de Guerry de Champneuf, the director of Criminal Affairs in France stated "there is the influence of climate and seasons, as the crimes against persons are always more numerous in the summer.

Table 4.10
Time of Violent Incidents, Percent Distribution 1994-1996

Time of Incident	*Violence per cent*
6:00 am-8:59 am	9.57
9:00 am-11:59 am	15.5
12:00 pm-2:59 pm	16.57
3:00 pm-5:59 pm	20.32
6:00 pm-8:59 pm	12.29
9:00 pm-11:59 pm	15.5
12:00 am-2:59 am	8.55
3:00 am-5:59 am	1.7

Source: Compiled By Author from Police Records, Kolkata.

Climate was believed by these nineteenth century writers to exert its influence in diverse ways. The warmer temperature of summer and the continuous warmth of the Southern latitudes were regarded as affecting the physical mechanism directly, heightening emotion, stimulating activity, and according to Lombroso, encouraging quarrels, brawls and stabbing affairs. The most abundant food supply and the minimum need for clothing was believed to account for the decrease in acts of criminal appropriation during the summer months and in the lush southern areas. Sex crimes which were reported to be at a maximum during May and June were regarded as related to an inherent crimes which were reported to be at a maximum during May and June were regarded as related to an inherent biological periodicity of sexual interest.[10] The criminal activity against women in Kolkata can be explained in terms of seasonal change. Kolkata experiences a typical hot humid climate as in most cities in South Asia. The winter season has pleasant weather, which lasts from November to mid February. The summer sets in by mid April and lasts till June. July to early September is the rainy season, which also happens to be the slack season for all business activities. E.G. Dexter's "Weather Influences: An Empirical Study of the Mental and Physiological Effects Of Definite Meteorological Conditions" gives some explanations for causes of certain crimes in certain seasons. "Rainy weather has ambivalent influences upon the organism. It puts people out of sorts, but also deprives them of the energy necessary to indulge their sulky moods. The number of crimes of violence is, therefore, minimized by rain. Dexter believed that the weather operates directly upon the emotional and physiological activities of the individual producing various anomalies of behavior."[11]

In the case of Kolkata, the seasonality of crime has been given in graphical form below. The diagram shows the average distribution of the incidence of crime against women between 1991-1996. In this it is evident that crime against women is highest between February and March and again between June and July. Crime is maximum in the summer season and before the rains. Winter months in Kolkata record a moderate number of cases. While, June, which is the peak of the summer season, has the highest number of cases. With the rains, the crimes committed against women slacken. Another feature, which can be noted here is that from October onwards till early January, Kolkata has numerous festivals and trade, hence, incidences of crime is relatively the unemployed able bodied youth low.

Diagram 4.6
Average Distribution of Crime 1991-96

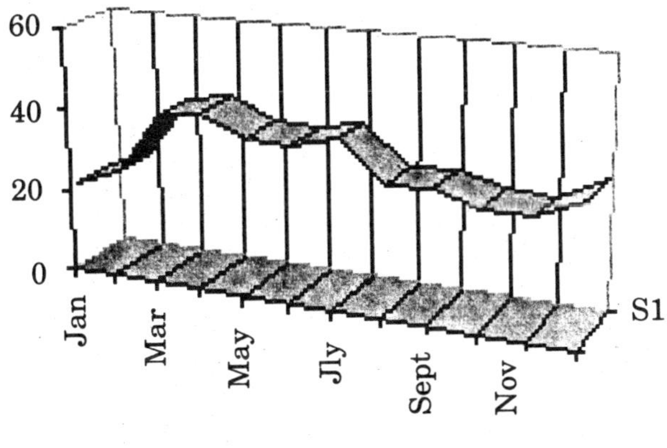

Source: Compiled By Author from Police Records, Kolkata.

The individual crimes such as murder, dowry death, rape etc. can be studied according to seasonal distribution in the diagram on Seasonal distribution of crimes in Kolkata 1996. Murder is highest during May and December, while dowry death is highest in May and July. This is due to the fact that most Hindu marriages take place in between December and June. Hence, the cruelty and death cases take place after this period. Rape cases as mentioned before take place mostly during the summers i.e. in June-July.

Due to large scale under reporting of crime, a content analysis of the Statesman newspaper was done from 1991-1996. From the newspaper reports, table 4.11 it is evident that in newspapers too Crime against women reporting is maximum in April and December. The maximum cases reported over 6 years are that of murder and rape due to the sensational nature of the offenses.

In table 4.11 it is possible to see that the reporting in the newspaper has been increasing over the years. However, most reported offences are in the form of murder or offenses that take place in high rent residential areas or the more sensational offenses in any part of the city.

Diagram 4.7
Seasonal Distribution of Crimes in Kolkata1996

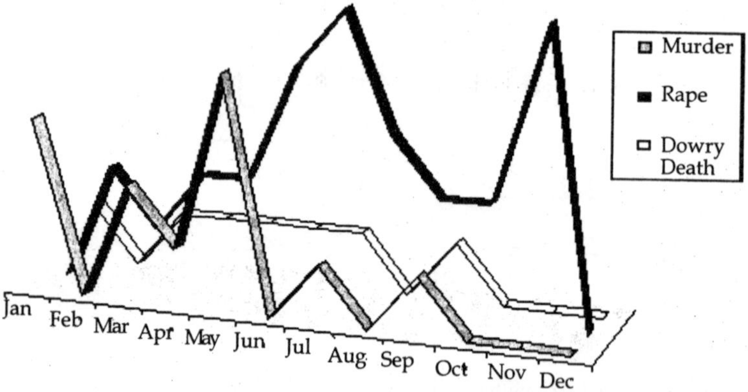

In recent years, another source of data information is with various non-governmental organizations working on women. Victims to avoid further trauma prefer meeting women and social workers involved with these social agencies as the police personnel are insensitive, rude and not responsive. The courts and the police further trauma tise the victims and makes the families take these unfortunate decisions where the cases have to be dropped midway. The case study on Kolkata makes it evident that crime is on the rise and it is of concern to the women as well as for the city. With the increase in population there has been a steady increase in crime. Kolkata has a mixed ethnic population. Hence, there are pockets where crime against women is concentrated. Like the Western Ecological model crime is more in the transitional zone, which has vast areas of slums like the ghettos or natural areas. Crime is also seen more in areas where there are unskilled labor or semi skilled industrial labor, more migrants, and low rent for housing, male non- working population and male illiteracy. The maximum case of crime against women in Kolkata is the Eastern Suburban Division. It is also evident from the maps

Table 4.11
Monthly Average of Crime Data from Statesman 1991-96

Crimes	Jan	Feb	Mar	Apr	May	Jun	Jly	Aug	Sept	Oct	Nov	Dec	Total
Murder	0.8	0.3	0.3	2.3	1	1	0.8	0.66	1.2	0.66	1.3	1.2	11.62
Rape	0.3	0.7	0.8	0.2	0.5	1	0.8	0.83	0.5	0.83	0.3	0.7	7.46
Kidnapping	0	0.8	0	0.7	1	0.2	0.16	0.2	0.33	0	0	3.63	
Cruelty	0	0	0.3	0	0	0.2	0.2	0	0.2	1.83	1.5	3.2	7.3
Abet. to suicide	0	0.3	0.2	0.2	0.16	0	0	0	0.2	0.16	0.5	0.2	1.79
Molestation	0	0.2	0.2	0.2	0.16	1	0	0.16	0.2	0.5	0	0	2.47
Eve teasing	0	0.2	0.2	0.5	0	0	0.2	0	0.3	0	0	0	1.31
Dowry death	0	0.2	0.2	0.2	0.16	0	0.2	0	0.5	0	0	0.2	1.46
others e.g. robbery	0.5	0.3	0.3	0	0.33	0.2	0	0.16	0.2	0.16	0	0.2	2.29
att. abduction	0	0	0	0.2	0	0	0	0	0	0	0	0	0.16
att. murder	0	0	0	0	0	0	0	0	0	0.16	0.5	0	0.66
Total	1.7	3	2.5	4.3	3.31	3.5	2.5	1.97	3.3	4.63	4.2	5.5	40.14

Source: Compiled By Author from Statesman 1991-1996.

that where there is a high density of population there is more crime against women. The most notorious areas for crime and density of population are Jorasanko (Sec. E), Amherst Street (Sec. F), Burtolla (Sec. C), Beniapukur (Sec R), Manicktolla (Sec O1), and Ultadanga (Sec O2). Hence, it is evident that areas of greater urban deprivation with low rent structure like slums have higher crimes against women.

Table 4.12

	Statesman 1991-1996					
Crimes	*1991*	*1992*	*1993*	*1994*	*1995*	*1996*
Murder	16	5	12	11	9	17
Rape	6	8	7	9	10	5
Kidnapping	2	2	9	5	3	1
Cruelty	0	1	1	2	1	39
Abetment to suicide	1	1	0	4	2	3
Molestation	2	1	3	4	2	3
Eve teasing	1	1	3	2	0	1
Dowry death	2	0	2	2	2	1
others e.g. robbery	1	1	4	2	4	1
attempted abduction	1	0	0	0	0	0
attempted murder	1	1	0	0	1	3
Total	33	21	41	41	34	74

Source: Compiled By Author from Statesman 1991-1996.

However, portions of the study have been incomplete due to the lack of proper data and incomplete data as found in the Crime Index and copies of FIRs. Only six cases of eve teasing have been found in the police records between 1981 and 1996. Out of these 5, were in 1981 and only one in 1996. Hence, crime reporting is not very authentic. However, one must agree that data on crime is most exhaustive in the police records.

The present study is an apt example of a study in the Developing country where there is high male population in the cities, high illiteracy, high non-working population etc. In the next chapter, a study on crime against women in a Developed country has been attempted. As compared to the example in the developed country the case of Kolkata projects underreporting and limited data. The police on their part need to take special note that all crimes are equally dangerous and need to be registered. Burking and reporting an incident does not solve the problem and nor does it project a good image of them. What the personnel in uniform need to do is to make the women of the city trust them and report those unreported incidences more so that the virus can be eradicated from its roots. There is also a need to make improvements in data collection and computerization of data, without which exhaustive research is impossible and hence improvements in the system to combat crimes against women.

References

1. Jean Racine, ed. *Kolkata 1981*, (New Delhi, 1986) p.1.
2. R. Ramachandran, *Urbanization and Urban Systems in India*, (New Delhi 1989), p. 194.
3. M. Mohanty, *Geography of Urban Crisis and Conflicts in the Third World: A Comparative Study of Kolkata and Dhaka*, Thesis, JNU, SIS, 1991, p.146.
4. Jean Racine, ed., *Kolkata 1981* (New Delhi) 1986, p.135.
5. I.M. Gomme, *The Shadow Line: Deviance and Crime in Canada* (Toronto, 1993) p. 50.
6. *Ibid.*, pp. 51-52.
7. *Ibid.*
8. M.D. Smith and others, *Sociological Perspective*, Vol. 35, No. 4. 1992, p. 552.
9. David Herbert, *The Geography of Urban Crime*, (London,1982) p. 22.
10. Joseph Cohen, *The Annuls of The American Academy of Political and Social Sciences*, Vol. 217, 1941, p.30.
11. *Ibid.*

5

Crime in Toronto City

Over the years Toronto has gained the reputation of being the best and the cleanest city in the world. This is a city with a potpourri of cultures from all over the world due to its immigrant population. It is a city, which is multi – cultural, which has a high quality of life and a strong economy, supported by a healthy social environment. Toronto is the financial capital and has the highest population in Canada. It is a relatively safe place to live . Yet many women who live in Toronto feel unsafe. The police statistics tell us that Toronto the Good is a relatively peaceful and law – abiding city. As compared to the other North American urban areas, Metro Toronto has the lowest rate of violent crimes. The majority of crime is directed against property, not people.[1]

However, as seen earlier that crime against women is quite different from crimes against people. Often the nature of crimes are such that the victims are unable to register a case with the police. Hence, the police statistics do not give a clear picture in the case of crime against women. Victims of sexual assault are often reluctant to register a case with the police due to poor and insensitive treatment. There have been surveys like the Urban Violence Against Women Survey which has clearly brought out the fact that 56 per cent of urban Canadian women feel unsafe walking alone on their own after dark in their neighbourhoods. This perception of fear to a certain extent is due to the imbalance of power between the two sexes. The women are the victims of negative portrayal by the media, unequal economic power and social status in Canadian society.

Before embarking on the case study on Toronto, it is important to understand the city first. The quality of good life in Toronto is due to its well – supported network of social welfare. The city has gone through periods of boom and recession. During the boom of the mid 1980's several new jobs were created in Toronto. During recession in the early 1990's, more than half of the jobs lost in the country were in the Toronto region. Over 176000 jobs disappeared here between 1989 and 1992; mostly in the clerical sector (- 90000) and in manufacturing. By 1995, and despite renewed economic growth in the country and strong growth in much of Southern Ontario, those jobs had still not been recovered. Preliminary estimates suggest that employment in the Greater Toronto Area is still some 42000 jobs below the pre – recession peak.[2] Although some residents are prospering, income polarization is increasing. Metro's poverty rate is almost 19 per cent, more than double the rate for the rest of the Greater Toronto Area (GTA). Metro's economic recovery has been slow and unemployment remains high, especially for youth. Many of society's most vulnerable groups, including poor children, seniors and single parent families, are concentrated in the Metro portion of the Greater Toronto Area. Because of Metro's high social costs, the pressure to raise taxes or cut services in difficult economic times are strong. As services deteriorate, social conditions worsen and fear of crime accelerates, and those who can will flee the city to the suburbs outside of the Metro, along with businesses seeking lower taxes. As experience from some United States cities have shown, this can trigger a viscious circle of higher taxes, out – migration, reduced assessment, fewer dollars to pay for social services, increased need, and significant erosion of the social environment for all residents.

The Metropolitan Toronto police has its jurisdiction over Metro Toronto, Etobicoke, East York, North York, York and Scarborough. Hence, the GTA comprises of six municipalities. In a research produced by United Way of Greater Toronto, it was seen that the society's most vulnerable groups are concentrated in the Metro. Relative to the rest of the GTA,

Metro has a high number of seniors and single parent families. Metro has only 50 per cent of the GTA's total population, but has 70 per cent of all the single parent families and 67 per cent of all the seniors.[3] As Toronto is a large financial capital of Canada, there is a large immigrant population. This growth in population, coupled with the recent economic recession, has led to unemployment and less social benefits and has led to a disparity among several groups such as single parent families' etc. This poverty and recession has also affected women and children who have been victims of violence. Increasingly, women escape violence only to enter a life of poverty. And because of restrictions to legal aid, more women are being pressured to enter into mediation with their abusive partners, despite the fact that mediation is inappropriate and even dangerous in situations where violence has been used.[4]

For the over all well – being, there must be both social and economic development in a city. If there is a negative trend in economy as well as in the social environment then the social fabric of the society may be in danger.

Crime in the City : The Macro Study

As mentioned earlier crime in a society and especially crime against women is an effect of the pressures of urban life and the deteriorating social fabric in families. In Toronto there has been work on violence against women in 1982 by Task Force on Public Violence against Women and Children by the regional government. This Task Force later resulted in the creation of an advocacy agency, the Metro Action Committee on Public Violence against Women and Children, more popularly known as METRAC. METRAC through its study was able to find the perceptions of fear of women in their neighborhoods. Most women were wary of parking garages (48 per cent), streets (42 per cent), public transit (40 per cent), parks or ravines (27 per cent). Besides women were also wary of dark poor lightening 61 per cent at night and 10 per cent during daytime; deserted areas 39 per cent at night and 20 per cent during daytime etc. Over the recent years several reports on violence against women have been published such as The Safe City Report: Municipal Strategies for Preventing Public Violence against Women, The Toronto Transit Commission (TTC), etc.

In 1996, the Assaulted Women's Helpline in Metro received over 18000 calls from abused and assaulted women. In that same year, Metro police reported 5330 cases of domestic violence. These cases included murder (3), attempted murder (3), sexual assaults (73), assaults (4022), harassment, threats and intimidation.[5] Besides data from such societies, in 1982, the Canadian Urban Victimization Survey was able to project to a certain extent the gravity of the situation in Toronto as 0.92 per cent of the interviews were conducted in Toronto. The Victimization Survey is noteworthy for what it reveals about women's perception of their personal safety. However the most complete form of statistics about violence against women is available with the police, although as mentioned before, this is not the complete picture.

The study on Toronto is based on primary data collected from Police Headquarters in Toronto, taking 22 parameters of crime over a period of seven years from 1991 to 1996. In the case study on Calcutta a study between 1981 and 1991 was possible. However, for Toronto, the Toronto Metropolitan Police does not keep data which is more than 7 years old. The present study also shows the relation between crime and the demographic variables in the city. The incidences of crime have been limited to those provided in the police records. Since the media plays an important role in today's society, a content analysis of the popular newspaper. The Toronto Daily Star was studied for the above-mentioned period of time.

The statistical data provided by the police was quite exhaustive. However, as mentioned earlier, the police records do not project a complete picture of the crime situation. Due to the nature of offences, the victims often do not register cases with the police due to embarrassment and sometimes due to the insensitive nature of the police personnel. In the case of the study on Calcutta eight parameters of crime were taken into account. The Toronto, MTPS when contacted gave 22 parameters of crime, which they felt dealt exclusively on violence against women.

Table 5.1 at a glance shows the nature of incidences of crime against women. The absolute figures have been taken in this case as to understand the seriousness of the offenses in the city.

The maximum offences are in the form of assault cases followed by assault with weapon causing bodily harm, sexual confinement and sexual interference of person less than 14 years etc. The reporting of assault cases is extremely high. Infact in 1991 data itself, the assault cases are 70.60 per cent of the total incidences. Where as assault with weapon causing bodily harm is 11.69 per cent and forcible confinement is (1.33 per cent) and sexual assault is (12.28 per cent) in 1991. In all the years, i.e., between 1991 and 1996, assault cases are highest.

Table 5.1
Incidences of Crime in Toronto 1991-96

Crimes	*1991*	*1992*	*1993*	*1994*	*1995*	*1996*
(1)	*(2)*	*(3)*	*(4)*	*(5)*	*(6)*	*(7)*
Assault	8802	10527	10928	10825	10332	9185
Assault with weapon cause body harm	1458	1649	1562	1456	1495	1547
Aggravated assault	108	87	96	79	76	193
Unlawfully causing bodily harm	4	8	1			
Abduction of person under 14	53	10	8	11	8	11

(Contd.)

(Contd.)

(1)	*(2)*	*(3)*	*(4)*	*(5)*	*(6)*	*(7)*
Abduction of person under 16	9					
Incest	4	9	7		14	17
Sexual interference person <14 year	91	230	256	202	242	217
Invite sexual touch person <14 year	25	45	47	36	76	60
Sexual exploitation	43	48	43	53	35	41
Conspire to murder	2			4		
Kidnapping	28	27	25	37	23	19
Forcible confinement	166	243	249	237	207	268
First degree murder	17	10	4	5	9	13
Second degree murder	11	9	9	12	9	2
Attempt to murder	26	18	11	26	15	
Aggravated sexual assault	9	6		8	4	6
Sexual assault with a weapon	79	88	75	50	64	71
Sexual assault	1532	1874	1982	1857	1804	1706
Manslaughter			1	1		
Harassment anti- stalking				971	1096	909
Sexual intercourse female <16 year						2
Total	12467	14888	15304	15870	15509	14267

Source : Compiled From Police Records Toronto.

In 1996 the assault cases were 64.37 per cent, assault with weapon causing bodily harm was 10.84 per cent and sexual assault was 11.95 per cent and forcible confinement was 1.87 per cent. In other words the overall crime has gone down significantly over the last couple of years. Assault cases have gone down by 11.10 per cent between 1995 – 1996, and the overall incidence of violence against women has gone down by 8 per cent over 1995 – 1996. The highest incidence of assault cases were reported in 1993, and compared to the total crime the highest incidence of assaults was also in 1993.

The Metropolitan Toronto Police which covers six municipalities, has an administrative setup of three police districts with a total of 17 police divisions and 209 patrol areas. The city map shows the Metropolitan Toronto Police Districts and Division Boundaries and the crime situation in 1996. The boundaries of patrol areas are coterminous with the streets. Hence, the maps of patrol areas were developed using the MapInfo software from the street map of the Census from Statistics Canada. The Census data was converted to the corresponding patrol area data and on the basis of which the socio-economic and various demographic characteristics have been compared with the incidence of crime against women. However, for the convenience of the study, the total patrol areas have been distributed amongst three divisions viz. Northwest, central and east.

While discussing the crime situation, it is imperative to talk about the population. As agreed on earlier, due to the growth of population over the years, it has led to social degradation as the resources in society cannot be equally distributed. The heaviest concentration of population density is in the municipality of Toronto which is composed of the police divisions of the Central division of subdivisions of 11, 12, 13, 14, 51, 52, 53 and 55. This central division has the largest population over a small area as compared to the other divisions. In table 5.2 the estimated population and the highest population of the area is evident.

Table 5.2
Area and Population by Division and District

Sub	*Division*	*Estimated Population*	*Area Division (sq. kms.)*
11	Central	95157	15.9
12	Central	89497	18.5
13	Central	136228	19.2
14	Central	151357	15.7
51	Central	62300	11.4
52	Central	65611	12.4
53	Central	131793	26
55	Central	115052	20.4
Total	***Central***	***846995***	***139.5***
41	East	218684	60.1
42	East	339208	127.2
54	East	128549	20.4
Total	***East***	***686441***	***207.7***
21	North West	55420	16.8
22	North West	129257	50.1
23	North West	146506	56.6
31	North West	185130	47.7
32	North West	190965	62.6
33	North West	179490	53
Total	***North West***	***886768***	***286.8***
Grand Total	**MTPS**	**2420204**	**634**

Source: MTPS 1995 Statistical Report.

The crime map of 1991 shows the incidence of crime against women in Toronto in 1991. It is evident from this crime map that the high density of population and high incidence of crimes against women are not corresponding. However, there are some pockets such as subdivisions 11 and 12, which have a reasonably high population, density and a corresponding high incidence of crimes. So is the case with patrol areas 4112 , 5401 and 3103.

However, in the case of crime map of 1996 shows the incidence of crime against women in Toronto, the focal areas are the same as those as seen in 1991. The core-peripheral areas remain the same with heaviest concentrations in patrol

Map 5.1

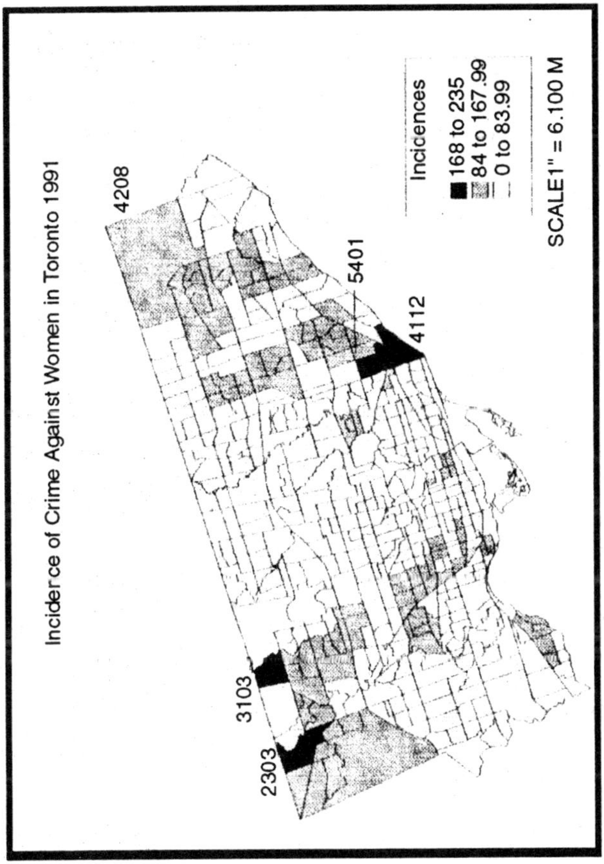

Source: Compiled by Author.

areas 2302 , 3103, 4211, 4213, 4111 and 4112. Crime against women therefore follows the social parameters of income, population and various other dynamics. While concentrating on the incidence of crime against women in 1991 and 1996, the different heads of crime and the patrol areas give a vivid picture of the crime situation. In 1991, the highest number of cases were reported in patrol area 2302, 3103, 4112, 4111 and 3107. The largest number of incidences of crimes against women are reported under assaults, followed by sexual assaults and assault with weapon causing bodily harm. Under assaults, the highest such cases were reported in the patrol area 2302 , followed by 3103, 4112, 4213, 3107 and 4111. The first patrol areas are in the Northwest and in the Eastern part of Metro Toronto. Patrol areas 4112 and 4111 and 4213 are in the Eastern Division. All the others are in the Northwest.

The second highest form of crimes is in the form of sexual assaults where cases are reported from unknown destinations. This is followed by 5207, 4111, 4208, 5401 and 5206. These areas are between the central and the eastern parts of the city. In case of assault with weapon causing bodily harm, 3103, 2303, 5107, 3107, 5102 and 4112 have the highest incidences. The details of this table are in table 5.3.

Table 5.3
Highest Incidences Under The Different Crime Heads in MTPS 1991

Crimes	*Patrol Areas*					
Assault	2,302	3103	4112	4111	4213	3107
Sexual Assault	unknown	5207	4111	4208	5401	5206
1st Degree Murder	4201	4208	3110	3106	5108	1401
2nd Degree Murder	5401	1401	1202	5102	1205	1201

(Contd.)

(Contd.)

1	*2*	*3*	*4*	*5*	*6*	*7*
Aggravated Sexual Assault	3110	5106	4203	1204	4115	5105
Sexual Assault with Weapon	2206	1205	2302	3110	5401	4213
Attempted Murder	4203	5401	2105	4108	3305	5403
Aggravated Assault	5202	5107	2101	1201	1402	4111
Assault with Weapon Cause body harm	3103	2302	5107	3107	5102	4112
Forcible Confinement	1205	1402	4208	5106	1108	5210
Kidnap	4208	1414	2310	1108	5102	unknown
Sexual Interference with person <14 year	5401	5406	3103	3112	4107	2305
Abduction of Person<14 year	4211	5503	5504	4108	1411	5108
Abduction of Person <16 year	5108	5405	3113	1416	3206	4215
Invite Sexual touch person <14 year	4214	5508	1409	1414	2304	1411
Conspire to Murder	1105	1205	4214	5508	1409	1414
Sexual Exploitation	1406	3105	3103	3106	4215	4102
Incest	2303	3105	2305	1105	1205	1406
Unlawfully Causing body harm	5108	3107	4205	3304	2303	3105
Total	2302	3103	4112	4111	3107	4213

Source: Compiled by Author.

Map 5.2

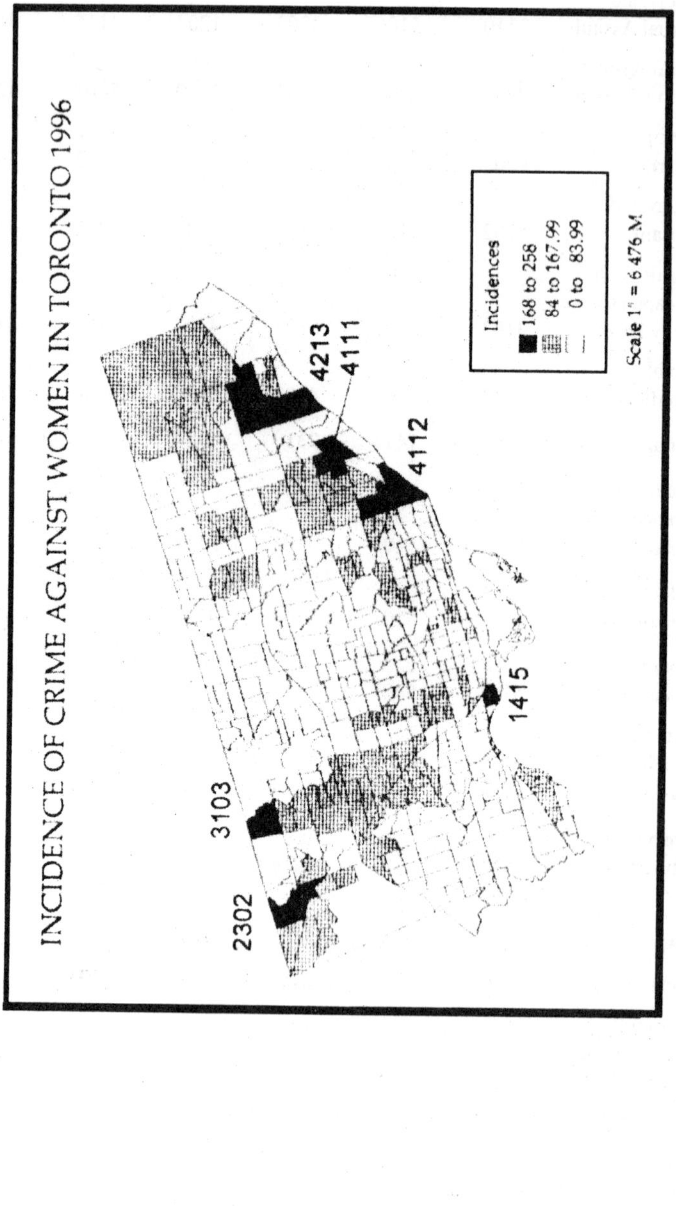

Source: Police Records, Toronto

However, at a glance it is certain that the highest incidences of crime and the various heads of crime are concentrated in the same area.

In case of 1996, the highest incidences of crime are evident as in the map. The highest cases are in the patrol areas 2302, 3103, 4211, 1415, 4111, 4112, and 4213. The focus of the highest concentration has not changed much. In table 5.4 it is evident that in the case of the highest incidences in 1996, are those of assault cases, while the highest number of reported cases in 1991 are concentrated in 2302, 3103, 4112, 4111, and 4213.

Table 5.4
Highest Incidences Under The Different Crime Heads in MTPS 1996

Crimes	*Patrol Areas*					
1	*2*	*3*	*4*	*5*	*6*	*7*
Assault	2302	3103	4112	1415	4213	4111
Sexual Assault unknown	3103	4213	5401	2303		2302
1st Degree Murder	3103	4112	1206	5213	1201	5407
2nd Dcgrcc Murder	1101	5509	3103	4112	1206	5213
Aggravated Sexual Assault	1305	5107	3202	1109	5518	5108
Sexual Assault with Weapon	4115	1417	1401	1407	1206	3305
Attempted Murder	4211	5401	1203	4111	5107	1201
Aggravated Assault	4111	3103	5106	2302	1305	5108
Assault with Weapon Cause						

(Contd.)

(Contd.)

body harm unknown		1415	4208	4201	2202	1207
Forcible Confinement	4201	2307	5214	4108	1407	2303
Kidnap	3103	1206	unknown	5401	4201	2303
Sexual Interference with person <14 year	3103	unknown	3105	4112	5411	1403
Abduction of Person <14 year	3103	unknown	3105	4112	5411	1403
Abduction of Person <16 year	2310	2302	3305	3108	3101	unknown
Invite Sexual Touch person <14 year	1305	4112	1206	3110	5102	3105
Conspire To Murder	1402	4112	1305	3110	1202	4107
Sexual Exploitation	1402	4112	1305	3110	1202	4107
Incest unknown		2302	1415	5213	4208	1402
Unlawfully Causing body harm	5206	5102	unknown	2302	1415	5213

Source: Compiled by Author.

However, in 1991, patrol area 3107 has fewer incidences of such cases while patrol area 1415 has higher incidences. In case of sexual assault and ordinary assault cases, the areas are similar to those of 1991. In both sexual assault cases as well as assault with weapon causing bodily harm, the highest incidence of reporting is in unknown areas. In other words, the victim possibly did not report such incidences or the actual crime took place in an area unknown to the victim.

From the above discussion it is evident that the Northwest and eastern part of the city has maximum incidence of cases. These areas fall under North York and East York and Scarborough. A small area of crime concentration is along the Humber River area along the Etobicoke – Toronto area. The level of poverty has also increased, especially in Metro's suburbs: the poverty rate in Etobicoke, North York and Scarborough has increased by 22 per cent between 1986 – 1991. It is evident that the incidence of offences are mostly in the peripheral areas of the city and not at the core. Attempts at explanation of the significant similarities in trends shown by the many studies of rural – urban crime distribution reveal almost the entire range of social and psychological theories. Certain obvious factors enter into the picture in a variety of ways.[6] While taking the city as a whole it is seen that there are areas with high concentration of population but these may not be the same areas with high incidences of crime. The highest incidence of crime against women is in the outer periphery to the core and the extreme peripheral areas.

Through the method of location quotient, it is possible to understand a particular crime occurrence in a specific area as compared to the rest of the city. In the case of incidences of assault the highest number of cases are in patrol areas 3203, followed by 2106, 4115, and 2203. 3203 is in the Northwest division of the city. The location quotient index used:

$$\mathbf{LQ} = \frac{\dfrac{\text{percentage of assault to total crime in a patrol area}}{\text{Total percentage of crime in a patrol area}}}{\dfrac{\text{Percentage to total assault in the city}}{\text{Total percentage of crime}}}$$

The highest incidence of assaults in 1996 was in 2302. However, by location quotient method the highest cases compared to the crime in the area and as well as compared to the city is 3203. Hence, the deductions here are more accurate while taking on a comparative scale.

In case of sexual assaults, the highest number of such cases used by location quotient are reported in unknown areas followed by 5311 and 5305 as compared to the incidences in 3103, 4213 and 5401. In case of assault with weapon causing bodily harm, the highest location quotient is in 5108, 4111, and 1417. If noticed closely, it will be obvious that even by the location quotient method, crime is more concentrated in the periphery than the core.

From date available from E-state it is seen that income of males earning less than $1000 who are 15+years of age, are mostly concentrated in between King Street West and Wellington Street West near the Union Station, followed by the area around the Kew Gardens (again near the Harbour Front) and the area around the Elm Street area, which is again a downtown area. This comes under 55th and 52nd Divisions. Another area where there is alot of low-income males is in between the 55th and 51st Divisions around the Donlands Parkway and Danforth Avenue area. The crime maps of 1991 and 1996 show that there are more crimes in these areas. However, no conclusion can be derived without further study, whether low incomes amongst males lead to more crime against women. The total immigrant population in the city is found mostly in the peripheral areas of the city as larger immigrant populations prefer to settle in low sent areas.

The Theory of Crime

While discussing the subject of crime and the urban environment, it is important to see the contributions of the Chicago School and whether the model can be used in the case of Toronto. On the basis of these observations, Chicago sociologists developed explanations for a variety of social phenomena, including deviance and crime. As discussed earlier in the chapter on Kolkata, contained within the Chicago model are a macro theory (human ecology) and a micro theory (differential association).[7] The Chicago model was a typical example of the early 1900's. The Chicago model emphasized on the fact that recent immigrants and the poor people predominantly occupied the city. (See diagram of concentric model).

Diagram 5.1.

The Chicago Model

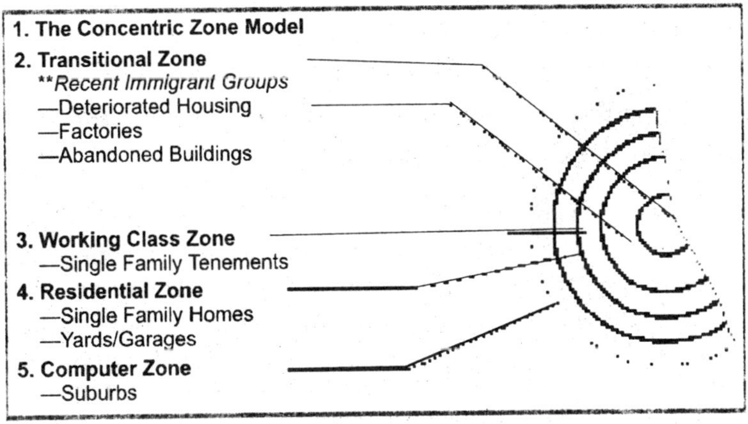

The city also grew by the process of invasion and succession as seen in the plant kingdom. The dominant communities occupy favorable sites, which are areas of more property values, away from the industries and with a cleaner environment. Sociologists argued that all these intricate relationships form a social system, or "web of life". They believe that the normal conditions of this complex system are equilibrium and order. They envisaged change as an evolutionary process involving the gradual adaption of people and groups to alterations in the characteristics, either of one another of their physical surroundings. When species become incompatible with one another or when the nature of the environment changes, some forms of life inevitably suffer or perish. In the world of nature, plants produce oxygen that are vital to the survival of animals. Animals produce carbon dioxide that is equally essential to the survival of plants. This mutually dependent relationship among plants and animals exemplifies symbiosis. The slow destruction of large masses of plant life, through industrial expansion and pollution, however, undermines this equilibrium. The ultimate loss of food and shelter caused by acid rain, for example, is dramatically changing the nature of animal and bird life in affected areas. The demolition of urban slums represents an analogous change in the physical surroundings of city dwellers. The elimination of housing affordable to disadvantaged class and ethnic groups requires both their adaptation and relocation. An important point emphasized in the ecological approach is that change in one part of the system invariably affects other system components.[8]

According to Environmental Criminologists, the land values at the core are much higher due to the small space, and high density of population. This area is ideal for commerce and governmental offices. While towards the outer core there are residential areas and workshops, this is the transitional zone with lower property values. The peripheral areas have relatively inexpensive residences. Beyond the third zone are the suburban areas with contemporary satellite cities which caters to the middle class and beyond that to the affluent society, due to their higher rate of mobility.

In case of Toronto, it is evident that the inner core which would extend from the Central Business District around Bloor Street in the north to the Union Station in the south, Sherbourne in the east to Bathurst in the west. It is obvious from the maps of 1991 and 1996 that the incidence of crime is greatest in the transitional zone. One such transitional belt is along the Humber River and the other along the Don Valley area. This belt is an area where property owners believe that the buildings in this sector will eventually be torn down to make room for industrial and commercial expansion, they do not maintain the buildings. Residential areas in this zone deteriorate as higher status residents flee to the suburbs. Their low rents make these dilapidated and rundown dwellings attractive to improvised ethnic and immigrant populations. Many have simply followed the routes and networks established by relatives and friends who are themselves recent immigrants from the same countries. Newer immigrant groups also have little association with those groups living in more traditional immigrant reception areas. The result of this new suburbanization has been the emergence of distinctive ethnocultural landscapes, social spaces and new commercial services and facilities in such diverse suburban locations as Markham, Brampton and Missasagua around Toronto, and Richmond and Surrey in Suburban Vancouver.[9] The other area, which has a large number of incidences, is in the third zone, which has inexpensive dwellings of the working class as explained by Burgess in 1925. This area also has a large migrant population as in areas 2302, 3103, 4208, and the surrounding areas of North York. This area is an off shoot of the transitional zone. While examining the geographical distributions of deviant and criminal activity in Chicago, Clifford Shaw and Henry Mckay (1969) noted that rates of non – conformity and illegal conduct are highest in the transitional zone. They contend that the industrial growth and urban expansion erode the traditional social controls inherent in the family, the church, and community , and they argue that this erosion is particularly severe in the transitional zone. Areas where social controls are weakened or severed are "disorganized" and consequently susceptible to increased levels of deviance.[10] Shaw and Mckay felt that social disorganization occur due to the combined impacts of industrialization and urbanization. Due to the increase in the population, immigrant labourers who bring in various cultures to the zones, suffer from conflicts. According to them, primary social relationships are difficult to maintain in a transitional zone.

On the other hand Sutherland's differential theory which is complementary to the ecological theory says that criminality is a learned social behavior. With more exposure to an unconducive atmosphere, people may adopt criminal instincts.

As far as employment is concerned, the city of Toronto has the largest number of jobs and job opportunities, which the suburbs especially the older suburbs have fewer opportunities. This is largely due to the manufacturing losses in industries. Hence, from the maps we find that the peripheral areas of the city have the largest concentration of crime, than the core. It is certain that areas that are plagued by social and economic deprivation also experience more deviance and criminal activity. When the social fabric of a neighbourhood collapses, there is more crime and hence, crime against women is high.

The Micro Study

As seen in the last section, the peripheral areas of the city have higher crimes against women, than the core. This is a reversal from the usual in crime and population density trends in general. However, while studying table 5.5 it is seen that the highest concentration of incidence of crimes is in the Central division with 43.73 per cent of the crimes, followed by the North West division of 29.23 per cent incidence. Both these areas however have a large concentration of population. The area is largest in the North West part, followed by East division and then Central. These three classifications are according to the Annual Report 1996, as published by police headquarters Toronto.

Table 5.5
Dynamics of the Major Police Division Boundaries 1991

Divisions	*per cent Area*	*per cent crime Incidence*	*per cent of Prop.*	*per cent personnel*
North West	47.56	29.23	33.54	28.75
Central	22.23	43.73	42.36	49.25
East 30.2	26.29	24.09	21.09	

Source: Compiled By Author.

Table 5.6
Socio-Economic Matrix of Patrol Areas with the Highest Crimes 1991

Patrol Area	*Pop. density*	*incid-ences*	*%male pop*	*%immigrant Pop*	*<than grade 9 schooling*	*unemployed males15+*	*<$1000 males15+*	*$10,000 family income*
2302	4532.5	235	50.36	46.33	10.66	4.33	1.33	2
3103	2584.28	212	50.21	53.5	19.5	4.5	0.5	2.5
4112	15552.38	183	47.69	32.6	10.2	2	0.6	1.6
4111	2192.04	166	47.31	39.66	12.33	3	0.66	1.66
3107	2908.06	155	50.12	60	26	4.5	1	2
4213	2000.96	152	47.69	41	7.75	3.75	1.25	2.5

Source: Compiled by Author.

Table 5.7
Ethnic Composition In Selected Patrol Areas
1991(in percentage)

Pat. Area	*Single Origin*	*British*	*French*	*Italian*	*Canadian*	*Chinese*	*East Indian*	*Black*	*Others*	*Multiple Origin*	*Citizens*	
											Canadian	*Non-Canadian*
2302	83.36	13.67	0.86	8.95	4.58	1.93	14.19	13.08	26.08	15.19	66.93	31.63
3103	87.32	8.66	0.58	23.31	3.82	4.17	5.27	13.47	28.07	12.3	71.15	28.39
4112	73.37	26.71	1.45	3.4	9.27	5.81	1.74	4.03	20.96	26.38	86.2	13.55
4111	81.04	25.48	1.67	6.5	7.07	5.74	2.62	3.84	28.11	41.02	58.76	14.96
4213	78.34	21.07	1.17	2.18	7.68	1.83	6.24	5.62	32.54	20.85	73.8	25.39
3107	89.41	6.79	0.83	42.77	2.56	5.3	1.91	6.45	22.65	10.24	75.49	24.13

Source: Compiled By Author.

It is also evident from table 5.5 that the police personnel are concentrated maximum in the Central area followed by the Northwest. This no doubt shows that resources that are available with the police are used according to the requirements of an area. There is prior planning and a close coordination between the ground realities and the policy decisions.

The patrol areas under the Central and North Eastern divisions have the highest incidence of crimes. It is evident that division 14, followed by divisions 55, 52 and 51 have the highest aggregate of crimes. In division 14 the largest number of incidences is in patrol area 1415, and 1402 in 1991. Incidentally, patrol area 1415 has a high incidence as compared to the whole Metro Toronto. The patrol area also has a high percentage of males, immigrants, a relatively high number of males and families with low incomes.

Another patrol area which has a high incidence of crime is 5107 which also falls under Central division. There are 141 cases under 5107, with a relatively high density of population, large number of male population, and immigrant population and a large percentage of unemployed males above 15 years of age and a large number of population with less than grade 9 level of schooling. This area is near Gerrard Street and Dundas Street. Incidentally Gerrard Street is well known for its large Indian immigrant population, while patrol area 1415 is near the Lake Shore area, the Elm Avenue which has been mentioned in the earlier section.

Since division 14 has the highest aggregate of offences, in Central police division, Diagram 5.2 shows that there is a positive correlation between the immigrant population and the incidence of crimes against women in 1991.

It is believed that immigrants especially the women are more susceptible to such offences, as they have less access to justice, due to language and cultural barriers. Racial and ethnic minority women fear to report cases to the police as they are skeptical about their response to their complaints or they fear that their men may be dealt with more harshly. Besides this through a set of interviews, it was evident that ethnic minorities

Diagram 5.2

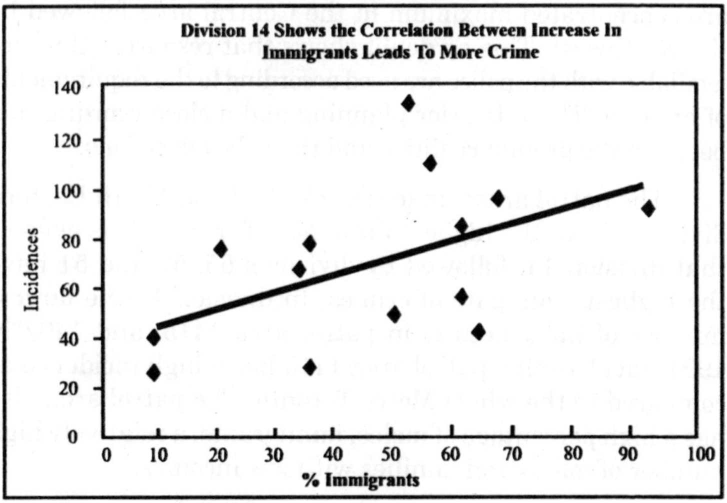

Source: Compiled By Author.

Diagram 5.3

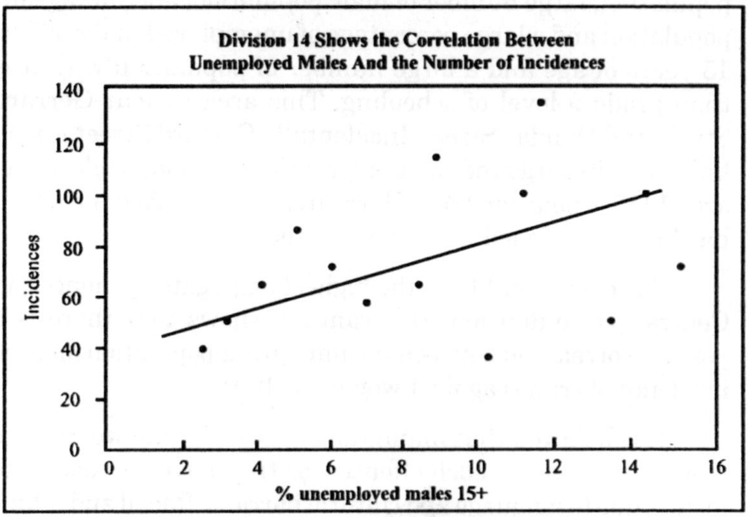

Source: Compiled by Author.

and immigrants especially the Asian community brings with them certain customs that are practices back at home. While interviewing the social workers at the Rexdale Community Center (at Rexdale) it was realized that they were dealing with several cases of dowry deaths and dowry harassment cases.

Through the Spearman's Rank correlation method, it was also proved that there is a definite positive correlation between unemployed males above the age of 15 years and the incidence of crimes against women in division 14.

Unemployed males are often immigrants with low educational qualifications. Cantor and Land (in 1985) conducted a study where they argued that unemployment influences crime both negatively by decreasing criminal opportunity (availability of targets and suitable chances for crime) and positively by motivating toward crime to people who are affected adversely by economic downturns.[11] However, further research is necessary to find the exact relationship between unemployment and crimes against women. The low economy and resource crunch and job layoffs could be a reason for the violence, frustration, rising unemployment and social stress.

Table 5.6 shows the patrol areas with the highest incidence of crimes against women in the Metro. Patrol area 2302 falls in the Northwest division. This area is on the border of division 31, which also has a high incidence of crime. Area 2302 is along the river Humber with large expanses of parkways etc. The crime in this area is mostly assaults and assaults with weapons causing bodily harm.

The next area is 3103, which has the infamous Jane Street running through it. This area also has several large open expanses and both 2302 and 3103 are on the outer most limit of the Metro. In patrol area 3103 too, the nature of offenses are the same. Most of the cases along Jane Street were committed by unknown men on the victims as seen in the content analysis of the Toronto Daily Star. The other areas are patrol areas 4111 and 4112. Both these areas are along the Lake Shore area. While patrol area 3107 is an extension of patrol area 3103. As in table 5.6 it is seen that all the six patrol areas have a high percentage of male population, with patrol area 2302 showing the highest figures. Besides this all the areas have a high immigrant population, and a population with low level of schooling. The number of unemployed males above 15 years of age and the income structure is average as compared to the data of the Metro.

In table 5.7, the ethnic composition of the six patrol areas has been given. Patrol area 2302 has a high percentage of members of the East Indian and Black community. However, most have Canadian citizenship.

Patrol area 3103 has a large Italian and Black community. However, it is certain that all these patrol areas have a large immigrant community.

Social Variables and Crime

Crime is evident not only as a social context, but also takes place in time. Besides this there are several social factors which are evident in criminal acts. It is important to know the nature of the criminal and victim to fully understand the nature of crime a city. From table 5.8, it is evident that the total incidents of crime against women takes place mostly in the age group of 16 to 30 years, followed by 31 to 45 years and then between 0 to 15 years.

Table 5.8
Age of Victims Under Different Crime Heads 1996 (Percentage)

Age Group	*victims*		*sexual assaults*	*assault with weapon cause body harm*
0-15	14.34	5.93	4.21	1.29
16-30	40.16	26.71	4.9	4.19
31-45	27.01	19.45	1.61	3.16
46-60	6.56	4.87	0.35	0.69
above 60	2.3	1.73	0.18	0.21
unknown	9.63	6.19	0.72	1.5
Total	100	64.88	11.97	11.04

Source: Compiled by Author.

In other words the most mobile population is more prone to attacks, and violence. The age group of 16 to 30 years is also the group which are single. They suffer attacks in the form of date rapes, attacks from common – law – husbands' etc. Most of such attacks are in the form of assaults, sexual assaults and assault with weapon causing bodily harm. In the case of the age group of 31 to 45, the crimes are similar to those of the earlier case. As noted earlier, the maximum crimes are in the form of assaults.

Diagram 5.4
Percentage Distribution of Violent Incidences

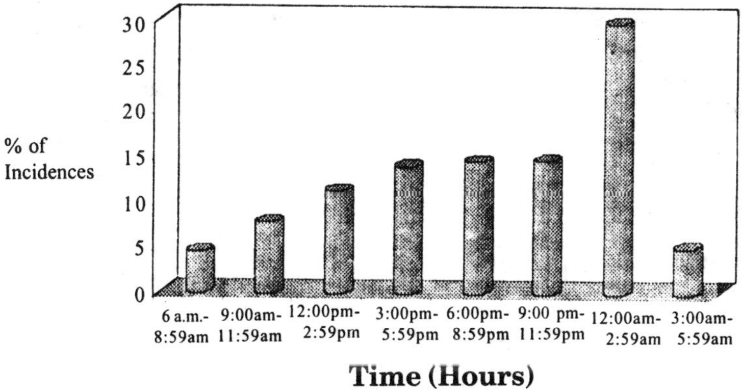

Source: Compiled by Author.

As far as the time period is concerned, the large number of incidents of crime are reported around 12:00 am and 2:59 am, followed by 6:00 pm – 8:59 pm and 9:00 pm – 11:59 pm. Therefore, it can be assumed that most of these cases take place after working hours. The details are evident in diagram 5.4.

Through research, the geographical and temporal variations in crime rates have been interpreted in relation to the social situation. Nineteenth century studies have shown that seasons have also influenced crimes. Concerning his data de Champneuf stated, there is the influence of seasons, for whereas the crimes against persons are always more numerous in the summer, the crimes against property are more numerous in winter-so of the crimes committed in the south, the crimes against the person are far more numerous than those against property, while in the North the crimes against property are in the same proportion, more numerous than those against the person.[12] Lombroso, Ferri etc also corroborated that in Italy, France and Germany, violent crimes against person were higher during the summers.

Diagram 5.5, shows that there are two peak periods of crime in Toronto, both incidentally during the summer. The first is in May – June and the second in August – September. However, there is a slight slide during June – July in 1996. It is believed that long summer's heightens emotional and stimulating activity. Sex crimes are maximum between May – June. Hence, the case of Toronto does conform to the international fluctuations of crimes during the different seasons.

Diagram 5.5

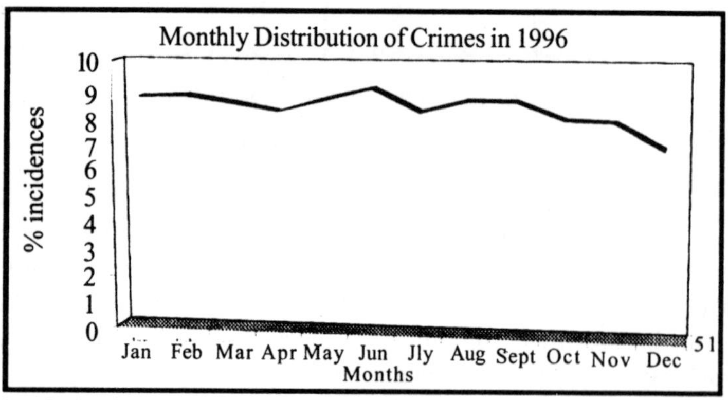

Source: Compiled By Author

The crime data provided by the police was supplemented by a content analysis of the well-recognized Toronto Daily Star. Details of various types of crime were recorded. As in the case of Calcutta, the Toronto Daily Star too is involved reporting the more sensational crimes of the decade like the Bernado – Homolka case. The media (as seen in Diagram

5.6) reported maximum number of cases from Toronto area, followed by Scarborough.

Diagram 5.6

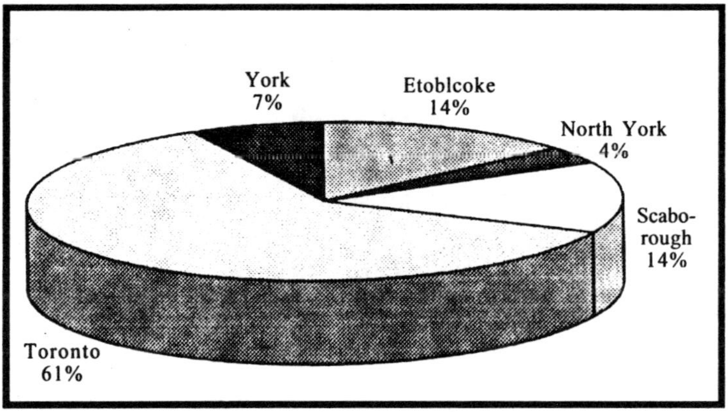

Source: Compiled by Author from the Toronto Daily Star, and Etobicoke.

As far as the reporting of offences are concerned, it is evident from table 5.9 that reporting of offences as a whole is going down.

Table 5.9
Toronto Daily Star 1991—1996

Crimes	*1981*	*1991*	*1992*	*1993*	*1994*	*1995*	*1996*
Assault	18	12	11	10	8	8	4
Attempt to murder	1					2	
Murder	18	24	15	5	13	10	13
Rape	15	6	2	2	3	2	
Sexual Assault	1	32	14	8	14		8
Snatching	1						
Kidnap		6	3	4	1	6	2
Stalking							1
Total	54	80	45	29	39	28	28

Source: Compiled by Author

The largest offences reported in any year are murder cases, followed by assaults and kidnapping cases. The relationship of the victim and accused is also important for any socio – economic study. From table 5.10, it is evident that the largest number of accused are either unknown or

Table 5.10
Victim-Accused Relationship and the Type of Crime 1995 - 1996

Percentage to total number of incidents							
Relationship	*per cent Violence*	*Murder*	*Attempt Murder*	*Assault*	*Kidnap*	*Sexual Assault*	*Stalking*
Acquaintance	12.69	9.09	1.81	1.81			
Father	1.79			1.81			
Husband	9.09	5.45		3.63			
Partner	3.62	1.81	1.81				
Son	1.81			1.81			
Unknown	43.49	9.09		10.9	7.27	14.54	1.81
Unidentified	29.07	16.36		1.81	7.27	3.63	
Total	101.56	40.8	3.62	21.7	14.52	18.17	1.81

Source: Compiled By Author from the Toronto Daily Star.

uni-identified men. Only 12.69 per cent are acquaintances. Amongst the acquaintances, 9.09 per cent were husbands or 3.62 per cent are common law-partners. When individual cases such as murder is taken into consideration the accused are mostly unidentified and unknown men. Amongst acquaintances, the rate of husbands murdering wives is the highest. Same is the case in assault cases, where husbands are the main culprits. However, in several assault cases, all the accused were unknown as reported in the Toronto Daily Star.

In the Toronto Daily Star too, the summer season sees the maximum number of reporting as in the case of the police records. In table 5.11, from the reporting of the Toronto Daily Star, it is found that maximum cases of offences reported were murder cases unlike police reporting where assault cases were

Table 5.11
Monthly Average of Crime Data From Toronto Star 1991-1996

Crimes	*Jan*	*Feb*	*Mar*	*Apr*	*May*	*Jun*	*July*	*Aug*	*Sept*	*Oct*	*Nov*	*Dec*	*Total*
Assault	0.66	0.66	1.16	1.2	0.83	0.5	0.83	0.66	1.2	0.83	0.2	1.2	9.77
Kidnap	0.16		0.16	0.5	0.16	0.2	0.33	1	0.5	0.16	0.7		3.79
Rape	0.33	0.33	0.16		0.33	0.2	0.5	0.16		0.16		0.2	2.29
Murder	1.33	0.5	0.83	0.8	2.33	1	0.5	1.16	1.8	0.66	0.7	0.8	12.46
Sexual Assault	1.33	1.33	1.33	0.7	0.5	0.5	0.83	1.83	1.5	1	1.5	1	13.31
Attempt to murder		0.16			0.16								0.32
Stalking								0.16					0.16
Total	3.81	2.98	3.64	3.2	4.31	2.3	2.99	4.97	5	2.81	3	3.2	42.1

Source: Compiled By Author from the Toronto Daily Star.

highest. Sexual assault cases were also reported in large numbers. However as in the police data, there are two peak periods of crimes against women, namely May and August during the summers. These two periods was also the time when there was maximum temperature fluctuations and weather change. May is the time for approaching summers, while August is the end of the summers and approach of the winter season.

The study on Toronto also included a set of interviews involving people from different walks of life, who felt that the situation of crime against women had deteriorated over the last five years. While others felt that the reporting had increased due to the awareness amongst the women. As for the prevention of more congestion with higher density of population with a higher rate of crime, about 72.72 per cent of the interviewees felt that highly populated areas have more crime against women. While the rest felt that there is no such correlation. However, from the case study, it is evident that where there is high incidence of crime against women, there is not necessarily high density of population. 54 per cent of the interviewees also felt that women who were not from an economically stable background reported cases more than women who came from affluent homes. However, it is also felt that since violence is a learned behaviour, when a child sees a parent abusing and harassing the other, the child has every chance of adopting such traits.

Another feature during the course of the interview, it was felt amongst 45.45 per cent of the interviewees that there is no correlation between male population and crime against women. However, further research in this is necessary before any conclusion can be drawn. In the course of the research it was found that in Toronto where there are more unemployed males, there is more crimes against women. A Violence Against Women Survey in 1993 in Canada brought to light several facts. Through a survey of the Canadian Center for

Justice Statistics in 1993, it was realized that 31 per cent of the major assaults were committed by unidentified men on the victims. In the course of the study on Toronto, from the newspaper reporting between 1995 – 1996, it is evident that maximum assaults are committed by the spouse while maximum violence as a whole is committed by unknown and unidentified men. As for the time period, for violent incidents, as per the Uniform Crime Reporting Survey 1993, it was found that all major assaults on women were committed maximum between 12:00 am to 2:59 am and maximum incidents take place after 6 pm . Through the study on Toronto, too similar results have been arrived upon.

In Toronto several women's organizations are involved in the development of the status of women, Women's Safety Audits, development and educational workshops etc. The Safety Audit, which was started by METRAC in 1989, has given fruitful results. The Safe City Committee in 1991 campaigned for safer parks, safer underground garages and developed training materials for the Planning and Development for self-education workshops. The Safe City has contributed towards controlling public violence against women as definitely public violence in the form of attacks by unknown, identified men is a common feature in the Toronto crime scenario.

A healthy city requires both economic prosperity and social stability. It is imperative to develop a healthy social environment in neighborhoods, which are more prone to criminal activity and social violence. The case study of Toronto is a typical example from a Developed country where there are large immigrant populations, high level of literacy and high income. The data provided by the police in Toronto was quite exhaustive, yet as per people's perception it is only a part of the story on crime against women. There are several untold ones as women in Toronto too prefer to take support and help from women's organizations as a visit to the police for them may be traumatic. However as in the case of Kolkata, the study on Toronto too, has some common features, which will be discussed in the chapter on Comparative Study between Kolkata and Toronto.

References

1. Municipal Strategies for Preventing Public Violence against Women, September 1988, pp. 1-2.
2. L.S. Bourne and A.E. Olvet, *New Urban and Regional Geographies in Canada: 1986-91 and beyond (Toronto),* July 1995, p. 41.
3. *Ibid.*
4. *Locked in Left Out,* Ontario Association of Interval and Transition Houses, 1996, pp. 25, 31.
5. *The* Safe City : Municipal Strategies For Preventing Public Violence Against Women, (1988), p. 2.
6. *Metro Toronto: A Community At Risk,* United Way of Greater Toronto, (July 1997), p. 3.
7. I.M. Gomme, *The Shadow Line Deviance and Crime in Canada,* Toronto, 1993, p. 49.
8. *Ibid.,* p. 51.
9. *Ibid.*
10. *Ibid.,* p. 52.
11. M.D. Smith and Others *Sociological Perspective,* 1992, Vol. 35, p. 552.
12. R.H. Beattie, *The Annuls of the American Academy,* Vol. 217, p. 30.

6

Special Problems: Sexual Assaults and Domestic Violence

While studying the nature of crimes against women in the micro areas of Calcutta and Toronto, it is obvious that Sexual assaults, whether they are cases of molestation or rape or just passing lewd gestures or remarks and domestic harassment or battery are of the maximum magnitude amongst the total offenses. These two types of offences however as they are getting more media attention and with the building up of awareness, women are reporting these offences as they become more confident that these offences are not taboos but need to be reported.

Sexual Assaults

It is believed that one in four Canadian women is sexually assaulted and in India the Crime in India statistics show that over 60,000 women were abused in the year 2000. Statistical evidences on incidences of rape and other forms of sexual assaults are mostly based on available police records. More often this is just the tip of the ice bug and not a due representation of the problem due to the cultural and social stigmatisation associated with the event. Women are more likely not to report rape if there is little support from their families, law enforcement agencies and the health sector.

In the Asia-Pacific region although statistics is difficult to find, the Asian Women's Resource Exchange compiled from various sources, the rape situation in some selected countries of the region.

Large scale studies of rape and sexual assault are scarce. Those that do exist however, consistently report high prevalence rates. Research conducted in industrialised countries has shown that the likelihood of a women being raped on having to fight off an attempted rape is high. Research in developing countries suggests that rape is an ever-present threat and reality for millions of women. Six separate investigations suggest that between 14 per cent and 20 per cent of women in the United States will experience a complete rape at least once in her lifetime.

In a random sample of 420 women in Toronto, Canada, 40 per cent reported at least one episode of sexual intercourse since the age of 16.

Country	*Reported cases of rape 1997*	*Legislative reforms on rape*	*Rape crisis services/centres available*
Bangladesh	753	No	Yes
Fiji	18	No	Yes
Japan	1854	No	Yes
Lao PDR	48	No	Yes
Malaysia	1323	Yes	Yes
Philippines	794 (Jan-Apr.)	Yes	Yes
Thailand	140 (Jan-Aug)	in process	Yes

Source: Asian Women's Resource Exchange.

Although rape and sexual assault may be perpetrated by strangers, evidence from many services indicates that a high percentage of rapists are acquaintances, friends, relatives and those in positions of trust or power. Another consistent finding is the high percentage of young, and often very young, rape victim as shown in the table below*.

Statistics on Sexual Crimes

Country	*Attacks known to victims*	*Victims aged 15 or less per cent*	*Victims aged 10 or less*
Peru (Lima)	60	—	18
Malaysia	68	58	18
Monico city	67	36	23
Panama city	61	40	—
Papma New agvinee	—	47	13
Chice (Santiago)	72	58	32
U.S.	78	62	29

* Heise L. Violence Against Women: the hidden health burden. World Health Statistics quarterly, 1993, 46 (1): 78-85.

Many sexual assaults are perpetuated by more than one attacker. "Gang rape", where two or more men subdue and penetrate their victims, is not uncommon. Women are also subject to what has been termed as "non-contact" several abuse in which, for example, men expose their penises or make obscene telephone calls. Where non-contact abuse has been studied, it has been discovered that a high percentage of women have experienced this type of abuse; in some cases up to 50 per cent of all women questioned.

Based on a survey by METRAC, the present situation in Canada reads as follows:

Statistical Sheet: Sexual Assault

General

- Fifty-one per cent of all Canadian women have experienced at least one incident of sexual or physical violence. Close to 60 per cent of these women have survived more than one incident of violence. (Statistics Canada 1993, 1, 3)

- Of all women who are sexually assaulted, 69 per cent are assaulted by men that they know. (OWD 1995,1)
- According to the Violence Against Women Survey (VAWS), 39 per cent of Canadian women reported of having being sexually assaulted since age 16. (Johnson 1996, 50) Nineteen per cent reported of having been sexually assaulted by strangers. (Statistics Canada 1993, 1)
- According to the same study, 25 per cent of women experienced unwanted sexual touching *and* another 24 per cent of women experienced violent sexual attack. (Johnson 1996, 50)
- Of all incidents of sexual assault, 24 per cent took place in the victim's home, 20 per cent in the perpetrators home, 10 per cent in someone else's home, 25 per cent in a car, and 21 per cent in a public place. (OWD 1995, 3)
- Thirty-eight per cent of women who have been sexually assaulted were assaulted by their husbands, common-law partners, or boyfriends. (OWD 1995, 3)

Reporting of Sexual Assault

- According to Statistics Canada, only 6 per cent of sexual assaults are reported to the police. (OWD 1995, 1)
- Only 1 per cent of date rapes are reported to the police. (OWD 1995, 5)

Sexual Assault and Young Women

- Sixty-three per cent of all sexual assaults reported to the police involve girls under the age of 18. (Russell 1996)
- Fifty-four per cent of girls under the age of 16 have experienced some form of unwanted sexual attention. Twenty-four per cent have experienced rape of coercive sex, and 17 per cent have experienced incest. (Holmes and Silverman 1992; Russell 1996)

- Four out of five female undergraduates reported that they had been victims of violence in a dating relationship. Twenty-nine per cent of that number reported incidents of sexual assault. (OWD 1995, 1)
- Girls are two or three times more likely to experience sexual abuse than boys. (Johnston and Saenz 1997)
- Sixty per cent of Canadian college-aged males report that they would commit sexual assault if they were certain that they would not be caught. (OWD 1995, 2)
- Thirty-one per cent of sexual assaults occur in dating and acquaintance relationships. (OWD 1995, 2)
- Twenty per cent of Toronto secondary school students reported that they had experienced at least one form of assault in a dating relationship. (OWD 1995, 5)
- In a Canadian study, 25 per cent of all female post-secondary students in 1993 had been physically and/or sexually assaulted by a male date or boyfriend. (Johnson 1996, 115)
- In this study, 1 in 5 male students surveyed said that forced intercourse was all right "if he spends money on her", "if he is stoned or drunk", or "if they had been dating for a long time." (Johnson 1996, 120)
- In 51 per cent of all incidents of dating violence reported by Canadian women, the perpetrator was under the influence of alcohol. (Johnson 1996, 128)

With Disabilities

- Eighty-three per cent of women with disabilities will be sexually assaulted during their lifetime. (OWD 1995, 1)
- The rate of sexual abuse of girls with disabilities is four times that of the national average. (Razack 1994)

Aboriginal Women

- Eight in 10 Aboriginal women in Ontario reported having experienced violence. (Ontario Native Women's Association 1989, 17)
- Up to 75 per cent of victims of sex crimes in Aboriginal communities are female under 18 years of age; 50 per

cent of those are under age 14, and almost 25 per cent are younger than 7 years of age. (Mclvor and Nahanee 1998, 65)

Women Living in Poverty

- Women with low household incomes, low levels of education and/or who are unemployed are at higher risk of being sexually assaulted than women in general. (Johnson 1996, 108-109)

Sexual Assault: Dispelling the Myths

Myth: Sexual assault is not a common problem.

Fact: Sexual assault is experienced by Canadian women every day—at home, at work, at school and on the street. The *Violence Against Women* survey found that over one-half (51 per cent) of Canadian women have experienced at least one incident of sexual or physical violence. Of these women, almost 60 per cent were the targets of more than one such incident. In a 1998 survey, 56 per cent of female victims reporting sexual assault of 169 police forces in Canada were under 18 years of age. Several studies have shown that women with disabilities are at a high risk of being abused. Research has found that 40 per cent of women with disabilities have been assaulted, raped or abused. Further, it is estimated that 83 per cent of women with disabilities will be sexually assaulted in their lifetime.

Myth: Women lie about being sexually assaulted, often because they feel guilty about having had sex.

Fact: Women rarely make false reports about sexual assault. In fact, sexual assault is a vastly under-reported crime. According to Statistics Canada, only 6 per cent of all sexual assaults are reported to police. Only 1 per cent of all "date/acquaintances rapes" are reported to police.

Myth: Sexual assault is most often committed by strangers.

Fact: Women face the greatest risk of sexual assault from men they know, not strangers. A 1998 study found that 33 per cent of female victims of sexual assault age 18 and over were assaulted by a friend or a casual acquaintance; 25 per cent by a family member (including a spouse or ex-spouse). When a women knows the men who sexually assaults her, it is less likely that it will be recognised as a crime, even by her. These sexual assaults are no less a crime than those that are committed by strangers.

Myth: The best way for a woman to protect herself from sexual assault is to avoid being alone at night in dark, deserted places, such as alleys or parking lots.

Fact: 80 per cent of sexual assaults occur in the home and 49 per cent of sexual assaults occur in broad daylight. Most sexual assaults do not fit the 'stranger-in-a-dark-alley' stereotype. Currently, there is a trend towards non-consensual drug-induced sexual assaults.

Myth: Women who are sexually assaulted "ask for it" by the way they dress or act.

Fact: The idea that women "ask for it" is often used by offenders to rationalize their behaviour. It also blames the victim for the crime, not the offender. Victims of sexual assault report a wide range of dress and actions at the time of the assault. Any women of any age and physical type, in almost any situation, can be sexually assaulted. If a women is sexually assaulted, it is not her fault. No woman ever "asks" or deserves to be sexually assaulted. Whatever a woman wears, wherever she goes, whoever she talks to, "no" means "no". It's the law. A drug-induced sexual assault is non-consensual and therefore also means "no".

Myth: Men who sexually assault women are either mentally ill or sexually starved.

Fact: Men who sexually assault are not mentally ill or sexually starved. Studies on the profiles of rapists reveal that they appear to be "ordinary" and "normal" men who sexually assault women in order to assert power and control over them.

Myth: Men of certain races and backgrounds are more likely to sexually assault women.

Fact: Men who commit sexual assault came from every economic, ethnic, racial, age and social group. The belief that women are more often sexually assaulted by men of colour or working class men is stereotype rooted in racism and classism. Men who commit sexual assault can be doctors, teachers, employers, co-workers, lawyers, husbands, or relatives of the women they assault.

Myth: It's only sexual assault if physical violence or weapons are used.

Fact: The Criminal Code definition of sexual assault includes a number of acts ranging from unwanted sexual touching, to sexual violence resulting in wounding, maiming or endangering the life of the victim. Most sexual assaults are committed by a man known to the victim. The man is likely to use verbal pressure, tricks, such as administering drugs without the victim's consent, and/or threats during an assault.

Myth: Unless she is physically harmed, a sexual assault victim will not suffer any long-term effects.

Fact: Any sexual assault can have serious effects on women's health and well being. A Canadian survey found that nine out of ten incidents of violence against women have an emotional effect on the victim. Women who have been sexually assaulted feel anger, fear and can become more cautious and less trusting. Women who have experienced a history of victimization are at high risk for developing lifetime mental health problems. It is estimated that 30 per cent of sexually assaulted women contemplate suicide.

Myth: Women cannot be sexually assaulted by their husbands or boyfrineds.

Fact: Under the law, women have the right to say no to any form of sex, even marriage or dating relationship. The Canadian Panel on Violence Against Women found that 38 per cent of sexually assaulted women were assaulted by their husbands, common-law partners or boyfriends. Although sexual assault within relationships has been illegal in Canada since 1983, few women report such incidents to police. Women experience long-term negative effects of partner sexual assault and the traumatic consequences of the sexual assault may even be more significant than those of non-partner sexual assault.

However, most often perpetrators of several violence and traditional societies are bound by myths which are related to sexual assault. These myths are not area specific but are true in the context of South Asia, Canada and other developed and developing countries.

Source: Ontario Women's Directorate: Sexual Assault: Dispelling thoughts.

Inspite of incamera trials in several countries for rape victims; victim counselling, many women prefer to keep violence a secret. Women are reluctant to report the crime to the family or police as often unmarried women are forced to marry their attachers; some may be murdered or even prosecuted for committing such as offence.

Moreoften women are taken to be objects as they have little or no power in society. Any form of violence that is thrust on a women is based on the concept of control and power over her. The diagram that has been prepared by the Domestic Abuse Intervention Project in Minnesota has successfully used the dynamics of power to show how violence is used to intimidate women.

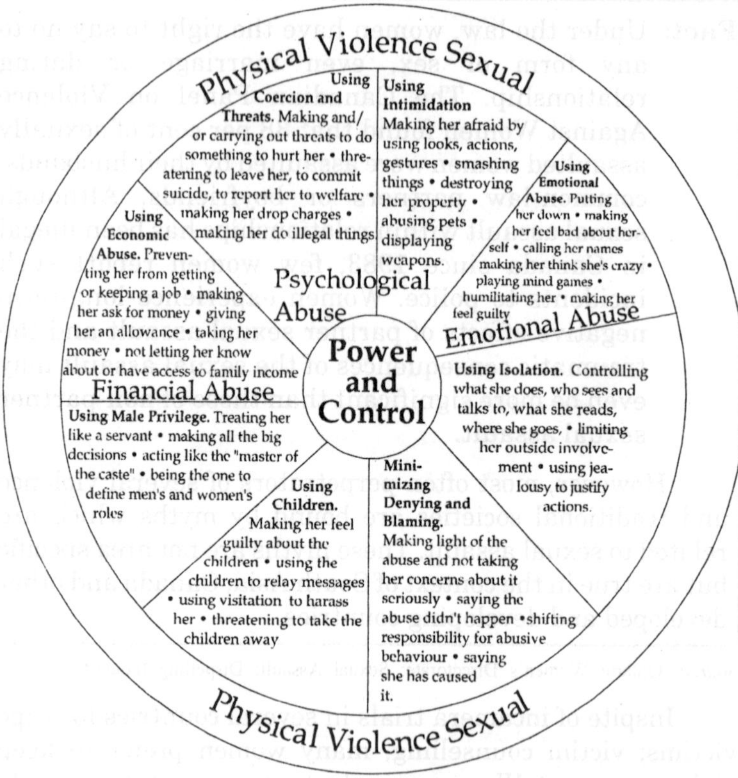

Source: Domestic Abuse Intervention Project, Minnesota, U.S.A.

As seen in the diagram on power and control, rape is used as a political weapon of repression and is widely committed and seldom denounced. Rape and sexual assault of women in situations of conflict have been viewed more as the spoils of war than as illegitimate acts that violate humanitarian law. Not until the international outcry rose in response to reports of mass rape in the former. Yugoslavia did the international community confront rape as a war crime and begin to take steps to punish those responsible for such abuse. Rape nonetheless has long been mischaracterised and dismissed by military and political leaders—those in a position to stop it—as a private crime, a sexual act, the ignoble act of the occasional soldier; worse still, it has been accepted precisely because it is so common place.[1]*

In early 2001, three Bosnian Serb men were found guilty of rape of Bosniac women and girls, some as young as 12 years and 15 years of age in Foca, Eastern Bosnia—Herzegovina, classified as a crime against humanity and a war crime. Two of the accussed were also found guilty of sexual enslavement as a crime against humanity by holding women and girls capture in a number of de factor detention centres in and around Foca. Many victims subsequently disappeared. The Foca verdict taken by the International Criminal Tribunal recognised that the sexual violence suffered by the women formed part of a widespread and systematic attack against a civilian.

Human Rights Watch investigations in the former Yugoslavia, Peru, Kashmir and Somalia reveal that rape and sexual assault of women are an integral part of conflicts, whether international or internal in scope. We found that rape of women civilians has been deployed as a tactical weapon to terrorize civilian communities or to achieve "ethnic cleansing," a tool in enforcing hostile occupations, a means of conquering or seeking revenge against the enemy, and a means of payment for mercenary soldiers. Despite the prevalence of rape in war, according to the United Nations Special Rapporteur on Violence Against Women, "[Rape] remains the least condemned war crime. Throughout history, the rape of hundreds of thousands of women and children in all regions of the world has been a bitter reality."

Our investigation of rape in Haiti under the former military regime led by Lt. Gen. Raoul Cedras revealed that rape may also serve as a tool of political repression much as it has been a weapon of war. Women activities, the members of the opposition or, in many instances, the female relatives of opposition members were the focus of such attacks. Individuals were attacked in their homes, on the streets, or in detention.

---

* The Human Rights Watch-Global report on women.

As with rape in conflict, rape as a means of suppressing and rooting out political opposition has long been hidden—both because sexual attacks on women are not viewed as political and because such abuse often is carried out by the only authorities in a position to provide remedies.

Of all the abuses committed in war or by repressive regimes, rape in particular is inflicted predominantly against women. Although men are also raped, efforts to document human rights abuse reveal that women are overwhelmingly the targets. Despite its pervasiveness, rape has often been a hidden element of strife, whether political or military, a fact that is inextricably linked to its largely gender-specific character. That this abuse is committed by men against women has contributed to its being narrowly portrayed as sexual or personal in nature, a characterization that depoliticizes sexual abuse in conflict and results in its being ignored as a crime.

Yet rape in conflict or under repressive regimes is neither incidental nor private. It routinely serves a strategic function and acts as a tool for achieving specific military or political objectives. Like other human rights abuses, rape serves as a means of harming, intimidating and punishing individual women. Further, rape almost always occurs in connection with other forms of violence or abuse against women or their families. Under Haiti's brutal former regime, for example, police or paramilitary troops raided the homes of families accused of supporting then exiled President Jean-Bertrand Aristide, killed or detained some family members, looted families' property, and raped one or more of the women they found. In the conflict in the former Yugoslavia, combatants have raped and beaten women while shooting or taking their family members away to concentration camps. Women who are raped are often murdered or left to die by their attackers; Peruvian soldiers who served in the security forces have

---

* The Human Rights Watch Global Report on Women's Human Rights Delhi, OXFORD UNIVERSITY PRESS, New Delhi.

recalled gang-raping and then murdering civilian women. Far from being an isolated sexual or private act unrelated to state agents' violent attacks on others, rape often occurs alongside other politically motivated acts of violence.

Soldiers in Bosnia-Herzegovina rape women of particular ethnic identities as part of their campaigns to drive these women, their families and communities out of the country. Women have also been abducted from their homes and forced by the military into prostitution. In the former Yugoslavia, non-Serbian women report being taunted by their rapists that they will be forced to carry and give birth to Serbian babies.

In Japan, the comfort women were the 200,000 girls and women of Korea and Philippine origin who were forced into prostitution by the Japanese government. Till date, they have not been provided any compensation in spite of international pressures. It is believed that of the many survivors who were detained in the programme for 3 to 5 years, most of them were raped between 5 to 20 times a day.

Social Scientists in South Asian countries do not limit the reasons of rape to power dynamics only, but also include other psychological and socio-cultural environment of the offenders such as lack of proximity to women; social taboos which makes the offence more illusive.

However, the nature of victimization of the victims are complete with psychological, physical and social consequences. Researchers in the 80's and 90's felt that women are victims of rape even before the crime takes place as most women fear rape which is a source of mental anxiety to the victim. The possibility of being victimized troubles many people. This perpetual fear includes a continuing state of psychological stress which leads to resorting to several safety precautions which is turn seriously restricts their freedom especially moving alone.

It is also a fact that women who have gone through the crime wary of reporting the case due to the repeated interviewing of the victim unlike in victims of other offences. The post attack trauma of the victim is much more than the attack itself. Apart from the official response of the police which in many instances have been a repeat in the offence for the victim and her family, the social stigma is also great.

The conducive factors which increase women's willingness to report rape:

- laws protecting confidentiality and disclosure of survivers name.
- public education about acquaintence rape
- expanding counselling and advocacy services.
- Accessibility of abortion services for rape services.
- Mandatory HIV/AIDS testing for those indicted for rape.
- Confidentiality from testing for HIV/AIDS or STDs.

Source: National Victims centre and crime victims research and treatment centre 1992.

The above reasons are the conducive conditions for women to report the offence. In order to address rape, the concerns of rape survivors have to be taken seriously. Police personal, religions authorities and health workers need to be sensitised while dealing with rape victims. In some countries government agencies and NGO's have taken the initiative to set up crisis centres for rape survivors in collaboration with the different sectors of the community. Moreover, countries which have recently passed laws or reformed their penal codes to broaden the definition of rape have done so as an outcome of the lobbying efforts of women's groups. The challenge to make sure that the law is not prejudicial against women regimes, and that the law is properly enforced to ensure the protection of women. By providing suitable legal support and health services, it is hoped that the responsibility of dealing with rape would fail on society rather than on women, survivors and their families would then feel encouraged to come forward to report rape.

World Health Organisation in 1997 reviewed the Commonwealth government initiatives to combat violence against women has pointed to the relative paucity of campaigns dealing with rape and sexual assault, as compared, for example with wife-battering and sexual harassment. However, women's groups in many countries are offering support across a range of women's issues, including rape and sexual assault, alongwith domestic violence and child sexual abuse.

- *Survivor groups and rape crisis centres* have been set up in some countries where women can work together to try and overcome their trauma.
- *Special rape crisis rooms* have been set up in hospitals in El Salvador and police stations in the United Kingdom for victims to be examined and questioned in privacy.
- *Woman police officers* have been recruited and trained specifically to deal with victims of rape and sexual abuse in Bangladesh and Malaysia.
- *Theatrical performances followed by discussions* in school and community settings are exploring issues relating to rape in Jamaica.
- *Rape crisis telephone lines* have been established in many countries, providing anonymous counselling and support for victims
- *Complaints about violent sexual themes* on television and radio and in the press are fuelling public debate on these issues in Jamaica.

Domestic Violence

Crime against women traditionally includes rape, kidnapping and abduction, dowry, death, torture, molestation, sexual harassment, importation of girls, cases under the Immoral Traffic (Prevention) Act, Sati Prevention Act, Dowry Prohibition Act, Indecent Representation of Women (Prevention) Act. In 2000, a total of 141373 such cases were reported. Of these violence that take place within the four walls which is in the form of dowry death, torture and dowry harassment has amounted to 55649 cases as against 53586 cases reported in 1999 (as increase of 3.7 per cent).

This situation is not limited to the women of the Southern continents, but is a problem for women in developed countries where women have more access to finances and education and are more empowered. Yet it is certain after seeing the crime statistics that patriarchy unites man everywhere in their domination of women.

The recently released Delhi crimes against women by the Crime Against Women Cell has confirmed that there are more rapes, more cases of eve-testing and molestation in Delhi in 2003 than in 2002. The police personnel explain the rise in these crimes due to the sensitisation of police personnel, lodging of FIRs, more investigation of cases and more success in arresting the guilty.[2]

Crimes Reported to Delhi Police (2004)

	2003	2002
Rape	490	429
Molestation	489	446
Eve-teesing	1599	976
Dowry death	130	135

The Crime Against Women Cell in Delhi was formed in 1983 to look into cases of dowry deaths. Netu it area of work was indened to include all crimes related to women. In 2003 alone, the call received 8161 complaints of marital discord and dowry harassment. Of these more than 2315 cases are pending[3] have proved successful and has removed the stigma from reporting by the family and the society.

More and more women learn about the law and as they and the society slowly get empowered try to break away from the bonds of a murderous marriage and try to seek relief. However, only they wake up to the fact that the laws are inadequate and archaic. The police, the judiciary use non-contemporary methods to settle disputes over custody of children, marital property, return of streedhan and maintenance.

The absence of adequate civil courts lead many women to seek police help and exploit section 498A to secure divorce or settlement. A conviction of an errant husband under Section 498A1PC does not give the women divorce. She has to approach civil court and also pursue the criminal case filed in a police station. If she is economically dependent on the husband and if he is imprisoned, the question of maintenance may not arise. So, women use section 498A IPC to redress all material grievances for a quicker and advantageous settlement.[4]

Woman who opt to go away from her marital home and report an offence does not obtain relief quickly. Her trauma gets relieved through reporting to the police or while seeking protection for herself or children; but she has no where to go. Even the prospect of returning to her parental home means that she gains social disapproval; the husbands go to all extent to dispose off the property in her home or those held jointly; after she is deprived of the custody of her children or the right to meet them. The nightmare is relived several times over. This often makes her agree to situations where she is made to compromise. This is the situation in most places in South Asia and is not uncommon in the developed nations.

International statistics shows the following

* Around the world, at least one in three women have been coerced, into sex or abused in some way—most often by someone she knows. One women in four is abused during pregnancy (UNPF, Sept. 2000).
* Violence against women and girls is widespread—one woman in three will experience violence during her lifetime, most often at the hands of someone she knows. Each year 2 million girls are at risk of genital mutilation, and up to 5,000 women and girls are the victims of so-called "honour" killings. (United Nations Population Fund, September 2000 and summary)

* The number of girls and women have been undergone female genital mutilation is estimated at between 100 and 140 million. It is estimated each year, a further 2 million girls are at risk of undergoing FGM. (World Health Organisation, Fact Sheet No. 241, June 2000)
* The brothels of India hold between 100,000 and 160,000 Nepalese women and girls, 35 per cent were taken on the false pretext of marriage or a good job. (Radhika Coomaraswamy, UN Special Report on Violence Against Women, Gustavo Capdevila, IPS, April 2, 1997)
* Every minute in the United Kingdom, police receive a call from the public for assistance for domestic violence. 81 per cent of these are female victims attacked by male perpetrators. (Economic and Social Research Council's Programme on Violence, Royal Holloway, September 28, 2000)
* At least 60 million girls who would otherwise be expected to be alive are "missing" from various populations, mostly Asia, as a result of sex-selective abortions, infanticide or neglect. (United Nations Study on the Status of Women, 2000)
* 70 per cent of the men and women interviewed in a Kenyan survey said they knew neighbours who beat their wives. Nearly 60 per cent said women were to blame for the beatings. Just 51 per cent said the men should be punished. (Kenyan Women Rights Awareness Program survey, 1997)
* In 1999 37 per cent of women homicide victims were killed by present or former partners, compared to 6 per cent of men. This totals 92 women-1 every 3 days, or 2 women per week. (Criminal Statistics England and Wales 1999. London: Home Office, 1999)
* 69 per cent of women inmates compared to 27 per cent of women in general have suffered from physical abuse by an inmate partner in an adult relationship. (Jane Laishes Mental Health, Health Services, Canada, December 1997).

* A study of more than 2,500 women in London, UK found that women who were physically and sexually abused in childhood are at increased risk of victimization in adulthood. (The Lancet, August 11, 2001)
* Domestic violence accounts for almost a quarter (23 per cent) of all violent crimes. (The British Crime Survey: England and Wales. London: Home Office, 2000)
* In March 2000, Pakistan's Human Rights Commission reported that, on average, at least two women were burned every day in domestic violence incidents. (Human Rights Watch)
* Approximately 70 to 90 per cent of Pakistani women experience spousal abuse. ("Crime or Custom?: Violence Against Women in Pakistan," Human Rights Watch, August 1999)
* Millions of women are denied reproductive choices and access to health care, contributing each year to 80 million unwanted or mistimed pregnancies and some 500,000 preventable pregnancy-related deaths. Nearly half of all deliveries in developing countries take place without a skilled birth attendent present. (United Nations Population Fund, September 2000 and summary)
* Somewhere in America a women is battered, usually by her intimate partner, every 15 seconds. (United Nations Study on the Status of Women, 2000)
* On average, more than three women are murdered by their husbands or boyfriends in the United States every day. (Bureau of Justice Statistics Special Report, "Intimate Partner Violence and Age of Victim, 1993-99," October 2001)
* Boys who witness their fathers' violence are 10 times more likely to engage in spouse abuse in later adulthood than boys from non-violent homes. (Family Violence Interventions for the Justice System, 1993)
* Domestic violence often does not consist of a single incident; it is instead a continual state of victimization. ("Domestic and Sexual Violence Data Collection,"

National Institute of Justice and Bureau of Justice Statistics joint report, July 1996)

* Approximately 50 per cent of the homeless women and children in the United States are on the streets because of violence in their homes. ("A Report on the 1988 National Survey of the Shelters for the Homeless," U.S. Department of Housing and Urban Development, 1989)
* Domestic violence occurs in approximately 25-33 per cent of same-sex relationships. (NYC Gay and Lesbian Anti-Violence Project, October 1996)
* Pregnant or recently pregnant women are more likely to be the victims of homicide than to die of any other cause.[5]

The 1999 General Social Survey on spousal violence found that spousal violence measures are the prevalence of violence in intimate relationships across the country. The GSS findings reveal that the rates of spousal violence experienced by men and women were only slightly different—8 per cent for women and 7 per cent for men in relationships five years prior, and 4 per cent for both women and men in their current relationships.

In a country where 3.4 wives are murdered for every one husband killed (Locke, 2000), and where previous statistics reveal that 98 per cent of sexual assaults and 86 per cent of violent crimes are committed by men (Johnson, 1996); where women constitute 98 per cent of spousal violence victims to sexual assault, kidnapping or hostage taking (Fitzgerald, 1999), and where 80 per cent of victims of criminal harassment are women while 90 per cent of the accused are men (Kong, 1996), the GSS findings do not capture the full extent of violence against women perpetrated by men.

Limitations and Findings

- The GSS is a telephone survey excluding respondents who do not speak any of the official languages; people with speech disabilities; Aboriginal and homeless peoples, and poor people living in households without a telephone. This means that women who are in transition, who are homeless, and who may be escaping their abusive partners are not included in the survey. Hence, women who are most vulnerable and have experienced multiple forms of violence are not taken into account.

- The GSS involves respondents' responses to questions concerning their experiences of violence and emotional abuse which they have been subjected to by their partners in the previous 12 months and 5-year period prior to the survey. However, the rates for emotional abuse are not calculated in the rates for spousal violence—they are kept separate even though in reality, emotional abuse and physical violence are intertwined, one often preceding and accompanying the other.
- Although the GSS is a victimization survey in that it asks respondents to identify their experiences of violence as opposed to the crime reporting surveys which are based on police reports of violence, the GSS has its own limitations. This includes the assumption that respondents are able to articulate their experiences of violence and are in circumstances that permit them to make such disclosures. Further, the GSS only asks respondents about the violence they have experienced from their partners in their last 5-year and 12-month periods. In contrast, the Violence Against Women Survey (VAWS, 1993) asked women about the violence they had experienced since the age of 16.
- Unlike the VAW Survey, also conducted by Statistics Canada, the GSS does not measure the full spectrum of violence to which women are subjected. The GSS spousal violence rates do not include emotional abuse rates, although these are measured separately. Neither do they include the kind of data on sexual harassment obtained in the VAW Survey or other surveys. These surveys report that 8 in 10 victims of incidents of harassment reported to the police were female and 9 out of the 10 accused were males (Kong, 1996).

- The GSS module of questions on violence simply lists the different forms of violence ranging from minor acts such as having something thrown at you, to more severe forms such as being choked or beaten. However, the module does not tap into the dynamics of violence which cohere around power and control. Instead, the questions seem to equalize all actions as forms of violence. The survey does not take into consideration how violence may be used to exercise dominance or how violence may be used as a form of self-defence and retaliation. The intentions and context surrounding the violence are ignored.
- Despite these limitations, the GSS results reveal the true severity of violence against women. Not only were women beaten, choked, threatened with a weapon and sexually assaulted in significantly large numbers as compared to men, the consequences of the violence they suffered were multiple and extensive. As the GSS results show, women were more fearful of their lives, their children's safety, and suffered from sleeping problems, depression/anxiety attacks, and low self-esteem as a result of the violence. Women also reported being physically injured and were 5 times more likely to require medical intervention as compared to men who reported experiencing violence.
    - More than twice as many women as men reported being beaten;
    - 5 times as many women as men reported being choked;
    - Almost twice as many women as men reported having a gun or knife used against them;
    - More than 6 times as many women as men reported being sexually assaulted;
    - 4 out of 10 women are afraid for their lives, as compared to 1 out of 10 men;
    - 4 times as many women as men reported being threatened, harmed or having someone close to them

being threatened or harmed;

- More than twice as many women reported having their property damaged or their possessions destroyed as compared to men; and,
- 4 times as many women as men reported being denied access to family income.

- The GSS on violence only captures a small section of the continuum of violence experienced by women everyday. It does not take into consideration the socio-economic and political context in which women live-a context symbolized by the pervasive objectification, sexualization, and devaluation of women as it occurs in the media, within the labour force, and in the increasing numbers of women who are become poor. Neither does it capture the full range of violence meted out to women who cross normative boundaries, or who are at the intersections of various kinds of oppressions. It does not take into consideration the extreme forms of violence, as in homicide, where other statistics reveal that for every 1 husband killed, there are 3.4 wives killed by spouses.[6]

Domestic Violence Worldwide

- Family violence and abuse affects all of us; no one is immune to violence.
- Abuse occurs in all forms of relationships including: parent-child, caregiver-client, adult child-parent, dating, gay and lesbian, marital and common-law and sibling.
- Since the age of sixteen, 51 per cent of Canadian women report having experienced at least one incident of physical or sexual violence.
- Nearly three in ten Canadian women (29 per cent) who have ever been married or lived in a common-law relationship have ever been physically or sexually assaulted by a marital partner at some point during the relationhip; 21 per cent of these women were

assaulted during pregnancy.

- Of 22,000 victims of spousal violence reported to a sample of 179 Canadian police agencies in 1997, 88 per cent (19,575) were female and 12 per cent (2,679) were male.
- Children witnessed violence against their mothers in almost 40 per cent of violent marriages; in many cases of children witnessing violence, the violence was so severe that the women feared for their lives (52 per cent) and/or were injured (61 per cent).
- Nearly one quarter of women (22 per cent) who have experienced wife assault never told anyone about the abuse.
- Violent men are three times as likely as nonviolent men to have witnessed spousal violence in childhood, and women who were raised in similar circumstances are twice as likely to be victims of spousal violence.
- Between 1978 and 1997, 1,485 females and 442 males were killed by their spouses in Canada. A total of 90,792 women and children were admitted to 413 shelters for battered women across Canada in 1997-98.
- In 1996, children under 18 represented 22 per cent of victims of assaults reported to a sample of 154 police agencies; children represented 60 per cent of all victims of sexual assault and 18 per cent of all victims of physical assault.
- Of sexual assaults by family members reported to police, girls were victimized in 79 per cent of cases (1,662); while boys were victims in 21 per cent of cases (440).
- The degree of risk of sexual abuse of persons with disabilities is "at least 150 per cent of that for individuals of the same sex and similar age without disabilities."
- In 1997, older adults accounted for 2 per cent of victims of all violent crime reported to a sample of 179 police agencies; of these, 53 per cent reported

sustaining some type of injury.

- Almost 25 per cent of violent incidents against older persons reported to a sample of police in 1997 were perpetrated by family members; and while more older men were victimized by their adult children (41 per cent) than by a spouse (28 per cent), older women experienced violence by adult children (40 per cent) and spouses (40 per cent) in equal 13 proportions.

Dowry: A Traditional form of Violence

The dowry system and marriage in India both Hindu and Muslim and also sometimes Christian marriages too are interlinked.

In the early stages of a marriage, a new bride who is being mis-treated by her husband's family may not seek help from her own parents because they will already have counselled her that a period of adjustment to her new situation may be needed. If she does not complain, unless the abuse is repeated or extreme, most parents would probably be reluctant to intercede on her behalf with the in-laws or husband. This reflects the Hindu norm that once a girl is married, her parents have only limited rights to a say in her new family's personal affairs. They might also hope that some mutual adjustment might occur between the bride and her new family so that there would be a reduction in harassment and ill-treatment. If the girl returns to her parents' house because of quarrels with her husband, this brings shame on her parents' family and prevents the marriage of any of her sisters. Moreover, she cannot take part in any religious ceremonies without her spouse. For all these reasons an abused wife may not expect much support from her parents and may only get support in more extreme cases.

These marriage arrangements reflects the generally subordinate and powerless position of younger women, and patterns of domestic violence in India are indicative to this position. In particular, there are certain forms of victimization in India and that would be almost unheard of in western society: female infanticide, dowry deaths (bride burning) and sati[7]. The last, sati, is different from the first two in that the widow "chooses" to commit suicide on the death of her husband.

The Dowry System

The dowry system is deeply rooted in Hindu culture and is the customary practice of giving gifts in cash and kind by the bride's family to that of groom (Goody and Tambiah, 1973). These gifts may be given before the marriage or at any time afterwards and include such things as appliances and furniture as well as cash and jewellery.[8] The cost of the dowry may impose a significant additional burden on the bride's parents, who also have to pay for a customarily elaborate and expensive wedding. The amount of the dowry is determined by the groom's family status, his level of education, his occupation and his income. Grooms who are physicians, engineers, lawyers, foreign-educated or working abroad are often preferred and command the highest dowries.

Despite its religious origins, the dowry settlement has all the characteristics of a market transaction. Some scholars suggest that the practice of giving dowry follows from a system of inheritance that excludes the female children and, by settling some of the family's wealth upon the daughters before the parents' death, to some extent compensates for the discriminatory effects of the system[9]. The nature and purpose of the dowry practice should therefore be considered in the context of property rights under a system of exclusively male inheritance (Harrel and Dickey, 1985; Paul, 1986; Upadhya, 1990). However, D'Souza and Natarajan (1986) have argued that the spread of the dowry practice from upperclass Hindus to the middle and lower classes, as well as to other religious groups, is evidence of its real purpose in compensating for women's low economic value. This seems all the more true because the spread of the practice has been accompanied by a subtle change in the conditions of the dowry, which increasingly is seen as a gift made to the groom and his family rather than as an amount of capital belonging to the bride.

Nature of Dowry Deaths

When not satisfied with the dowry, the bridegroom and his parents may humiliate, harass and physically abuse the bride. They may even murder her in order to arrange a second marriage. In some cases, also falling under the definition of dowry deaths, the bride might be driven to suicide.

Although brides may be murdered in a variety of ways, dowry deaths are popularly known as bride burning. In fact, many dowry deaths are by burning. One of the reasons is that such deaths can be easily concealed as accidents. In most Indian homes, kerosene is used as fuel for stoves and accidents are frequent. As the fire may destroy any evidence of violence, it can be difficult for the authorities to prove malicious intent.

Drowning is also a frequently used method of murdering the bride. Such deaths are facilitated by the wells that exist in many parts in India to provide drinking water. Since these are the sites of many accidental and suicidal deaths, murders are easily concealed. Likewise, because insecticides (organophosphorous compounds) and poisonous plants are widely available there is a high incidents of accidental and suicidal poisoning, which facilitates concealment of a murder through poison.

Essentially the same three methods—burning, drowning and poisoning—are used by brides driven to suicide. This makes it difficult to compile accurate statistics about the proportion of dowry death due to homicide. In fact, most recorded dowry deaths are registered as abetment to suicide under section 306 of the Indian penal code (Kronholz, 1986). A further complication lies in the fact that the rate of suicide among women is on the increase. Suicides by women are mainly due to family quarrels, especially problems with in-laws and with spouses and in many of these quarrels dissatisfaction with the dowry may play a part even if it is not the principal cause.

National level dowry death statistics are not reported in India. Devi Prasad (1990) notes that there was a total of

1649 dowry deaths reported in 18 of the 22 states in 1987, but these figures are of suspect reliability and are likely to understate the problem substantially. For example, there is large unexplained variation between states in rates of dowry deaths (the rate for Assam was 0.15 deaths per million of the population, whereas for Delhi the rate was 13.9) and reported deaths for individual states show considerable annual fluctuations (in 1985 the figures for Bihar (3) and Andhra Pradesh (15) were very much lower than in 1987, respectively 120 and 98).

During recent decades there has been much greater recognition in Indian society that murder and suicide associated with disputes over dowries have become significant social problems. The Indian government has responded through legislation (The Dowry Prohibition Act 1961, amended in 1984) prohibiting dowry payments, but these laws are widely ignored, partly because the legal definition of dowry has a number of loopholes and also because the dowry system is seen to serve a valuable social purpose by many sections of society.

Factors have been consistently identified. One of the most important of these is that many families simply do not have the resources to make the large dowry payments that are expected that they had promised (Khan and Ray, 1984). This problem has become more acute as the practice of dowry, formerly confined to the upper classes, has increasingly been adopted by middle and lower middle class families as a route to improve social status (Ahuja 1987).

A second important contributory factor is the joint family system (Ahuja, 1987). As explained, wives commonly move in with their husband's family. If the family also includes a number of the husband's siblings, the probability of conflict between the bride and these individuals is greatly increased. Quarrels often center upon accusations of insufficient dowry payments. In these arguments, husbands do not always support their wives and when her parents live at a distance and cannot easily come to support her, she is even more isolated. In Khan and Ray's (1984) study, it was found that about 55 per cent of dowry victims were living at quite some distance from their parents.

Problems may be exacerbated by the economic situation of the husband's family. Some families try to meet their debts by extracting a large cash dowry in exchange for their son's hand in marriage. Others try to meet their ambitions, for example, by obtaining education abroad for their sons or building an extension to their house (Ahuja, 1987). In general, commentators believe that modernization and urbanization have resulted in a more materialistic society. Husbands and their families view the dowry as a way of satisfying their ambition to own electronic goods, scooters and even cars.

The economic situation of the wife's family is also relevant. The bride's family more frequently has difficulty in paying when there is a large discrepancy between the educational backgrounds of the bride and the groom and a large dowry has been demanded (Dasgupta et. al., 1984). The bride's family may make unrealistic promises about their ability to pay a large dowry. This may be particularly likely to happen when they are anxious to marry one daughter off quickly because there are several other waiting to be married. The only situation may be to pay the dowry in installments, which may make the groom's family dissatisfied and encourage them to pressurize the girl to bring the rest of what had been promised by her parents (Ghosh, 1984; Ahuja, 1987; Devi Prasad, 1990).

These economic discontents may be aggravated by a variety of other factors such as incompatibility between spouses, unrealistic expectations of life, alcoholic family members, and the bride being young, lacking in education and stranger to the husband's family (Gayford, 1978; Law Commission 1983; Ahuja, 1987; Gautam and Trivedi, 1987; Garg, 1990).

The dowry death rate in India is 2000; alarming as it shows 6995 cases as against 6699 cases, a clear increase 4.4 per cent. However, there have been fewer cases under the Dowry Prohibition Act of 2876 cases is 2000 as against 3064 cases is 1999. The highest number of cases of dowry are reported from Uttar Pradesh, Bihar, Andhra Pradesh, Orissa etc.

Recently the case of Nisha Sharma (2003) reported from Noida, Uttar Pradesh brought to the foreground that dowry is not limited to the poor or the rich. Even the upwardly mobile middle class face a huge number of problems. Nisha, a 21 year of software engineer put down her bridal foot and refused to marry the groom after he demanded a few more extra hundred thousand rupees and a car. The police had also acted swifty to book the groom under the rarely used laws against dowry. The message was clear made by Nisha—don't marry a man who demands dowry."

A study conducted in Delhi in 1986 by M.C. Paul found the following:

1. The cases of dowry demands were more in medium SES (Socio-economic status) households, followed by low and high SES households. Mostly the modern consumer and luxury goods like black and white and colour television, VCR, sofa set, fridge, stereo, motor cycle, car, etc. were expected and demanded as dowry.
2. Various types and forms of torture were inflicted on the women belonging to all categories of socio-economic status, because their families did not comply with demands for dowry. In decreasing order, slapping and fisting, taunts and abuse, battering without instruments, attempt to kill, denying of food and clothes, sexual harassment, and sexual assault were the crimes inflicted on women belonging to high SES households. In the case of women from medium SES families the dowry related crimes were slapping and fisting, taunts and abuse, battering with and

without instruments, denying of food and clothes sexual assault, attempt to kill and sexual harassment in decreasing order. More or less, the women belonging to low SES households reported the same as the medium SES women.

3. A majority of husbands as well as in-laws wanted dowry to 'show-off' to others. Women from medium and low SES families suffered from cruelty due to the vices of their husbands which included alcoholism, drug addiction, smack use, extra-marital sex relationships, etc. Dowry demand in cash for business purposes came more from medium SES houses and high SES homes. The problem of housing in Delhi being acute, a significant percentage of women from medium SES families in the sample were tortured in order to bring dowry for this purpose. Quite a good number of women belonging to low SES homes were tortured by their husbands and in-laws for dowry to marry their sisters-in-law.
4. A majority of women listed their husbands as the main culprits followed by their *sas,* the *debar, nanad, sasur, jeth* and *jethani,* were also responsible though to a lesser extent in decreasing order.
5. Most of the crimes inflicted on women were within the confines of their homes. The women said that they initially tolerated the crimes and minor injuries from their husbands and in-laws and tried to make adjustments. Only when the cruelty was unbearable they went to the Police Headquarters in order to complain. Almost all women reported that they were not aware of the law against dowry related crimes before their marriage. In fact, 63.3 per cent learnt about it later on from friends, relatives, neighbours and social workers of various women's organisations in Delhi. About 22 per cent said that their awareness came from mass media mainly television and newspapers. Only 15 per cent come to know when the women's organisations took up their cases.

6. Just about half of the respondents were fatalistic about dowry related crimes. However, about 43 per cent stated that when they were cruelly maltreated for dowry by their husbands and in-laws they felt insulted.
7. A majority (52 per cent) of women wanted to get back their dowry and wanted a divorce in order to sort out their problems. Of these, a significant percentage belonged to medium and low SES families. Quite a good percentage belonging to medium SES families wanted to live independently. This was not so among women belonging to low and high SES households.
8. It was seen that in two-third cases the demand for dowry was absent when the marriage was settled. The demand came after the marriage as a post-marital phenomenon. They were tortured for dowry for the following reasons. First, they were not able to bring adequate dowry after the marriage. Second, they were pressurised to bring dowry for different purposes at different times on different pretexts.
9. It was found that a majority (60 per cent) of women did not comply with the demand and even those who did comply partially were also not able to save themselves from torture.[10]

All these indicated that the thirst for dowry was unsatiable and the crimes against women were also perennial. The women could not fulfill the demand for dowry due to the reason that:

- they could not afford to bring dowry as their parents/ guardians were not in a position to do so;
- fulfillment of such demand even once meant more demand in future so they wanted to take a stand against this unlawful demand.

The respondents were used as 'pawns'. The respondents stated that they were given the feeling by their husbands and in-laws that lots of women were available in the marriage market because there was a demand for employed men. By and large, marriage in India was arranged as per the traditional prescriptions. The economic compulsions of 'modern' acquisitive society was synchronised as per one's desires and experiences. It was likely that these attitudes and desires had made the asymmetrical marriage in 'modern' India, a commercial deal. Moreover, a widow cannot marry as easily and as frequently as a widower. Women who questioned the propriety of husbands and 'in-laws' unlawful demand of dowry faced the brunt of torture in their in-laws' homes. The respondents complained that man-woman equality, human dignity, respect for each other etc. were sacrificed at the 'altar of avarice' in the present 'modern' society of Delhi metropolis. They said passing of laws against dowry related crimes were of little help.

In view of the imposing and sobering realism of the findings of the present study it may be said that dowry related crimes against women can be tackled if proper education and employment opportunities are provided equally to men and women. And along with it a socio-cultural crusade by men and women is the need of the hour. The crimes against women on account of dowry cannot be checked if the present system perpetuates and expands.

The well known activist lawyer, Ms. Indira Jai Singh defined domestic violence as behaviour that one person in an intimate relationship uses in order to control the other. Some of the common features of Domestic Violence are:

- Use of physical violence including hitting, punching, slapping, kicking, shoving, choking or biting.
- Use of intimidation or manipulation to control the woman and her children.
- Forcible sex, forcing a woman to participate in sexual activities with others.
- Constant criticism of the woman and her abilities, especially as a spouse or partner, parent or employee.
- Preventing the woman from leaving the house or even communicating with others over the telephone or otherwise.

- Preventing the woman from visiting the family or friends and preventing her friends and family from having access to her.
- Preventing the woman from being gainfully employed or restricting such employment.
- Threats to hurt the woman, her children, family members, friends or himself.
- Destruction of personal property or throwing things around.
- Denial of access to personal property such as streedhan.
- Denial of access to family assets such as bank accounts, transport or control over finances.
- Humiliation or embarrassment of the woman in public.

The aspect of severe and progressively escalating physical and mental pain is the most obvious similarity between torture and Domestic Violence. Fear of death due to such violence is also an important factor of control in both torture and Domestic Violence. Physical beating, kicking, isolation, keeping a person for prolonged periods of time in darknes, depriving one of food, purely psychological methods such as instilling fear of death, threats to kill a loved one etc. are all methods common in both torture and Domestic Violence.

Similarly, it is necessary to point out that both torture and Domestic Violence often function along patterns of behaviour. Both, the torturer and the violent intimate, often alternate kindness with active and passive brutality, intersperse it with arbitrary and unpredictable punishment, and undermine the victims morale sustaining hatred for the perpetrator. All these methods work towards exhausting the endurance and manipulating dependency of the victim. These methods highlight the importance of the psychological aspects of torture and Domestic Violence. In other words, these aspects highlight the fact that both Domestic Violence and torture involve creation of an environment of domination through a process of acts and that considering either merely as sets of brutal acts undermines the true nature of such violence.

There is a distinct difference between torture and domestic violence. In the concept of torture, there are a range of types, and one of them is domestic violence. Especially in the Indian context, where the dowry system is intrinsically linked to Domestic Violence, one of the most important features is that of economic abuse. This makes it difficult for the woman to remove herself from the environment of Domestic Violence and ensures that status quo is maintained. Where the woman is gainfully employed, she is often denied access to her own income. Other means of economic abuse include the disposal or threatened disposal of personal and household effects that are important or necessary to the woman.

Although these acts have the effect of control and could be considered as acts causing mental pain, economic abuse does not squarely fit into the prevalent understanding of torture. It would, perhaps, be easier for cases where economic abuse is only an accompanying aspect of violence, where the other methods of violence are predominant, to be understood as torture. However, where economic abuse is the dominant factor it would be difficult to link Domestic Violence and torture.

The societal attitude towards Domestic Violence, especially in India, is another aspect of difference. Whereas torture is generally looked upon as an evil, Domestic Violence is not. In fact one may go to the extent of holding that Domestic Violence has societal backing. Consider the number of deaths that occur every day due to Domestic Violence, that the woman's younger sister is often forced to marry the person or into the family of the person who murdered her own sister, the fact that in most cases when a woman leaves the violent house and comes back to the house her parents live in she is actually sent back notwithstanding a threat to her life, and the fact that such leaving is considered bad by the community and that the woman's "value" lies in her ability to "adjust". It is also relevant to point out that the primary consideration when a woman finally leaves the violent house is "who will marry her/her sister now?" In such circumstances, treating Domestic Violence as a matter of force anud control of one person over another would be to absolve the rest of the society of their guilt.

The Trauma of Custody

Even though the definition of torture does not require that the person be in any sort of custody, the definition is based in the assumption that the person being tortured is in the captivity of the state. The understanding of torture is thus largely affected by the assumption that it usually occurs with the custody of the state. Whereas it is clear that in the case of Domestic Violence the woman is not the actual captivity of the state, it may be pointed out that the realities of Domestic Violence are frighteningly similar in this regard.

Firstly, there are cases where there is actual physical captivity, where the woman is not allowed to leave the house, is not allowed to speak to any one outside the house, even by telephone or post, either by actually physically restraining her movement or by threat of violence if she attempts to do so. The woman is not in a position to leave the violent relationship, and in many cases, she is not in a position to let any person outside the house know that she is being severely abused and her movements restricted.

Even in cases where the woman is not so physically restrained in most cases it is impossible for the woman to leave the house. This is especially true in the Indian context. In cases where the woman has escaped to the house of her parents she gets no support. In most cases she is told to "adjust" and is sent right back to the violent spouse. She is told that it is largely her fault that she was beaten up or abused and that it is up to her to behave in a manner that would not provoke such "anger". As such women are not only denied potential support structures in times of need but are also burdened with the guilt of not having fulfilled their responsibilities. This happens even in cases where there has been a serious threat to the woman's life. Unfortunately the threat is only understood in its seriousness after the woman has been killed or has been driven to suicide. One reason for this attitude is the importance given to the "institution" of marriage and family values. The pressures to be the perfect wife/daughter-in-law are enormous. The main reason, however, may be seen in the economic implications to the family. Where a family saves money and valuable goods over years for the dowry to be given at the woman's marriage, a separation is seen as a waste. Further, the parents are not in a position to repeat the exercise of saving a dowry. The woman is expected to be grateful for the marriage and is promptly sent back.

It is also necessary to recognise that in the Indian Context the norms of particular communities, such as caste and religious communities, are also a common hurdle to contend with. Whereas a consciousness of caste can be an important source of support in certain circumstances, the pressures of living in a closely knit community, where every member has knowledge of the everyday experiences of the other, is another restriction that makes escape from the violent environment impossible. Most often both the man and woman belong to the same community or caste. Often the parties happen to be closely related by blood and are for all practical purposes a part of the same extended family. Reaching out for help thus amounts not just to going against the idea that a family matter should be resolved within the four walls of the house but also to challenging the sanctity of the community. Another important aspect of such caste consciousness is the secrecy attached to "private" matters by the members of the community. This is reflected in the fact that in locating evidence that would be necessary for a case one may come across many hurdles due to such an attitude. People who would know about the relationship and would be potential witnesses often do not co-operate.

Another aspect that needs to be understood is the manner in which the education and career opportunities of women, especially middle class women are restricted by social structures in urban India. In the absence of support from other sources such as the family this additional drawback often implies that a woman has no choice but to remain within the relationship as economic independence is difficult if not impossible. Even where it is possible, the stigma that goes with challenging the structure of family makes the option unviable if not impossible. Further, there is the risk of severe violence and even death to contend with. This implies that not only does the woman have to earn enough to pay for a place to stay, she has to earn enough to find a place that is safe.

The fear a woman has with respect to the losing custody of her children if she tries to break away from the relationship or tries to take any other action is an important factor that adds to the effect of captivity. Not only has there been fear that taking the children with her would be illegal in some way but also the fact that economic independence would have to include the ability to support the children. Leaving the children the perpetrator not only leaves the children insecure but also deprives the woman of what is often her base for emotional support. The recent Gita Hariharan case in which the Supreme Court held that the mother is also the natural guardian alongwith the father should go a long way in dealing with the this aspect.

The captivity, actual or constructed, in the case of Domestic Violence is thus of a more complex and serious nature than the custody with respect to the understanding of torture.

Interpretation of Intention

The next aspect of the definition of torture, it may be recalled is that of "intention". The meaning of the term intention in this context may be understood from the fact that the drafters rejected the suggestion of restricting the concept to "deliberately and maliciously" inflicted pain. Other than defences such as insanity, grave and sudden provocation, mistake of fact, self-defence etc., all of which are established legal concepts. The concept of intention in the definition of torture is sufficiently wide to include acts of Domestic Violence.

Interpretation of "Particular Purpose"

The definition of torture in the UN Convention requires that the suffering be inflicted for the purposes of obtaining information or a confession, as a punishment for an offence, to intimidate a person or for any other reason based on discrimination.

There is no doubt that the particular purpose requirement provides clarity to the context of torture. However, the question that is important in the context of reconceptualisation of Domestic Violence is whether the requirement of purpose implies showing of specific or conscious intent. In the absence of judicial pronouncement in this regard it may be argued that the purpose requirement implies a study of the functions and impact of the violence. In such a construction, there would be no problem in understanding Domestic Violence as based on "discrimination of any kind". The fact that the CEDAW recently clarified that "violence against women is a form of discrimination" and the recent judgements of the Supreme Court attempting to apply the CEDAW despite the indifference on the legislature in this regard brightens up the possibility that a reconceptualisation of Domestic Violence as torture would be fruitful. The other possible purpose that could be invoked in the case of Domestic Violence is that of intimidation. It may be argued that besides the obvious effect of intimidation on the woman in a particular case, an act of Domestic Violence would amount to intimidation of women as a class. The fact that violence, especially where it is of a recurring nature, may occur at any time is another aspect that adds to the intimidating aspect of Domestic Violence.

Further, there is no doubt that certain forms of Domestic Violence would fall within the other recognised purposes. For example, where the violence is linked to jealousy and is interrogative in nature the act would satisfy the purpose of eliciting information. Similarly, where violence is committed as a "punishment", the purpose requirement would be fulfilled.

The "Public Official"

The definition of torture requires that the act should be "by or at the instigation of or with the consent or acquiescence of a public official or other person acting in an official capacity". Torture has been seen as a special case requiring the intervention of the international community because where the offender is the state the citizen cannot depend on the state machinery for redress. It has been argued that Domestic Violence cannot be included in the definition of torture, as it does not have such a character. The obligations of the state, under domestic and international law, serve as sufficient basis for the inclusion of Domestic Violence in the understanding of torture. This argument gets support from the development in domestic Indian jurisprudence with respect to the enforceability of fundamental rights provided in the Constitution. Apart from the provisions that explicitly provide rights that may be enforced against non-state parties case law has clearly extended the application of fundamental Rights against private parties. International intervention is justified on various grounds and there is definitely no lack of such justifications in the context of Domestic Violence.[11]

Overall, thus, it is possible to conceptualise Domestic Violence as torture within the present understanding.

Response of the Indian State to Domestic Violence

In the last two decades the state has been increasingly sensitised to women's issues. This may be seen in the fact that there has been legislative recognition of cruelty within the domestic sphere. The amendments to the Indian Penal

Code in order to include Sections 498A and 304B, the amendments to the Indian Evidence Act to include Sections 113A and 113B and the amendments to the Dowry Prohibition Act are all part of this development.

Similarly, there has been increasing sensitivity of the judiciary in the last decade or so. Cases such as *Visakha v State of Rajasthan, Gita Hariharan v RBI, Rupan Deol Bajaj v KPS Gill, Goutam Kundu v State of West Bengal* etc. are example of this. With respect to Domestic Violence, the courts have had to deal largely with matters linked with dowry harassment and dowry death. In dealing with these cases the courts have been open to a wide understanding of what constitutes cruelty. The Supreme Court has, in numerous cases stressed that cruelty need not be physical at all and that the mental aspects of cruelty are of importance. In the case of *E. Balakrishnama Naidu v. State of Andhra Pradesh* the husband was accused of causing the death of his wife and that he had earlier subjected her to cruelty by taunting her with the fact that she had to be gotten children as yet. Although the accused was able to get an acquittal on technical grounds that court recognised that such taunts could constitute cruelty.

The broad interpretation of the term cruelty may also be seen in the case of *Mukund Martand Chitnis v Madhuri Mukund Chitnis* where the accused suspected the chastity of the woman right from the first day of their marriage and the husband resorted to character assination and mudslinging and even filed a false complaint of theft against the wife. This led to the filing of 2 separate complaints of defamation under S. 500, IPC. In addition, a complaint under S. 498-A, IPC was filed. While the accused was convicted of cruelty and defamation by the High Court, on the Supreme Court's suggestion the matter ended in an amicable settlement.

Another case where the court has emphasised not on physical cruelty but on emotional aspects of ill-treatment is that of State of *West Bengal v Orilal Jaiswal* where a woman had allegadly committed suicide, the Court partly reversed the High Court decision acquitting the accused husband and his mother of charges under Sections 498A and 306 of the IPC. The Supreme Court reversed the High Court and convicted the accused under section 498 of the IPC. This is an outstanding vindication of the law under section 498A for it states very clearly, that "cruelty" can be not only physical but also, and mainly, mental cruelty. The Court held that repeatedly telling a woman that she was an *"alakshmi"* (woman of evil luck) at a time when she had lost a child was an act of mental cruelty.

As such, criminal law in India makes an appreciable effort in understanding the problem of Domestic Violence. The courts are in a position to address Domestic Violence in a wide range of cases ranging from dowry death, to physical abuse, to mental cruelty.

This development is a welcome departure from the hesitation that the state earlier showed with respect to the intervening in cases of subjugation with the family. The "public/private divide" is thus on its way to being obliterated.

However, owing to the cultural context within which the laws have to apply, it has been seen that the use of criminal law is not an effective strategy. As such, the law has not been as effective as it is capable of being.

The question thus is whether such a reconceptualisation has the potential for being an effective manner of bringing international focus to Domestic Violence.

Domestic Violence is definitely of a different nature, in the Indian context as compared to what may be broadly considered the western context. Perhaps due to the deep link between Domestic Violence and financial motives in India (the dowry system and dowry linked violence being the most articulate examples) the method of violence is organised. It is necessary to recognise that in the Indian context, the societal backing of the commission of Domestic Violence are powerful and that simple strategies are insufficient in dealing with the problem. We have already experienced the unsuitability of the criminal law in this regard, even where it is dealing with the most obvious forms of cruelty. The reaction in the Indian context must be comprehensive and sensitive to all the specifics of our culture(s). The prevalence of economic abuse, the nature of familial reaction, the pressures of caste and religious communities, the phenomenon of migration to urban centres and the consequent change in the predominant family structure etc. among other aspects need to be considered seriously. This is perhaps impossible in a context where conceptualisation of the problem for the purpose of international definition is a restricted process.

At the same time it is necessary to consider the fact that there exists in the international regime a lop-sided balance of power between the developed and "developing" nations. The principles and assumptions that go into the making of the instruments are often unsuited, if not alien to our context. The relevance of considering this aspect of the human rights regime lies in the nature of the exercise of inclusion of Domestic Violence into the concept of torture. Whereas it may seem that the experience of Domestic Violence and torture are very similar in the western context and that the ingredients of the definition of torture address all the aspects of the experience of Domestic Violence, the same cannot be said in the Indian context. Utilising this restricted definition of torture for the purpose of activating the state machinery will definitely affect the manner in which the state understands the problem, notwithstanding local advocacy. This may just cause the further invisibilisation of various forms of violence.

It may be argued that the same may happen if the international regime were to recognise Domestic Violence as a distinct violation of human rights. The difference between the two strategies, however, lies in the fact that in including the concept within torture, the attempt will be to expand an already existing concept. Such an exercise definitely restricts the ability to address all the various contexts in which Domestic Violence occurs the world over. On the other hand, an exercise of defining Domestic Violence as a distinct human rights violation offers greater possibilities, although the entire process of evolving a global consensus would be long and complicated.

There is consensus that the international community should recognise Domestic Violence as the heinous violation that it is. The international community should recognise the grave implications and complex nature of Domestic Violence with as much seriousness as it has with respect to torture. However, in the process it should not make the process of elimination of such violence any less effective than it can be.

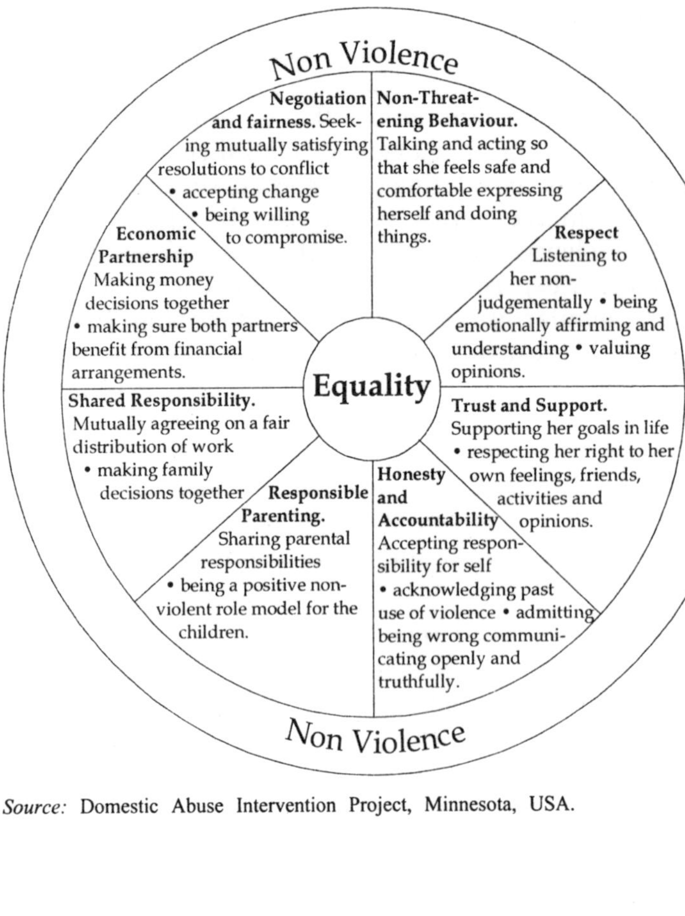

Source: Domestic Abuse Intervention Project, Minnesota, USA.

All this leads to the question as to why domestic violence at all takes place which borders on gruesome torture?

There is scope beyond violence which has been expressed in the form of the non-violence and equality cycle by the Domestic Abuse Intervention Project in Minnesota, USA. Concepts such as negotiations, equal sharing platforms, respect, trust and support may help in resolving situations.

In South Asia, the situation is quite pregnant with hope. On Sept. 19, 2000 the Indian National Human Rights Commission has suggested that maintenance may be increased to Rs. 5000 as a maximum limit. The Supreme Court directives and guidelines on the Visakha judgment, Sheela Barse cases have been a silver lining over a dark cloud.

The Domestic Violence (Prevention) Bill is a significant step forward in recognising the problems of women, children and other family members living in an atmosphere of violence. When it is finally enacted, it will provide protection against domestic violence by obtaining protection, residence and monetary relief orders. However, it does not cater to the longstanding demand of women for appropriate linkages between civil and criminal law to make section 498A effective. The proposed bill will provide some sort of balm to the aggrieved. This law with its enactment must be coupled with setting up of more family courts to deal with divorce, maintenance, child custody and also the emphasis must be placed on speedy and discreet trials.

References

1. The Human Rights Watch–Globnal Report on Women Delhi, Oxford University Press, 1995.
2. The significantly large number of sexual harassment cases reported from Tamil Nadu and Andhra points out to the fact that awareness campaigns have proved successful and has removed the stigma from reporting such cases to the family and society.
3. HT, Jan 10, 2004 "more crimes against women in 2003".

4. Crime Against Women: Violence Within and Without, Tejdeep Kaur Menon, The Hindu, Sunday Sep. 1, 2002.
5. Journal of the American Medical Association, March 2001.
6. Loche, Daisy, "Family Homicide." The Family Violence in Canada: A Statistical Profile, pp. 39-44. Ottawa, ON: Statistics Canada, 2000.
7. Ahuja, R. (1987) Crimes Against Women, Rawat Publications, Jaipur, India.
8. Victimisation of Women: A Theoretical Perspective on Dowry Deaths in India, Mengai Natrajan.
9. Tambiah, SJ (1973) Dowry and Bridewealth and the property rights of women. In Bridewealth and Dowry Goody, J. and Tambiah, S.J. pp. 59-169, Cambridge University Press, London.
10. Social Change: Dec. 1992.
    - Women Aid International: Women and violence, http://www.womenaid.org/press/info/violence/womenviolence.html
    - Gordon Young, Mapping Mayhem: The Geography of Crime, *Computoredge* August 2003.
    - John Markovic and Christopher Stone:Crime mapping and the policing of democratic societies; Vera Institute of Justice, March 2002
    - Nancy LaVigne, (Crime Mapping Research Center, NIJ, Washington, DC), Western Society of Criminology ,1999 Meeting Proceedings.
    - World Population prospects 1950-2050, UN 2001, Department of Economic Affairs, Population Division, New York.
    - Population Division, Department of Economic and Social Affairs, United Nations Secretariat, New York 2002.
11. Jai Singh, Indira excerpts from paper on Domestic Violence which was presented at an international conference in India in 1999. (pp. 223-230).

7

Women, Social Legislation and Enforcement in India and Canada

Women's Rights and Social Legislation in India

Each year, hundreds of women suffer because of cruelty by the patriarchal society. Yet these cases have low conviction rates due to the inefficiency of the law enforcement agencies and the dismal laws which are present in society. Roop Kanwar's Shah Bano's petition for maintenance, Ameena's plight and Anjana Mishra's ordeal for justice, cases of brutality during riots as in Gujarat has brought to the fore the condition of the women in Independent India where the women's laws and social legislation is apparently very sound.

The Indian constitution both in its fundamental rights and directive principles has provisions for protecting the interests of women. It tries to ensure that men and women are treated equally. Yet at several junctures it agrees to the fact that women have been ill-treated in society. Hence to remove this injustice and to re-introduce equality, the constitution allows the state to make special provisions favoring women. Article 39(c) of the constitution ensures the women are not exploited in society and not forced to work which may be unsuited to their age and strength. Again Article 51A(e) of the Constitution provides that the citizens must ensure, the dignity of the women is preserved. Somehow, these enactments in effect remain on paper only. They are like a token gesture.

There have been several women's campaigns, however, the questions of power balance between men and women and women's and women's economic rights within the family and society have seldom been raised. The concept of the good' and the bad women in society have been categorized and the conservative notions of women's chastity, virginity and the image of the Indian women have been glorified. The society has failed to uphold that women are first and foremost human beings and not merchandise.

In the recent past there have been several campaigns such as the rape campaign, Sati Bill, and Immoral Traffic (prevention), women's inheritance laws etc. which have drawn strong public pressure on the judiciary. Today India has several laws for the women. Some of the preventive measures for violence against women under the Indian penal code (IPC) are as follows:

(i) rape (Sec 376 IPC)
(ii) Kidnapping and abduction for different purposes (Sec 363-373 IPC)
(iii) Homicide for dowry, dowry deaths or their attempts (Sec 302/304-B IPC)
(iv) Torture, both mental and Physical (Sec 498-A IPC) including misappropriation of Streedhan.
(v) Outrage of Modesty (Sec 354 IPC)
(vi) Sexual harassment in the form of a word, gesture or act to insult the modesty of a woman (Sec 509 IPC), also Obscene acts and songs (Sec 294 IPC)
(vii) Abetment to suicide (Sec 306 IPC) (The Indian Penal Code is given in detail in Appendix 11)

In this case it is important to note that no where in the IPC words molestation or eve-teasing is used. In popular literature these two words are frequently used. There are crimes which fall under Special Laws such as

(i) Commission of Sati (prevention) Act 1987
(ii) Dowry Prohibition Act, 1961

(iii) Immoral Traffic (Prevention) Act 1956

(iv) Indecent Representation of women (prohibition) Act, 1986.

In the course of this study eight important parameters of crime have been identified in Kolkata and Toronto. In case of the Special Laws in India, the Dowry Prohibition Act, 1961 has been scrutinized. The campaign on rape is perhaps a classic example of the impact of public pressure on the judiciary. It is felt that public pressure is a better safeguard to ensure justice than ineffective enactments.

Reforms In Rape Laws:

The subject rape falls under chapter (XVI) Offense affecting the human body, under sexual offenses. The two sections identified are IPC 375 and IPC 376. Section 375 of the IPC deals with rape. Section 375 states a man is said to commit rape who except in the case hereinafter excepted, has sexual intercourse with a women under circumstances falling under any of the six following descriptions:

First - Against her will;

Secondly - Without her consent;

Thirdly - without her consent, when her consent has been obtained by putting her or any person whom she is interested in fear of death or of hurt;

Fourthly - with her consent, when the man knows that he is not her husband, and that her consent is given because she believes that he is another man to whom she is or believes herself to be lawfully married;

Fifthly - with her consent, when, at the time of giving such consent, by reason of unsoundness of mind or intoxication or the administration by him personally or through another of any stupefying or unwholesome substance, she is unable to understand the nature and consequences of that to which she gives consent;

Sixthly - with or without her consent, when she is under sixteen years of age.[1] Further, the section explains what constitutes penetration; Penetration is sufficient to constitute the sexual intercourse necessary to the offence of rape.[2]

There are some exceptions to this law. If example, there is intercourse between a man and his wife who is less than fifteen years of age then it is a rape. The state of Manipur has some exceptions. In clause five, instead of the word sixteen, the substitute word is fourteen and instead of age fifteen in sexual intercourse between men and wife in Manipur it is thirteen. Going by the guidelines of the above law, at this stage Susan Brownmiller's work (1995) which has been well acclaimed, defined rape as a sexual invasion of the body by force, an intrusion into the private, personal inner space without consent - in short, an internal assault from one of several avenues and by one of several methods - constitutes a deliberate violation of emotional, physical and rational integrity and is hostile, degrading act of violence that deserves the name of rape. In rape, invasion may be through the mouth or rectum with batons, sticks or even fingers which are substituted for the natural thing.[3] While explaining the Indian laws on rape, it is evident that there are several lacunae. It is necessary to explain a couple of terms within section 375, such as against her will. That is the act is done against the will of the women when she is fully conscious, capable of consenting and is aware of what is being done and resists or objects the act. The word consent has an important role to play in sexual assault. The laws emphasize that consent should be obtained before the sexual intercourse and she should be under no duress. A sleeping woman or a person retained or intoxicated is incapable of giving consent. The consent of a girl below 16 is not considered a valid consent because the law presumes that the young girl is incapable of consenting due to her lack of understanding of the implications of her consent.[4]

The word consent and submission is often confused by people. Consent means submission, but submission does not at any cost mean consent. Consent should not at any cost be due to fear or threat. Often the courts judge consent based on the injuries on the body of the victim. This is definitely a very lob-sided view of our society where the aims of proof is on the victim. Past sexual history is scrutinized to judge whether victim has a tendency to give consent or is habitual to sexual intercourse. The onus of the investigation lies on the victim the women. At this juncture it is important to point out-that IPC 375 does not explain what is penetration or the instrument of rape which has been mentioned by Brownmiller. Indian Law does not mention here any word such as marital rape. In this case section 375 does mention in the sixth clause that if the wife is less than 15 years of age then it will be adjudged as a rape. However, the overall age of consent is sixteen years.

There is tremendous contradiction in the law as our Indian laws vouch for the fact that a woman is an adult at the age of 18 and marriage is lawful at the age. However, sexual consent as seen under IPC 375 is 16. Then how does the Indian Legislation and conservative, traditional society agree to this discrepancy. Then what happens to the people who fall between age 16 (age of consent) and age 18 (age for lawful marriage.) Then does our Indian law also cater to pre marital sex amongst the women? If age of lawful marriage is 18 then why does IPC 375 state that sexual intercourse by a man with his wife who is less than 15 years is rape. Then the law does permit marriage of minor girls. Without doubt that the assumption of law being that a man has a right to sexual intercourse with his wife and she does not have the right to refuse her consent to it. The law is also promised on the assumption that the married woman is the property of her husband. Nevertheless married women are raped by their husbands and suffer this extreme form of violence without any legal remedy. Absence of a remedy in Indian Law against the offense of marital rape is alarming and is a major area which needs law reform.[5]

In a rape case, the absence of injury on the accused goes against the commission of the crime. Moreover, in several landmark judgments it has been stated that the existence of injury to the vagina does not necessarily justify the crime. The prosecution in a rape case must prove that the women had sexual intercourse. The man accused of rape was the one who committed the offence; the act of sexual intercourse was done without her consent or the consent obtained by threat fraud, deception, intoxication etc.; the accused had sexual intercourse with a girl below 16 years of age; the husband had sexual intercourse with his wife below 15 years of age; and above all there was wife. The defence usually argues that the women did consent; she was of loose morals; had previous sexual relations with other people; her age ascertained was wrong; her story was fabricated; no injuries have been found on her person; the F.I.R. was not promptly filed.

In practice getting justice for rape almost entirely depends on the credibility of a women. Section 376A on the other hand specifies the punishment for rape, when a man has intercourse with his wife during separation by decreed. However, there have been several cases where a man is known to rape his wife before a separation or even for the custody of the children. This is used as a convenient weapon of violence to practice dominance. In such cases the punishment is only for two years. Sections 376 IPC emphasizes the punishment for rape. There are four sub-clauses for this section. The normal punishment for rape case is a minimum of 7 to 10 years imprisonment and minimum life imprisonment and fine. It is interesting to note that maximum life imprisonment is 14 years. An offender who harasses a women, destroys her personality, may go practically scot-free. When a police officer commits a rape the punishment is rigorous imprisonment for not less than 10 years or imprisonment for life, plus a fine. However, the crime has been defined area wise i.e. if it is committed within the premises of a police station to which he is appointed or if the women is in his custody or that of his subordinate. The same rule applies for a public servant such as a member of the management or staff of a hospital, jail, remand home, women's or children's institutions; if a person commits rape on a pregnant women or on a girl under 12 years of age or a gang commits rape on a women.[6]

However, if a public servant or a superintendent or manager of a jail, remand home or women's or children institutions, takes advantage of their official position and seduces the victim though this may not be rape, the offender may be imprisoned upto 5 years with fine. The same is the case with a member of the management or staff of a hospital. Attempt to rape falls section 511 IPC, the offender only gets half the full term of an accused rape case.

The struggle for the anti-rape campaign triggered off with the infamous Supreme Court judgment in the Mathura case in 1972. Prior to this case the media highlighted only gruesome cases. With the incidents of the Mathura case (1972), the Ramazabee and (1978) and Maya Tyagi case (1980), the media as well as the common people realized that there were some severe problems. Amazingly all the cases took place in police stations, committed by the guardians of law. These cases in the long course have been able to bring the word rape to the forefront, which was considered a taboo previously. Mathura a 16 years old tribal girl, was raped by two policemen within a police compound. The session's court acquitted the policemen on the fact that since Mathura had eloped with her boyfriend she was habituated to sexual intercourse and hence she could not be raped. Further the court held that there is a world of difference between sexual intercourse and rape. The High Court convicted the policemen and held that mere passive or helpless surrender induced by threats or fear cannot be equated with desire or will. The Supreme Court set aside the high court judgment and acquitted the policemen and held that since Mathura had not raised any alarm, her allegations of rape were untrue. Her consent was not a consent which could be brushed aside as submission.

One of the major thrusts in the anti-rape campaign is the word consent. The major demand was that the onus of proving consent should shift from the persecution to the accused. The other major demand was that in a rape trial a women's past sexual history and general character should not be used as evidence. The response of the government was that a Law Commission was set up. The commission made the following suggestions:

1. The present definition of rape given under section 375 IPC must be amended to include fear of injury, either to body, mind, reputation or property as a reason for submitting to sexual intercourse. Consent obtained by creating such a fear in the women is not a legal consent.
2. Age of consent by a woman must be raised from 16 to 18 keeping in line with the minimum age of her marriage. Sexual intercourse of husband with his wife below 18 years of age must be considered as rape.
3. A women should have the right to be accompanied by her relative or friend when she goes to the police station.
4. Except in unavoidable circumstances a woman should not be arrested after sunset and before sunrise. In case of urgent need of arrest between sunset and sunrise, the police officer must inform his superior officer and get his permission.
5. An officer in charge of a police station, who refuses to record the commission of a cognizable offense reported to him must be punished with imprisonment up to one year, or with fine, or with both.
6. A public servant who knowingly disobeys the law regarding the attendance of women for investigation must be punished with imprisonment up to one year or with fine or with both.
7. Printing and publication of any matter related with a rape case conducted in a court in camera must be declared unlawful. Any person who prints or publishes

such matter without the permission of the court must be punished with fine up to Rs. 1000.

8. Any person who assaults a minor girl under 16 years of age in an obscene manner must be punished with imprisonment up to 3 years or with fine or with both.
9. The person accused of rape and the victim must be referred to a registered medical practitioner for medical examination without delay.
10. The medical practitioner, without delay, must examine the accused or victim and give a report of the examination with the reasons for the conclusion he arrived at.
11. If a statement of a girl under 12 years of age, against whom a sexual offense is alleged to have been committed, is to be recorded, it must be done by a female police officer and, in her absence, by an authorized women representative of an organization engaged in the welfare services for women.
12. When male officer records a statement made by women, her relative or friend or a representative of a women's organization must be allowed to remain present.
13. A women's past sexual history should not be taken into consideration.[7]

On December 1983 the Bill was finally placed in the Lok Sabha. Women's groups, which had vociferously attacked the bill, were not even aware of the content of the revised bill and that it was being presented in Parliament. Without much fanfare the bill was pressed and become known as the Criminal Law (Amendment) Bill 1983. The act did not scrap the provision which were criticized but made them slightly milder. The publication of rape trials was made into a bailable offence. The provision about past sexual assault did not figure in the new bill. The bill, which was passed, was limited in scope as compared to what was promised by the Law Commission's report. Although, the bill was inadequate, it was welcomed that the courts would follow the spirit of the amendment and give women a better deal in rape trials.[8]

The year after the amendment, started off with an extremely negative view of women's sexuality.

A schoolteacher had seduced a young girl but when she conceived, he refused to marry her. The girl filed a complaint that the consent was given under a false promise of marriage and hence it was not a valid consent and the act amounted to rape. The Calcutta High Court held the view that failure to keep a promise to marry at a future date to which a grown girl consents to sexual intercourse and continues to indulge in such activity until she becomes pregnant, it is an act of promiscuity. This judgment was relied upon in several later cases where girls were duped into sex under a false promise of marriage to acquit the accused.[9] In another case in 1989 a minor girl was raped at a bus stand by a 21 years of youth, the Delhi High court pointed out that there was no rape as the youth had injury mark only on the body and not the penis. In this case, the court took an extremely negative stand as the minor was nine years old.

Although the 1983 amendment did take a strong stand against paedophilia and custodial rapes, in practice the judgments meted out by the courts have often been pro-accused. Hence, today the rape laws are again being questioned. A new definition is necessary for rape. The laws must do away with the age-old notion of chastity, womanhood and the key word virginity. The concepts of the good and the bad women must be done away with and women must be seen as a human being and not as objects. At several junctures, the word rape has been thought to be a constricting term. Instead it should be replaced by the word sexual offences as the punishment can be given according to the degree of injury. The concept of penis penetration is a concept, which is negative. Instead penetration of foreign body by assault and violating the inner space of a women can be brought in as emphasized by Brownmiller. Instead of further stringent punishment the victim can be given monetary compensation. The in camera trials also have their negative effect as public consensus plays an important role on the Indian judiciary. However while recording the statement of the victim, total privacy must be given; delicate handling by a women officer while the victim is reporting; in child victims, i.e. preferably the statement should be taken at home. Help should also be taken from psychiatrists. However, in India this is difficult, as expertise is only available in large towns and cities. But whether monetary compensation is enough for a rape victim is also a debate which is worth taking note of. But the most important point of the whole debate is that there is absolute need for speedy enforcement of law. For too often such cases get bogged down in self-hearted investigations and difficulties in securing evidence.[10]

While conducting fieldwork in Kolkata, the F.I.R. seemed extremely poorly recorded. The name of the victim and her place of residence in most cases were recorded. Other than that all other details were often found lacking. The women officers were found insensitive and cases are registered mechanically.

It is evident that the onus of investigation should shift to the accused instead of the victim. The law needs redefining and the word marital rape must be introduced. The victims must be supported in society and both the law enforcement agencies and judiciary must give a sympathetic ear.

Dowry: Unique in South Asia

Dowry is a unique form of murder of a women or harassment of a women and her family (pre-marital) over a period of time for economic gain by the husband and his relatives. Sec 304 B IPC deals with dowry death. However, the killing may not be direct. The victim may be forced to kill herself due to extreme forms of physical and mental torture. In this case the IPC 306 and 307 IPC (attempted to murder) may be applied. Though the Dowry Prohibition Act was passed in 1996 to combat the age-old practice, very few cases are actually reported and the accused punished. It is difficult to uproot this social evil. The first step the government took to cure this evil was the improvement of property rights on women under the Hindu Succession Act in 1956. As this was found inadequate, the Dowry Prohibition Act was passed. The common pattern is the harassment of brides by their parents-in laws for more dowry. Ultimately, the women are driven to suicide or are murdered in circumstances which resemble an accidental fire in the kitchen. The Dowry Prohibition Act 1961, falls under Special Laws, which says that any person shall be punished with jail term which may extend to six months or with fine or with both. It is also an offence to demand dowry, directly or indirectly from the parents or guardian of a bride any dowry. He shall be punished in the same manner. An agreement for giving or taking of dowry is void and cannot be enforced. Dowry is defined as any property or valuable security given or agreed to be given either directly or indirectly (a) by one party to a marriage to the other party to the marriage or (b) by the parents of either party to a marriage or by any other person, to either party to the marriage or to the other person; at or before or after the marriage. This does not include dinner or meher among the Muslims. The law was improved through certain amendments in 1984. In 1983, the principal Criminal Acts were amended to control bride- burning related to dowry.

Section 304 B Dowry death says (i) where the death of a women is caused by any burns or bodily injury or occurs otherwise than under normal circumstances within seven years of her marriage and it is shown that soon before her death she was subjected to cruelty or harassment by her husband or any relative of her husband for, or in connection with, any demand for dowry, such death shall be called dowry death, and such husband or relative shall be held responsible for the cause of her death.

Whosoever commits dowry death shall be punished with imprisonment for a term which shall not be less than seven years but which may lead to imprisonment for life.[11] The Dowry Prohibition Act of 1961 was full of loop holes. The Act laid down had a very narrow definition of dowry. The L.V.

Jhadhav vs Shankerao case enabled the Supreme Court to clearly define dowry. There was high drama at the wedding of Anita, a science graduate of Pune. The bridegroom and his father almost stopped the ceremonies and told the bride's father that unless he promised to pay Rs. 50,000, the function would be stopped. The wedding ultimately took place. The groom left for the US and the bride stayed in his house. Meanwhile she was pressed for money. The bride's father filed a case against the boy and his father under the dowry Prohibition Act, 1961. The Bombay High court interpreted the definition of dowry in a narrow sense. The question was whether the demand of money was a demand for dowry. According to section 2 of the Act, dowry means any property or valuable security given or agreed to be given by one party to the other. According to section 14, any person demanding dowry shall be punishable. The High Court ruled that there was no demand for dowry.

The Supreme Court overruled this verdict. We are of the opinion that having regard to the object of the Act, a liberal construction has to be given to the word dowry used in Section 4 to mean that any property or valuable security which if consented to be given or the demand being made, this become dowry within the meaning of section 2, the judgment said. It added we are also of the opinion that for property or valuables under section 4, it is to discourage the very demand for property or valuable security as consideration for marriage... There is no warrant for taking the view that the initial demand for giving of property or valuable security would not constitute an offence and that an offence would take place only when the demand was made again after the party on whom the demand was made agreed to comply it.[12]

However, earlier dowry death or dowry was believed to be a part of the violence experienced by Hindu women. However, the case study on Kolkata proved otherwise. There were several cases where Muslim women as well as Christians were tortured and murdered for dowry. In 1980, a bill was introduced in Parliament. The findings of the committee were that the definition of dowry was too narrow and vague; the act was not being vigorously enforced. The committee suggested that the words in consideration for the marriage ought to be totally deleted from the definition of dowry. It recommended that the gifts given to the bride should be listed and registered in her name. In case she dies during the first five years the gifts should revert back to her parents. In case she is divorced, the gifts should also revert back. The presents could not be transferred or disposed for a minimum period of five years from the date of marriage without the prior permission of the family court on an application made by the wife. These provisions were aimed at ensuring the bride's control over the gifts. The committee also recommended the appointment of Dowry Prohibition officers for the enforcement of the act.[13] Surprisingly, the bill gives the impression that our Indian women were given the right to exercise their power both in their paternal home as well as their marital home.

Unfortunately, the bill, which was introduced in 1984, failed to take into consideration some of the positive recommendations of the committee. The suggestion of imposing a ceiling on gifts in marriage openness did not find a place in the act. The important feature was the increase in punishment to five years and a fine up to Rs.10, 000 or the value of dowry whichever is more. But again the section did not apply to presents given to the bride or to the bridegroom. The one year limitation period was removed and it was now possible for the girl's parents, relative or a social work institute to file a complaint on her behalf. The requirement of prior sanction of the government for prosecuting a husband who demands dowry was dropped and dowry was made into a cognizable offence.[14] The Act was amended again in 1986. The fine was increased from Rs.10, 000 to Rs.15, 000, making the punishment more stringent. Another positive approach was how the onus of proving the offence was with the accused and offence of dowry became a cognizable, non-bailable offence. Besides this imposed a ban was also imposed on advertisements.

However, inspite of these amendments, nothing seems to have changed as every year the number of cases are increasing by leaps and bounds. The amazing fact is that the seven year time period, which is in the IPC within which if there is an unnatural death, then it is a dowry case. Amazingly in course of the field study in Kolkata, it became evident that the crime often takes place even after 15 years of marriage.

Along with section 304 B, it is necessary to include Sec 306 IPC i.e. abetment to suicide. If any person commits suicide, whoever abets the commission of such suicide, shall be punished with imprisonment of either description for a term which may extend to ten years, and shall also be liable to fine: Punishment - imprisonment for 10 years and fine cognizable -non-bailable.

A large number of dowry death cases are actually cases where the victim is forced to take the ultimate step of killing herself to end all misery. A large number of such cases have been seen in the course of the study in Kolkata. While on the course of domestic crimes or domestic violence another widespread violence is cruelty by husband or relatives of husband and misappropriation of Streedhan. These two crimes are correlated to the heinous crime of dowry death. To combat such offences, the Supreme Court directed the state of Rajasthan and Harayana to set up special dowry cells at the state level to investigate into unnatural deaths. This order was set due to the case of the Joint Women's program Vs State of Rajasthan. In the long run, this was a trend setter, as today all states have special cells for women known as Grievance Cell to deal with dowry related offences, section 498 A and misappropriation of streedhan etc.

Cruelty

Cruelty of a woman takes place within the four wall of her home, which is perpetrated by a close family member. Hence section 498 A is usually carried on as an appendix to the discussion on dowry. Here a conscious effort is made to evaluate them within the framework of domestic violence because they in fact deal with (or at least ought to deal with) the issue of domestic violence - cruelty and harassment of wives and wife murders. Out of every five cases, four cases of domestic violence, the accused are the women of the family. Till 1983 there were no specific provisions pertaining to violence within the home. Husbands could be considered under the general provision of murder, abetment to suicide, causing hurt and wrongful confinement. But these general provisions of criminal law do not take into account the specific situation of a woman facing violence within the home as against assault by a stranger. The offence which is committed within the privacy of the home by a person on whom the women is economically and emotionally dependent needs to be dealt with at a different place.[15]

It is extremely difficult to prove domestic violence by husbands and in-laws as there are no witnesses and it is over a period of time. This leads to mental trauma of the women and her children. The woman needs protection before and after the crime as the victim is living with the accused or in close proximity of the accused. The irony of section 498 A IPC is that it falls under chapter XXA which is a separate chapter in the IPC on cruelty by husband or relatives of husband. Amazingly this section has not been included in offences affecting the human body. The section states whoever, being the husband or the relative of the husband of a woman, subjects such women to cruelty shall be punished with imprisonment for a term which may extend to three years and shall also be liable to five years of imprisonment. Cruelty means (a) any willful conduct which is of such a nature as is likely to drive the women to commit suicide or to cause grave injury or danger to life, limb or health (whether mental or physical) of the women; or (b) harassment of the woman where such harassment is with a view to coercing her or any person related to her to meet any unlawful demand for any property or valuable security or is on account of failure lay her or any person related to her to meet such demand.

Punishment for such offences is imprisonment for three years with fine. The offence is cognizable if information relating to the commission of the offence is given to an officer in charge of a police station by the person aggrieved by the offence or by any person related to her by blood, marriage or adoption or if there is no such relative, by any public servant belonging to such a category as may be notified by the state government in this behalf.[16] The offence is non-bailable.

Through the study on Kolkata, it was evident that a large section of the women were victims of emotional and physical assault at home. In a large number of cases there was misappropriation of streedhan. In December 1996, the Supreme Court passed a judgment that even misappropriation of streedhan can invite trial. The court said an offending husband could be liable for action under section 406 of the Indian Penal Code if he converts the streedhan brought by her on her marriage, including jewellery and gifts etc. to his own use or willfully allows any other person to do so. The properties gifted to a woman before her marriage, at the time of marriage, at the time of farewell or bidai and after marriage constitute her streedhan. The court said persons who dishonestly misappropriated streedhan could be imprisoned for three years or fined or both[17]. This ruling is not only important to strengthen section 498A IPC but also for all dowry related offences. The above Supreme Court ruling will try to prevent loop holes existent in dowry and cruelty cases as the important item over which violence is mostly on the women is either due to property or money matters. For domestic violence, the government has amended the Criminal Acts twice during the decade first in 1983 and again in 1986, to create special categories of offences to deal with cruelty to wives, dowry harassment and dowry deaths. Fortunately, this section has a wide application as cases outside dowry can be included. The section is able to cater to the day to day needs of a large number of women.

In course of the Field Study on Kolkata it was evident that there is wide misconception amongst the police personnel (both male and female officer) as well as criminal lawyers that women misuse this section. Hence often the police try to bring about reconciliation between the two parties in question. Often procedure in a women's grievance cell is that the victim should give in a written petition. The victim is called to the cell and her statement is recorded. The accused in question are invited to the cell to give in their statement. The Grievance cell advises both the victim and the accused. After a couple of counsels if the issue is not resolved, a criminal case is started. It is important to note in this case, that the counsel sessions are conducted by women police officers (the rank of sub inspector.)

There is lack of trained personnel and psychiatrists. However, certain cases are handled by some women's organization who are definitely more sympathetic than the grievance cells. In several circumstances, the women i.e. the victims are forced to withdraw their petition as they are financially dependent on the matrimonial home as well as the grievance cells or the women's Organizations do not have proper shelter homes to protect the victim during the proceedings. At this juncture, the women are forced to withdraw the complaint as the husbands often make it a precondition for any negotiations. The women have to cross several hurdles. If she wants a separation or a divorce on the ground of cruelty, she would have to state a criminal case as well as a civil case against the husband. This leads to tremendous emotional pressure on the women as the person may be financially insecure. But this is not to imply that S498 A has no use for women. Most women find it extremely useful as a deterrent. Women may not be in a position to see it through to its logical end. But this is not to deny its usefulness in bringing husbands to the negotiating table. Since the offence is non- bailable, the initial imprisonment for a day or two helps to convey to the husbands the message that the wives are not going to take the violence lying down any longer.

Ultimately most of the criminal cases which are followed up are the ones where the woman has died and the case is followed up by her relatives.[18] It is obvious that dowry death, domestic violence is interrelated. The other sections of the IPC which may be used in these cases is S302 i.e. punishment for murder, section 306 abetment to commit suicide. Domestic violence is like a virus in our society. It is disheartening as the assault is from a known person who is very dear to a person's heart. The ordeal before and often the violence is borne by the women, hence, our law enforcement agencies should review the cases with a sympathetic ear.

During the field study it was found that several cases were registered under section 306 i.e. abetment to commit suicide. From the detailed case history it was found that the suicide was due to constant harassment of the women by the marital family. Those cases which were due to dowry and other family related violence have been included in the study. Besides this cases for misappropriation of streedhan have been included as cases of cruelty and torture. Hence the crime data from the police files and the data that was evolved in course of the study has varied.

Other Sexual Offences

Other sex related offence identified in the study are molestation, eve-teasing, and stalking. Unfortunately all three crimes have not been mentioned clearly in the Penal Code. During the course of interviews with police personal, at the level of inspector and sub-inspectors, they all seemed extremely ill versed with the contents of the laws on molestation and eve-teasing. However, section 354 IPC does constitute assault or criminal force to women with intent to outrage her modesty. Whoever assaults or uses criminal force on any woman, intending to outrage or knowing it to be likely that he will thereby outrage her modesty, shall be punished with imprisonment of either description for a term which may extend to two years or with five or with both. The imprisonment term in Andhra Pradesh is 7 years.[19] The crime is cognizable and bailable. This section is not well defined.

This law changes from one culture to another, it depends upon the country, the religion and the culture to which one belongs. The Supreme Court of India has held (State v. Major Singh, AIR 1967, SC.63) that any act done to or in the presence of a woman is clearly suggestive of sex that act can be considered as an offence under section 354 of IPC.

* An offence under this section is less serious than one of rape under section 375.
* An assault or criminal force committed with the intention of committing rape is not contemplated by this section.
* Here a woman includes a female person of any age.
* There can be no outrage of a woman's modesty where she is a willing party.
* Under this section both men and women can be guilty of the offence.
    1. The offence may rage from pulling a woman by her arm with a request for sexual intercourse.
    2. Molesting a woman.
    3. Forcing a woman to remove her clothes.
    4. Fingering the private part of women.
    5. Raising the skirt of a girl and sitting on her person.
    6. Stealthily touching, with a corrupt mind, the body of any women whether she is a child or mentally retarded or is sleeping or under the effect of an intoxicant.[20]

In court, it must be proved that the person assaulted was a female on whom criminal force is used to outrage her modesty. A charge of this nature is very difficult to prove, as there may be witnesses on several occasions. Police personnel over look the more grievous offence of rape and register it as outrage of modesty of a woman. Touching a women with criminal assault and violating, humiliating her like on several occasions it as is seen in the newspaper that a women is stripped and paraded in a public place e.g. the Maya Tyagi case (1988) and Phoolen Devi case etc. is a glaring example of not just an assault on her modesty but can be equated to rape. A sentence of imprisonment of two years is too less for offences of such degree. Hence, section 354 should be made more specific. All sex related offences should be defined under one law and punishment should be given on the nature of the crime.

Eve-teasing is another such crime which is neither readily reported nor recorded as often as both the victim as well as the police personnel feel that the crime is of a mild nature. Eve-teasing is equated to Section 509 IPC word, gesture, or act intended to insult the modesty of a women, whoever, intending to insult the modesty of any women, utters any word, makes any sound or gesture, or exhibits any object, intending that such word sound shall be heard, or that such gesture or object shall be seen, by such women or intrudes upon the privacy of such women, shall be punished with simple imprisonment for a term which may extend to one year or with fine or with both. The punishment is simple imprisonment for one year. The offence is cognizable and bailable.[21] The offence is at the discrepancy of the officer-in-charge of the police station where the crime has taken place as it depends on the officer as to how, he will interpret the law and the gravity of the crime.

In the long run it is seen that the punishment of imprisonment is often not meted out to the accused. Instead the state should run reformation schools, where the accused may be taught morality, employed to do some social work so that they are able to become more sensitive to social issues. The one or two year simple imprisonment may not be a good measure as the men who are mostly in their youth in such offences get a chance to associate with more hardened criminals. Besides, it is easier for them to go back to the mainstream from a reformation school than a prison. Laws should be stringent yet progressive.

Kidnapping and Abduction

The Indian Penal Code defines kidnapping and

abduction under sections 363 to 373PIC. Laws for women specifically falls under:

Sec. 366: Kidnapping, abducting or inducing woman to compel her to marriage.

Sec. 366 A: Procuration of minor girl (for illicit intercourse)

Sec. 366 B: Importation of girl from foreign country (for illicit intercourse)

Sec. 372: Selling minor for purposes of prostitution

Sec. 373: Buying minors for purposes of prostitution.

The other laws such as Sec 369IPC are not women specific but deal with children under 10 years of age. In Calcutta especially specific areas such as Burtolla Police Station have large number of abduction cases of procurement of foreign girls for prostitution especially from Nepal and Bangladesh. The laws in these cases are well defined. However, there is lack of implementation of law and order in the red light areas.

Other Laws

The other crimes against women such as Sati, prostitution and indecent representation of women are also rampant in the country inspite of revised social legislation. All three crimes now fall under special laws. The incidence of Sati of Roop Kanwar in Deorala (1987), Rajasthan caused furor amongst various sections in society and led to widespread protests demanding legislative protection in matters relating to the practice of Sati. The first legislation against the practice of Sati was promulgated in 1827. Later after independence, it was felt that the various Sections under IPC such as murder, suicide, abetment to suicide etc. would be adequate to deal with the problem. However, when the Commission of Sati (prevention) Act was passed, it has taken charge of the religious as well as social evils of our society.

Although, Sec 306 which is abetment to commit suicide, the article proved inadequate to arrest the accused as the accused were a part of a mob, which encouraged the woman to mount the funeral pyre. Although the Act was made to protect the victim the final irony of the Act is that in its zest to protect women's right, the act stipulated punishment to the victim. A women who attempts Sati is to be imprisoned for one to five years and fined Rs. 5000 to Rs. 20,000.22 Section 4 of the Act has widen the scope of the term abetment of Sati so as to bring within its clutches all those persons who directly or indirectly abet, aid or help in the commission of Sati. Those guilty of glorifying Sati may be punished with imprisonment up to seven years with fine. However, since the accused is usually a mob, it is difficult to punish the guilty, so often the women gets victimized all over again and this time with the guardians of law. It is most important to bring awareness and educate women, so that they can become economically independent and if the need arises, she can fight for her rights.

Another law which penalizes the victim than supports her is the prostitution law (1986). The women are taken into custody for the immoral act. Invariably the touts and customers as well as the brothel keepers go scot- free. These touts and brothel keepers give bail and assurance and the women are taken back to work in the full knowledge of the police. The prostitution laws do not at any stage prohibit the act. But a women who is a prostitute is prohibited from public place and hence they are force to occupy slum-like areas or are on the urban periphery of the city. However, if a young girl is confined, and is forced into prostitution, there are sections 366, 366A IPC which can adequately deal with such cases. The Immoral Traffic Prevention) Act 1988 recognizes that children or even men can be sexually exploited for commercial purposes. The law infact is more stringent. The younger the age of the person who is sexually exploited, the greater is the magnitude of punishment of her exploiters. The amendment also punishes those living on the earnings of prostitution of a child or minor. Inspite of amendment, there is abuse of the Act and the police are often unable to execute their work as efficiently as is required. In 2004 the

National Human Rights Commission has published a path breaking proportions study in 5 states to prove that the menace is reaching to epidemic populations unless the laws are strengthened or the law enforcement deals with the problem with toughnists.

During the course of the study on Kolkata, it was conveyed by several individuals during the interview that women are attacked and molested due to their provocative clothing which is in the form of jeans-tee- shirts, skirts or any western attire. It must be noted that the women who were attacked were either at home or by a person who was known to them. In these circumstances, the argument that the western attire provoked the perpetrator to attack is baseless. Hence style of clothing was not the reason for attack. The Southern part of Kolkata was pointed by several members of the police personnel as the area where women were provocatively attired as they came from liberal homes as unlike the conservative North Kolkata or the older Kolkata.

At this point it is necessary to highlight the bill of Indecent Representation of women (1986) which was introduced in Rajya Sabha by Margaret Alva. The Act came into effect from October 1987. The apparent aim of the Act was to prevent the depiction of the figure of a women in a manner which is derogatory to women or denigrating women or which is likely to corrupt public morality. The Act confuses the issue of indecent representation of women with morality by introducing the test of anything that which tends to deprive and corrupt. The act also does not specifically state that depicting women in positions of servitude is indecent representation. The vagueness of the definition has left the ground open for its misuse. The act taken to its logical end, it leads to women's segregation, curtails women's movement and manner of dressing, reinforces the concept of women's chastity and purity and compartmentalize women further as good and bad. It subscribes to and strengthens the patriarchal, reactionary and fundamentalist notions regarding women and their sexuality.

Survey on Social Legislation

Keeping in mind the rapid escalation of atrocities against women, it is necessary to look for comprehensive crime management for tackling various crimes against women and for dealing with female depersonalization trauma. Ram Ahuja (1987) has encouraged a more humanistic approach while dealing with sensitive issues and making adequate changes in the criminal justice system. There is a need for a better judicial system. There must be adequate changes in attitudes and values of the law enforcement personnel and the judiciary. There must be more family courts or Lok Adalats to disperse cases relating to sexual offences at the earliest. 50 persons from all walks of life (social activities, police personnel, journalists, advocates) were interviewed in Calcutta. About 64 per cent of the people felt that the social legislative laws were not adequate in tackling crime against women problem in the country. Out of 50 the total male interviewed, 50 per cent agreed that the legislative laws are adequate to tackle women and only 29 per cent women felt in the same way. The rest of the 71 per cent females agreed that there should be changes in social laws. In the case of dowry laws, 27 per cent felt that the dowry laws were adequate to help women, while 63 per cent felt that changes should be made especially as seven years time period which is given for an unnatural death after marriage is inadequate. Only women journalist of a leading newspaper house seemed quite unaware of the dowry laws although she was in charge of the crime beat. 75 per cent males felt that the laws are adequate to prevent dowry deaths and 85 per cent women want changes in dowry laws. In the case of crimes such as abetment to commit suicide and cruelty, 73%, felt that the laws were inadequate and the punishment should become more stringent.

All the women interviewed agreed that the punishment should be stringent while 75 per cent of the men felt that the laws were adequate. Another question asked was whether abetment to commit suicide should be equated to murder. All women again agreed for the above 73 per cent agreed with the question while 75 per cent men felt that abetment to commit suicide and murder are different degrees of crime. 63 per cent of the people interviewed felt that there must be further reform in rape laws while 8.5 per cent of the women agreed with more reformation, and inclusion of the concept of marital rape, one lady police officer felt that the concept of marital rape is included in IPC. This proves that the personnel are often not aware of the laws, hence execution of duty may lead to lopsided investigation of cases. 75 per cent of the men interviewed felt that the concept of marital rape is unnecessary in the Indian laws as it may lead to complications. In the case of eve-teasing, molestation all women wanted more stringent laws. 90 per cent of the people interviewed wanted more awareness on the part of the police and all agreed that stalking should be included in the IPC. 75 per cent of the men felt that the one and two years of imprisonment in the case of eve-teasing and molestation was adequate to punish the accused. 73 per cent of those interviewed felt that the law enforcement agencies were inefficient. 50 per cent of the males agreed while 86 per cent of the women agreed with this statement.

From the survey it is evident that women want more reforms, broader social legislation and efficiency on the part of police personnel and judiciary. The men on the other hand seemed happy with the system as they fear female dominance.

While examining and understanding the various crimes against women, it is evident that as victims go through the police, the Rescue Home and Court ordeals, they often feel depersonalized, lost, bewildered and neglected. Although sometimes they may find sympathetic, supportive individuals, within these institutions who help them, yet, the overall organizational structures of these institutions contributes to their feeling that persons associated with these institutions do not care much about them. The procedures are often mechanical, a matter of routine. The victims are shunted back and forth. Often they run from pillar to post in search of justice. There are a handful of professionals who work to help the victims such as the police, doctors, lawyers, magistrates and the personnel of the rescue homes. However, one very striking fact is that these groups of professional have a total lack of communication amongst themselves. Each group sticks to its own guns, unlike the victim who is already emotionally broken is further washed out in matters which are a part of the procedure to give the victim justice.

Crimes against women deserve a scientific study and the victims of these crimes require an objective approach in understanding the administrative procedures. There should be correct assessment of the violence as well as the offenders along with balanced treatment programs and preventive strategies. The social laws should be reviewed from time to time, as the needs of women change, the laws must also be dynamic.

Excerpts from the Indian Penal Code, 1860

Laws for protection of crime against women in India

90. Consent known to be given under fear or misconception

A consent is not consent as it intended by any section of this code, if the consent is given by a person under fear of injury, or under a misconception of fact, and if the person doing the acts knows, or has reason to believe, that the consent was given in consequence of such fear or misconception; or

Consent of insane person. If the consent is given by a person who, from unsoundness of mind, or intoxication, is unable to understand the nature and consequence of that to which he gives his consent; or *Consent of child*-unless the contrary appears from the context, if the consent is given by a person who is under twelve years of age.

294. Obscene acts and songs

Whoever, to the annoyance of others,

(a) Does any obscene act in any public place or

(b) sings, recites or utters any obscene song, ballad or words, in or near any public place, shall be punished with imprisonment of either description for a term which may extend to three months, or with imprisonment of either description for a term which may extend to three methods or with fine, or with both.

299. Culpable homicide

Whoever causes the death by an act with the intention of causing death or with the intention of causing such bodily injury as is likely to cause death, or with the knowledge that he is likely by such act to cause death, commits the offence of culpable homicide.

300. Murder

Except in the cases hereafter expected, culpable homicide is murder, if the act by which the death is caused is done with the intention of causing death or

Secondly if it is done with the intention of causing such bodily injury as the offender knows to be likely to cause the death of the person to whom the harm is caused, or

Thirdly if it is done with the intention of causing bodily injury to any person and the bodily injury intended to be inflicted is sufficient in the ordinary course of nature to cause death or

Fourthly if the person committing the act knows that it is so imminently dangerous, that it must in all probability cause death or such bodily injury as is likely to cause death, and commits such act any excuse for incurring the risk of death or such injury as aforesaid.

302. Punishment for Murder

Whoever commits murder shall be punished with death or (imprisonment for life) and shall also be liable to fine.

304. Punishment for culpable homicide not amounting to murder

Whoever commits culpable homicide not amounting to murder, shall be punished with (imprisonment for life) or imprisonment of either description for a term which may extend to ten years, and shall also be liable to fine, if the act by which the death is caused is done with the intention of causing death, or of causing such bodily injury as is likely to cause death; or with imprisonment of either description for a term which may extend to ten years, or with fine, or with both, if the act is done with the knowledge that it is likely to cause death, but without any intention to cause death, or to cause such bodily injury as is likely to cause death.

304B. Dowry death

1. Where the death of a women is caused by any burns or bodily injury or occurs otherwise than under normal circumstances within seven years of her marriage and it is shown that soon before her death she was subjected to cruelty or harassment by her husband or any relative of her husband, for, or in connection with, any demand for dowry, such death shall be called "dowry death", and such husband or relative shall be deemed to have caused her death.

306. Abetment to suicide

If any person commits suicide, whoever abets the commission of such suicide, shall be punished with imprisonment of either description for a term which may extend to ten years, and shall also be liable to fine.

307. Attempt to Murder

Whoever does any act with such intention or knowledge, and under such circumstances that, if he by that act caused death, he would be guilty of murder, shall be punished with imprisonment of either description for a term which may extend to ten years, and shall also be liable to fine; and if hurt is caused to any person by such act, the offender shall be liable either to (imprisonment for life) or to such punishment as is here in before mentioned. When any person offending under this section is under sentence of imprisonment for life, he may if hurt is caused, be punished with death.

308. Attempt to commit culpable homicide

Whoever does any act with such intention or knowledge and under such circumstances that, if he by that act caused death, he would be guilty of culpable homicide not amounting to murder, shall be punished wtih imprisonment of either description for a term which may extend to three years, or with fine, or with both; and if hurt is caused to any person by such act, shall be punished with imprisonment of either description for a term which may extend to seven years, or with a fine or with both.

354. Assault or criminal force to woman with intent to outrage her modesty

Whoever assaults or uses criminal force to any woman, intending to outrage or knowing it to be likely that he will thereby outrage her modesty, shall be punished with imprisonment of either description for a term which may extend to two years, or with fine, or with both.

359. Kidnapping

Kidnapping is of two kinds: kidnapping from India, and kidnapping from lawful guardianship.

360. Kidnapping from India

Whoever conveys any person beyond the limits of India without the consent of that person or of some person legally authorized to consent on behalf of that person, is said to kidnap that person from India.

361. Kidnapping from lawful guardianship

Whoever takes or entices any minor under sixteen years of age for a male, or under eighteen years of age of a female, or any person of unsound mind, out of the keeping of the lawful guardian of such minor or person of unsound mind, without the consent of such guardian, is said to kidnap of such a minor or person form, lawful guardianship.

362. Abduction

Whoever by force compels, or by any deceitful means induces, any person to go from any place, is said to abduct that person.

363. Punishment for kidnapping

Whoever kidnaps any person from India or from lawful guardianship, shall be punished with imprisonment of either description for a term which may extend to seven years, and shall also be liable to fine.

364. Kidnapping and abducting in order to murder

Whoever kidnaps or abducts any person in order that such a person may be murdered or may be disposed off as to be put in danger of being murdered, shall be punished with imprisonment for life or rigorous imprisonment for a term which may extend to ten years, and shall also be liable to fine.

364A. Kidnapping for ransom

Whoever kidnaps or abducts any person or keeps a person in detention after such kidnapping of abduction and threatens to cause death or hurt to such person, or by his conduct gives rise to reasonable apprehension that such person may be put to death or hurt, or causes hurt or death to such person in order to compel the Government or any foreign state or international inter-governmental organisation or to do or abstain from doing any act or to pay shall be punished with death, or imprisonment for life, and shall also be liable to fine.

365. Kidnapping or abducting with intent secretly and wrongfully to confine person

Whoever kidnaps or abducts any person with intent to cause that person to be secretly and wrongfully confined, shall be punished with imprisonment of either description for a term which may extend to seven years, and shall also be liable to fine.

366. Kidnapping, abducting or inducing woman to compel her marriage etc.

Whoever kidnaps or abducts any woman with intent that she may be compelled, or knowing it to be likely that she will be compelled to marry any person against her will, or in order that she may not be forced or seduce to illicit intercourse, or knowing it to be likely that she will be forced or reduced to illicit intercourse shall be punished with imprisonment of either description for a term which may extend to ten years, and shall also be liable to fine; and whoever, by means of criminal intimidation as defined in this code or of abuse of authority or any other method of compulsion, induces any woman to go from any place with intent that she may be, or knowing that it is likely that she will be forced or seduced to illicit intercourse with another person shall be punishable as aforesaid.

375. Rape

A man is said to commit "rape" who, except in the case hereinafter excepted, has sexual intercourse with a woman under circumstances falling under any of the six descriptions:

First—against her will

Secondly—without her consent

Thirdly—with her consent, when her consent was obtained by putting her or any person in whom she is interested in fear of death or of hurt.

Fourthly—with her consent, when the man knows that he is not her husband and that her consent is given because she believes that he is another man to whom she is or believed herself to be lawfully married.

Fifthly—with her consent, when at the time of giving such consent, by reason of unsoundness of mind or intoxication or the administration by him personally or through another of any stupefying or unwholesome substance, she is unable to understand the nature and consequences of that to which she gives consent.

Sixthly—with her consent, when she is under sixteen years of age.

Exception—sexual intercourse by a man with his own wife, the wife not being under fifteen years of age, is not rape.

376. Punishment for rape

1. Whoever, except in the cases provided for by subsection (2), commits rape shall be punished with imprisonment of either description for a term which shall not be less than seven years but which may be for a life or for a term which may extend to ten years and shall also be liable to fine unless the women raped is his own wife and not under twelve years of age, in which case, he shall be punished with imprisonment of either description for a term which may extend to two years or with fine or with both: Provided that the court may, for adequate and special reasons to be mentioned in the judgement, impose a sentence of imprisonment for a term of less than seven years.
2. whoever
   (a) being a police officer commits rape—
1. with the limits of a police station to which he is appointed; or
2. in the premises of any station house whether or not situated in the police station to which he is appointed; or
3. on a woman in his custody or in the custody of a police officer subordinate to him; or

   (b) being a public servant, takes advantage of his official position and commits rape on a woman in his custody as such public servant or in the custody of a public servant subordinate to him; or

(c) being on the management or on the staff of a jail, remand home or other place of custody established by or under any law for the time being in force or of a woman's or children's institution takes advantage of his position and commits rape on any inmate of such jail, remand home, place or institution; or
(d) being on the management or on the staff of a hospital, takes advantage of his official position and commits rape on a woman in that hospital; or
(e) commits rape on a woman knowing her to be pregnant; or
(f) commits rape on a woman when she is under twelve years of age; or
(g) commits gang rape.

shall be punished with rigorous imprisonment for a term which shall not be less than ten years but which may be for life and shall also be liable to fine:

Provided that the court may, for adequate and special reasons to be mentioned in the judgement, impose a sentence of imprisonment of either description for a term of less than ten years.

Explanation 1—where a woman is raped by one or more in a group of persons acting in furtherance of their common intention, each of the persons shall be deemed to have committed gang rape within the meaning of this subsection.

Explanation 2—"women's or children's institution" means an institution, whether called an orphanage or a home for neglected woman or children or a widows' home or by any other name, which is established and maintained for the reception and care of woman or children.

Explanation 3—"hospital" means the precincts of the hospital and includes the precincts of any institution for the reception and treatment of persons during convalescence or of persons requiring medical attention or rehabilitation.

376A. Intercourse by a man with his wife during separation

Whoever has sexual intercourse with his own wife, who is living separately from him under a decree of separation or under any custom or usage without her consent shall be punished with imprisonment of either description for a term which may extend to two years and shall also be liable to fine.

498A. Husband or relative of husband of a woman subjecting her to cruelty

Whoever being the husband or relative of the husband of a woman, subjects such woman to cruelty shall be punished with imprisonment for a term which may extend to three years and shall also be liable to fine.

Explanation—For the purpose of this section, "cruelty" means—

(a) any willful conduct which is of such a nature as is likely to drive the woman to commit suicide or to cause grave injury or danger to life, limb, or health (whether mental or physical) of the woman; or

(b) harassment of the woman where such harassment is with a view to coercing her or any person related to her to meet any unlawful demand for any property or valuable security or is on account of failure by her or any person related to her to meet such demand.

509. Word, gesture or act intended to insult the modesty of a woman

Whoever, intending to insult the modesty of any woman, utters any word, makes any sound or gesture, or exhibits any object, intending that such word or sound shall be heard, or that such gesture or object shall be seen, by such woman, or intrudes upon the privacy of such woman, shall be punished with simple imprisonment for a term which may extend to one year, or with fine, or with both.

Social Legislation in Canada

Canada being a relatively new country, doesnot have age old practices and superstitions as India. The social legislation for women, though reformed in the eighties gives a certain amount of wider freedom to women in Canada. The Canadian Panel on Violence Against Women declares:

Equality and freedom from violence are rights of all women, and it is the responsibility of every individual, community, government and institution in Canada to work toward securing these rights.

- The elimination of violence will best be achieved through the adoption and rigorous application of a policy of zero tolerance.
- To this end we urge each person and every organization in Canada to commit to the equality and safety of women and implement the Zero Tolerance Policy.[22]

The Declaration given by the Canadian Panel aptly describes the Canadian Criminal Code.

However inspite of such broad outlook of Canadian society as reflected above, crime against women especially in the nature of domestic violence as well as sexual assault is rampant as seen in the case of Toronto.

The incident on December 6, 1989 when 14 women were murdered in Montreal is celebrated as a National Provincial and Civic Day of Rememberance and Action on Violence Against Women. Today the rememberance of this massacre has given new focus to the problem of women victimization. Women's campaigns for better laws since the 1980's have been able to achieve a certain amount of potency. However, women in Toronto still feel that the laws could be made more victim friendly in future. The struggle is still on to make the society more balanced. Some of the laws that protect women under the Canadian Criminal Code are given at the end of the chapter. As seen in the laws, they are not women specific.

It is evident that the Canadian laws have done away with gender bias in most instances to make the laws uniform. Some laws have been reformed in the eighties those such as rape laws and assault to accommodate domestic violence cases.

Sexual Assault

Sexual assault is defined very broadly under Canadian law. It ranges in severity from relatively minor acts of unwanted sexual touching to very serious sexual attacks resulting in injury or disfigurement to the victim. Victims can include males and females, as well as children and adults. Rape is not necessary component of sexual assault, although it falls within this definition. The crimes of rape and indecent assault were removed from the Canadian Legal books in 1983 and replaced with three new offences of sexual assault:

1. Sexual assault (maximum 10 years imprisonment)
2. Sexual assault with a weapon, threats to a third party, or causing bodily harm (maximum 14 years imprisonment)
3. Aggravated sexual assault resulting in wounding, maiming, disfiguring, or endangering the life of the victim (maximum life imprisonment).

The 1983 Criminal Code amendments to the old offences of rape and indecent assault constituted a major achievement by women's lobby groups. It was hoped that the new three-tier offence of sexual assault, along with its corresponding sentencing scheme and evidentiary rules, would make victims participation in the criminal justice system less painful and would also result in a higher conviction rate for this notoriously unpunished offence. The concept of rape was changed to sexual assault as in the old concept it was felt that women were objects or sexual property.

Several myths and misconceptions were evident in the old rape legislation. Prior to 1983, the law defined a rape

(a) A male person has sexual intercourse with a female person who is not his wife a. without her consent, or (b) with her consent if the consent (1) is extorted by threats or fear of bodily harm (2) is obtained by impersonating her husband, or (3) is obtained by false and fraudulent representations as to the nature and quality of the act (143).

Under this legal definition, rape was a gender offence, since the offender was presumed to be male and the victim female. The focus was on the sexual nature of the act, in that penetration was necessary in order for a rape to have occurred. Under this legislation, husbands could not be charged with raping wives. The key element in establishing the guilt of the accused in the rape cases was consent.[23] The old rape laws of Canada are similar to the rape laws in India today.

The trial was for the victim to prove whether she consented or not. In other words the victim had to prove her innocence in the trial. The past sexual history of the victim could be scrutinized in court. Medical and other psychological tests in the past taken by the victim could be used as evidence. In the process women had to ascertain her character and virtue in court. It came under the scrutiny whether the women were of good or bad character. In the old rape laws, it was found that there was no marital rape, as it seemed that rape was beyond the purview of the violence within the family.

In January 1983, the old rape law was replaced. Under the new legislation, the offence was degenderized. The sexual element of the offence of sexual assault was completely undefined. The courts gave various definitions of sexual assault. The word sexual was defined, meaning sexual characteristics, social norms of the meaning of sexuality. These definitions were however, felt by women's groups to be male - defined perspective of female sexuality.

The main aim of the 1983 law on sexual assault was to reflect the violence rather than the sexual nature of the offence. Women's group had impressed on the fact that four principals had to be embodied in the law: treatment of rape as a type of assault, creating tiers of sexual assault to parallel existing assault offences, abolishing spousal immunity, and limiting admissibility of past sexual history. The bill created by the government was called Bill c-52.

The concern with reducing the trauma of the trial for victims is reflected in changes to the evidentiary rules. Witnesses in criminal trial for other offences, for example, are not likely to be questioned as to their private sex lives or to be required to explain why they did not immediately report the offences. Nor is their testimony presumed untrustworthy if uncorroborated by other evidences, (Boyd and Sheehy, 1989). In other words, the testimony of the victim is important along with her character and movements.

One of the main objectives of the legislative reform was to shift the focus away from the sexual nature of the act and make its violent nature the main point of concentration. Thus, while the old rape law was included under Part (IV) if the Criminal Code, sexual offences, public morals and disorderly conduct, the new sexual assault legislation is included under Part (VI), Offences Against the Person and Reputation. One of the difficulties with the new legislation, however, is the absence of a clear definition of what constitutes a sexual as opposed to a common assault. In the absence of a statutory definition, it has been left to the courts to determine what comprises a sexual assault. [24]

Since rape has been replaced with the term sexual assault, there has been some confusion over the definition of the crime since Parliament did not define the term in the Criminal Code. The Supreme Court had to grapple with the issue in the R.V. Chase case. In the R.V. Chase case in 1987, the Supreme Court ruled that a sexual assault is differentiated from an assault by the part of the body touched, the nature of the contact, the situation and other circumstances surrounding the contact.

The case has been briefly described. The accused, Chase, was a neighbor of the complainant, a 15 year old girl. The case occurred in 1983 in New Brunswick. The complainant was alone at home with her 11 year old brother and 83 year old grandfather. The accused entered the house, seized the complainant around the shoulders and arms and grabbed her breasts. When she fought back, he said "come on dear, don't hit me, I know you want it. "The complainant said at the trial that: he tried to grab for my private, but he didn't succeed because my hands were too fast. Eventually, the complainant and her brother were able to make a telephone call to a neighbor and the respondent left. Prior to leaving, he said that he was going to tell everybody that she had raped him. The whole episode lasted little more than half an hour. The respondent was charged with the offence of sexual assault and was found guilty after trial in the Provincial Court. He appealed to the Court of Appeal for New Brunswick where his appeal was dismissed.[25]

The court had dismissed the case as the actions of the accused was taken as common assault only, as the breasts of a woman were defined as secondary sexual characteristics. In this case there was a lot of criticism involved. Women's groups tried to emphasize on the fact that a woman's perception of parts of her body is different to that of a man. A woman definitely feels that the touching of breasts is a sexual act. Hence, the structure and definition of the new offence of sexual assault presented a certain amount of vagueness.

When Chase was subsequently heard by the Supreme Court, in 1987, the Appeal Court decision was overturned. The Supreme Court held that breasts were indeed sexual, and defined sexual assault as an assault committed in circumstances of a sexual nature, such that the sexual integrity of the victim is violated. In its ruling, then the court has recognized that, while sexual gratification may be a relevant motivating factor, not all sexual assaults are committed for the purpose of sexual gratification .[26]

The Supreme Court's decision helped to clear the confusion and doubt in the Chase case. However, the meaning and scope of the word sexual was still unsolved.

In 1991, another set back occurred when the Supreme Court removed the rape shield law which was formed in the 1983 reform with the aim of preventing a victim's sexual conduct from being used to discredit her testimony. In 1991, the Supreme Court felt that for a fair trial it was necessary to look into the sexual history of the woman. This decision came as a result of the Seaboyer and Gayme case.

The Gayme case arose in different circumstances. The complainant was 15, the appellant 18. They were friends .The Crown alleges that the appellant sexually assaulted her at his school. The defense, replying on the defenses of consent and honest belief in consent, contends that there was no assault and that the complainant was the sexual aggressor. In pursuance of this defense, the appellant at the preliminary inquiry sought to cross - examine and present evidence of prior and subsequent sexual conduct of the complainant.

It was successfully argued that the rape shield law violated a fair trial. In response to this about 60 women's groups opposed the removal of the rape - shield law. However, the Parliament tabled Bill c - 49 in December, 1991. It was referred to committee after second reading on April 16, 1992. It was passed by the House of Commons and Senate, and came into force in August 1992. The Bill established guidelines to assist judges in determining when it would be permissible to admit evidence about a victim's sexual history. It also provided a definition of the concept of consent as it applies to sexual assault, and restricted the conditions under which the defense of mistaken belief could be used. For example, consent is not obtained when

- It is given by someone other than the victim.
- The victim is incapable of consenting due to intoxication or some other condition ;
- It is induced by abusing a position of trust , power, or authority;
- The victim indicates by word or conduct her lack of consent ; or

- The victim indicates by word or conduct that she has withdrawn her consent.

The last two conditions, specifying either word or conduct, were included in recognition of the unique vulnerability of disabled women to sexual assault and the fact that some disabilities prevent the articulation of lack of consent. The law also states that nothing in (the above lists) shall be constructed as limiting the circumstances in which no consent is obtained. In other words, the list is not exhaustive and the prospective may present other conditions to indicate absence of consent. With this change in the law, the focus shifts from determining whether the perpetrator used force or caused injury to determining whether the complainant articulated consent to engage in sexual activity. 27

This bill prevented the accused to use mistaken consent as a defense. The accused however cannot resort to drunkenness or recklessness as a defense mechanism. In 1994, in the case of R.V. Daviault, the Supreme Court overthrew the conviction of a man found guilty of sexually assaulting an elderly woman on the ground that the man was intoxicated. Since then, several cases have been acquitted on similar grounds. However, in 1995, Parliament passed amendments to the Criminal Code that disallow the drunkenness defense in violent offences requiring general intent, such as assault and sexual assault.

A special addition to the sexual assault laws were made to accommodate child sexual abuse. In 1988, the following offences were added:

1. sexual interference - sexual touching of a child under 14 years of age (maximum 10 years imprisonment)
2. invitation to sexual touching - inviting or counsel a child under 14 to be involved in sexual touching (maximum 10 years imprisonment.
3. sexual exploitation - a person who is in a position of trust or authority or with whom the child is in a

position of dependency and who is involved in sexual interference or invitation to sexual touching (child is between 14 and 18 years of age; maximum 5 years imprisonment.

4. incest - sexual intercourse with a person who is related by blood and who is a parent, child, brother, sister, Godparent, or grandchild (maximum 14 years imprisonment).

Prior to 1988 law for child abuse, in late 1980 the Badgley Committee was appointed by ministers of justice and National Health and Welfare in late 1980's. In broad terms, the mandate of the committee was to determine the adequacy of Canadian laws in protecting children and youths from sexual offences and to make recommendations for improving protection. In addition, the committee was instructed to determine the incidence and prevalence of sexual abuse against children and youths and to examine charge patterns and prosecution patterns of sexual offences committed against children and youths. Included in the mandate were the areas of juvenile prostitution and child pornography. The minister of justice introduced Bill c-53 in January 1981. This bill, which withered under criticism from civil libertarians, was designed to deal with the issue of child sexual abuse and to update the Criminal Code offence of rape to sexual assault. Under heavy criticism, the government outlined the role of the Badgley Committee in early 1981. In the Bill, the definition of child sexual abuse was incomplete. After Bill c - 53 died, it was replaced by Bill c- 127. This resulted in important amendments to the Criminal Code in 1982 and provided increased protection for women. This bill was followed by yet another Bill c - 15 where consent was further clarified. In 1986, a new version of the child sexual abuse offence, Bill c - 15 was first read in the House by the Legislative committee and ultimately it was proclaimed in January 1988 in its present form with the four offences added to its (as mentioned earlier).

Inspite of all the reforms in sexual assault cases, it is widely criticized that even today although a woman who is the victim, she is victimized not only by the accused but also during the trial. However, one very broad purview of the new law for sexual assault has been that husbands can come under the purview of sexual assault of wives. In other words marital rape laws have been approved.

During the survey of the women's groups they voiced their discontent about the legislation. In most occasions, the accuser gets acquitted. Often the gravity of the sexual assault cases is reduced in the courts and in turn the women are made to give testimony. It seems to the women that the sexual assault laws are to protect the men.

Domestic Violence

Domestic assault or violence, be it in India or Canada or anywhere in the world is of the same intensity and harshness. Till the early 1980's the Canadian society seemed oblivious to the fact that there was violence within the four walls of the home. However, in the recent past it has been noticed that physical assaults represent more than three-quarters of all violent offences and, as a result, have a major impact on the level of violence within society. In 1988, after the report of the General Social Survey was published, it indicated that an attack or incident involving the threat of violence was the type of crime of greatest concern with 43 per cent of those sampled identified violent assault as the crime they feared the most. These developments, combined with extensive media coverage of crime issues, have helped to produce a widespread perception among Canadians that crime, and especially violent crime, is on the increase.

The sad story of assault especially domestic assault in the earlier chapters is that the woman is assaulted by someone who she knows and possibly trusts. Wife assault cases have been able to focus on that fact that the Canadian society still has inequality. Till a very long time, women were believed to be the property of their husbands and hence rape laws for marital rape was not acknowledged since a long time. Wife beating was acceptable in England as the husband and wife relationship was that of guardian and ward. Clearly that the home is a refuge, a haven, a private domain is no longer true as violence is frequent in contemporary society.

The Canadian Criminal Code has identified three levels of assault:

First level or common assault

Second level or assault causing bodily harm

Third level or aggravated assault

A threatened assault or an actual assault that doesnot produce a serious physical injury is categorized as a common assault. The more serious second level assault requires the use or threatened use of a weapon, or the presence of injuries such as broken bones, cuts, and bruises.

Section 266 of the Criminal Code states that everyone who commits an assault is guilty of an indictable offence, or an offence punishable on summary conviction. This new section, introduced in 1983 under Bill c - 127, replaces what formerly was known as common assault. The new section creates a dual- procedure offence (the former section was a summary conviction offence) that allows police to arrest a person when they have reasonable and probable grounds to believe an assault was committed. Under the old section, the police could not arrest unless they witnessed the person committing the assault. For example, in domestic dispute situations involving assault of a wife, they did not have a power of arrest unless they had actually witnessed the assault or the wife had suffered bodily harm. Under the new section, police are able to arrest the aggressor, thereby avoiding the possibility of further assaults after they leave the scene.[28] Bill 127 clarified the definition and nature of assault, domestic situations were difficult find out as there were no witnesses. However, today due to awareness and with the support of several women's groups, the number of reported cases are going up. Much of the increase has been during the 1982 - 90 period. It is possible that previously there was under-reporting of cases.

Details on the legislation are provided at the end of this chapter on both India and Canada.

Survey on Social Legislation

Fifteen interviews were taken of people from different walks of life especially those working in non - profit organizations, women's cells, and police personnel. In 40 per cent of the cases, the people felt that the social legislative laws were adequate in Canada to tackle the present situation of rampant sexual assault cases and domestic assault cases. Amongst police personnel almost 80 per cent felt that the laws were adequate while 20% felt that the laws were adequate but poorly applied.

The women's groups especially could pin - point the flaws in the social legislation of the country. Most pointed out the fact that with the removal of the rape shield law, it makes the woman more vulnerable to attack. Victims after the traumatic experience were not in a position to face the assault of questions in court. Besides it has been found that when a victim is raped she is the one to give testimony as well. Many organizations have also expressed the fact that after a spouse threatens with a weapon to kill, the case is registered as a common assault. However, the threat may lead to dire consequences, like death of the victim as in common assault cases, the assaulter is not arrested. There should be mandatory arrest policy. Besides this in bail terms and conditions trespassing laws must be included. Along with this stalking is becoming a dangerous mode of threat perception to victims. There are several hundred stalking incidents in the city however, no laws have been formed. Hence, a reform is necessary. The current laws seem to provide short-term solutions. However, the laws should be reformed, in part to address long term solutions such as, anger control management, substance abuse management and parenting skill, all geared towards reducing repeated victimization.

Woman abuse according to Wendy Ross, Chair, Abuse against Women Committee at Peel Memorial Hospital, should be a health issue. The woman is mauled, bruised both mentally and physically from domestic assaults. According to Health Canada, one - half of Canadian women have experienced at least one incident of violence since the age of 16. These women avail of medical help and require hospitalization. Hence, at various points, women's groups have tried to emphasize that crime against women is not only a criminal offence but also a health hazard.

The most important short-term method to help women would be to execute the laws. The primary would be for police officers to respond to wife assault calls and charge the batterer. In the main Crown Attorney's adhere to the letter of the law in prosecuting cases of wife assault. However, only some of them engage in the specific activities outlined in directives that would ensure more consistent success in the prosecution of these cases. These activities include:

- holding meaningful pre - trial conferences with assaulted women to gain maximum cooperation from them and to prepare them better for their role as witness.
- Ensuring that the case is a strong one apart from the testimony of the assaulted woman (i.e. the case is not solely dependent on her testimony.)
- Preparing a sentencing report, with input from advocates for the assaulted woman, the assaulted women herself and the probation/ parole officer, that ensures the on going safety of the assaulted women and requests stronger penalties in the case of a repeated offence.
- Native and immigrant women, minority women, women who are disabled, women whose heritage language is not English and women who are not of Anglo culture have less access to and receive less protection from the justice system than white, able bodied, Anglophone, women. For example, native women are hampered both by the negative attitudes of police and because they live in remote locations.

> Racial and ethnic minority women fear that police attitudes will make response to their complaints less likely or, conversely, that the police will treat their partner more harshly.

The Government of Ontario made a five year commitment to the Joint Family Violence Initiatives in September 1986. The goals of the Joint Family Violence Initiatives are to;

1. reduce the incidence of wife assault
2. provide protection for victims and
3. provide a coordinated network of government and community services which deal effectively with family violence. The criminalization of wife assault was adopted as a fundamental strategy for reducing the incidence of wife assault.

The Initiatives are coordinated by the Interministeral Committee or services related to wife battering.[29]

It is important to clearly state the laws such as in sexual assault cases the parts of the body which are believed to show sexuality, should be clearly listed. This will reduce the discretion there may be while filing or preparing the charge sheet in a case. Besides this further reforms in the law especially sexual assault cases should take place. There should be a distinction between sexual assault and sexual penetration as often the accused gets a lesser sentence compared to the gravity of the case. Laws should be formulated in such a way as to protect the interests of the victim and not the male interests. Laws which are sympathetic to the woman can help to make the woman more confident and help them to assert their views in court. Until the laws of the land are fair and their execution correct, it will be difficult to bring more women to report cases.

From the above study it is certain that the judiciary has to make a positive impact in both India and Canada. The laws must grow and be changed according to the needs of the time. Laws should be able to cater to all sections of society and not be partisan in approach. However, in both India and Canada, it is evident since the 1980's laws for women are being made more progressive and according to the need of the times.

Excerpts from Martin's Annual Criminal Code 1997 Important laws for protection of women in Canada

1. Sexual Offenses:

Consent no defense / exception / exemption for accused aged twelve or thirteen / mistake of age 150.1 (1) Where an accused is charged with an offense under section 151 or 152 or subsection 153(1), 160(3) or 173(2) or is charged with an offence under section 271, 272 or 273 in respect of a complainant consented to the activity that forms the subject matter of the charge.

(2) Notwithstanding subsection (1), where an accused is charged with an offense under section 151 or 152, subsection 173 (2) or section 271 in respect of a complainant who is twelve years of age or more but under the age of fourteen years, it is not a defense that the complainant consented to the activity that forms the subject—matter of the charge unless the accused

(a) is twelve years of age or more but under the age of sixteen years;
(b) is less than two years older than the complainant; and
(c) is neither in a position of trust or authority towards the complainant nor is a person with whom the complainant is in a relationship of dependency.

(3) No person aged twelve or thirteen years shall be tried for an offense under section 151 or 152 or subsection 173(2) unless the person is in a position of trust or authority towards the complainant or is a person with whom the complainant is in a relationship of dependency.

(4) It is not a defense to charge under section 151 or 152, subsection 160 (3) or 173 (2) or section 271, 272 or 273 that the accused believed that the complainant was

fourteen years of age or more at the time the offense is alleged to have been committed unless the accused took all reasonable steps to ascertain the age of the complainant.

(5) It is not a defense to a charge under section 153, 159, 170, 171 or subsection 212(2) or (4) that the accused believed that the complainant was eighteen years of age or more at the time the offense is alleged to have been committed unless the accused took all reasonable steps to ascertain the age of the complainant. R.S.C. 1985, c.19 (3rd Supp.), s.1.

2. Every person who, for a sexual purpose, touches, directly or indirectly, with a part of the body or with an object any part of the body of a person under the age of fourteen years is guilty of an indictable offense and liable to imprisonment for a term not exceeding ten years or is guilty of an offense punishable on summary conviction.R.S>C>1985, c.19 (3rd Supp.) s.1.

3. Sexual Exploitation

153. (1) Every person who is in a position of trust or authority towards a young person or is a person with whom the young person is in a relation of dependency and who

(a) for a sexual purpose, touches, directly or indirectly, with a part of the body or with an object, any part of the body of the young person or

(b) for a sexual purpose, invites, counsels or incites a young person to touch, directly or indirectly with a part of the body or with an object, the body of any person, including the body of the person who invites, counsels or incites and the body of the young person, is guilty of an indictable offense and liable to imprisonment for a term not exceeding five years or is guilty of an offense punishable on summary conviction.

1. In this section, "young person" means a person fourteen years of age or more but under the age of eighteen years. R.S.C.1985, c. 19(3rd Supp.), s.1.

INCEST

155(1) Everyone commits incest who, knowing that another persons by blood relationship his or her parent child, brother, sister, grandparent or grandchild, as the case maybe, has sexual intercourse with that person.

2. Everyone who commits incest is guilty of an indictable offense and liable to imprisonment for a term not exceeding fourteen years.
3. No accused shall be determined by a court to be guilty of an offense under this section if the accused was under restraint, duress or fear of the person with whom the accused had the sexual intercourse at the time the sexual intercourse occurred.
4. In this section, brother, and sister, respectively, include half-brother and half-sister R.S., c.c-34, s.150; 1972, c.13. s10; R.S.C. 1985, c.27 (1st supp) s. 21.

Anal Intercourse

159(1) Every person who engages in an act of anal intercourse is guilty of an indictable offense and liable to imprisonment for a term not exceeding ten years or is guilty of an offense punishable on summary conviction.

Killing by influence on the mind

228. No person commits culpable homicide where he causes the death of a human being.

(a) by any influence on the mind alone or

(b) by any disorder or disease resulting from influence on the mind alone, but this section does not apply where a person causes the death of a child or sick person by willfully frightening him. R.S., c.c.-34, s.211.

Murder

229. Culpable homicide is murder

(a) where the person who causes the death of a human being

(1) means to cause his death or

(2) means to cause him bodily harm that he knows is likely to cause his death, and is reckless whether death ensues or not;

(b) where a person, meaning to cause death to a human being or meaning to cause him bodily harm that he knows is likely to cause his death, and being reckless whether death ensues or not, by accident or mistake causes death to another human being, notwithstanding that he does not mean to cause death or bodily harm to that human being: or

(c) where a person, for an unlawful object, does anything that he knows or ought to know is likely to cause death, and thereby causes death to a human being, notwithstanding that he desires to effect his object without causing death or bodily harm to any human being. R.S.,c.c-34, s.212

Classification of Murder

231(1) Murder is first-degree murder or second-degree murder.

(2) murder is first-degree murder when it is planned and deliberate.

(3) Without limiting the generality of subsection (2) murder is planned and deliberate when it is committed pursuant to an arrangement under which money or anything of value passes or is intended to pass from one to another, or is promised by one person to another, as consideration for others causing or assisting in causing the death of anyone or counseling another person to do any act causing or assisting in causing that death.

(4) Irrespective of whether a murder is planned and deliberate on the part of any person, murder is first degree murder when the victim is

- (a) a police officer, police constable, constable sheriff, deputy sheriff, sheriff's officer or other person employed for the preservation and maintenance of the public peace, acting in the course of his duties;
- (b) a warden, deputy warden, instructor, keeper, jailer, guard or other officer or a permanent employee of a prison, acting in the course of his duties; or
- (c) a person working in a prison with the permission of the prison authorities and acting in the course of his work therein.

(5) Irrespective of whether a murder is planned and

deliberate on the part of any person, murder is first degree murder, in respect of a person when the death is caused by that person while committing or attempting to commit an offense under one of the following sections:

(a) Section 76 (hijacking an aircraft)

(b) Section 271 (sexual assault)

(c) Section 272 (sexual assault with a weapon, threats to a third party or causing bodily harm)

(d) Section 273 (aggravated sexual assault)

(e) Section 279 (kidnapping and forcible confinement) or

(f) Section 279.1 (hostage taking)

(6) Repealed. R.S.C. 1985, c.27 (1st supp.) s.35.

(7) All murder that is not first degree murder is second degree murder.R.S.C. c-34, s.214; R.S.C.c-35, s.4; 1973-74, c.38s.2; 1974-75.c, 105,s.4; 1983-81-82-83, c.125, s.16; R.S.C.1985, c.27 (1st supp), ss.7 (2) (b), 35,40(2).

Murder reduced to manslaughter

232(1) Culpable homicide that otherwise would be murder may be reduced to manslaughter if the person who committed it did it in the heat of passion caused by sudden provocation.

(1) A wrongful act or an insult that is of such a nature as to be sufficient to deprive as ordinary person of the power of self-control is provocation for the purposes of this section if the accused acted on the sudden and before there was time for his passion to cool.

(3) For the purposes of this section, the questions

(a) Whether a particular wrongful act or insult amounted to provocation and

(b) Whether the accused was deprived of the power of self control by the provocation that he alleges he received are questions of fact, but no one shall be deemed to have given provocation to another by doing anything that he had a legal right to do, or by doing anything that the accused incited him to do in order to provide the accused with an excuse for causing death or bodily harm to any human being.

(4) Culpable homicide that otherwise would be murder is not necessarily manslaughter by reason only that it was committed by a person who was being arrested illegally, but the fact that the illegality of the arrest was known to the accused may be evidence of provocation for the purpose of this matter of this section.R.S., c.c-34,s-215.

Punishment for murder

235 (1) Everyone who commits first-degree murder or second-degree murder is guilty of an offence and shall be sentenced to imprisonment for life.

(2) For the purposes of Part XXIII, the sentence of imprisonment for life prescribed by this section is a minimum punishment R.S.C.c-34, s.218; 1973-74c.38,s.3;1974-75-76,c.105,s.5.

Manslaughter

236 Every person who commits manslaughter is guilty of an indictable offense and liable

(a) where a firearm is used in the commission of the offence, to imprisonment for life and to a minimum punishment of imprisonment for a term of four years; and

(b) in any other case, to imprisonment for life. R.S.,c.c-34,s.219 1995,c.39.

Assaults

264.1 (1) Everyone commits an offence who, in any manner, knowingly utters, conveys or causes any person to receive a threat.

(a) Without the consent of another person, he applies force intentionally to that other person, directly or indirectly;

(b) He attempts or threatens, by an act or a gesture, to apply force to another person, if he has or causes that other person to believe upon reasonable grounds that he has, present ability to effect his purpose; or

(c) While openly wearing or carrying a weapon or an imitation thereof, he accosts or impedes another person or begs.

(2) This section applies to all forms of assault, including sexual assault, sexual assault with a weapon, threats

to a third party or causing bodily harm and aggravated sexual assault.

(e) For the purpose of this section, no consent is obtained where the complainant submits or does not resist by reason of

(a) the application of force to the complainant or to a person other than the complainant;

(b) Threats or fear of the application of force to the complainant or to a person other than the complainant;

(c) Fraud; or

(d) The exercise of authority.

(4) Where an accused alleges that he believes that the complainant consented to the conduct that is the subject-matter of the charge, a Judge, if satisfied that there is sufficient evidence and that, if believed by the jury, the evidence would constitute a defense, shall instruct the jury, when reviewing all the evidence relating to the determination of the honesty of the accused's belief, to consider the presence or absence of reasonable grounds for that belief.R.S., C.c-34, s.244; 1974-75-76, c.93, s. 21; 1980-81-82-83, c.125,s.19.

Assault

266. Everyone who commits an assault is guilty of

(a) an indictable offence and liable to imprisonment for a term not exceeding five years; or

(b) an offence punishable on summary conviction

Assault with a weapon or causing bodily harm

267. Everyone who, in committing an assault,

(a) Carries, uses or threatens to use a weapon or imitation thereof, or

(b) causes bodily harm to the complainant, is guilty of an indictable offence and liable to imprisonment for a term not exceeding ten years or an offence punishable on summary conviction and liable to imprisonment for a term not exceeding eighteen months. 1980-81-82-83, c.125, s.19;1994, c.44, s.17.

Aggravated Assault

268(1) Everyone commits an aggravated assault who

wounds, maims, disfigures or endangers the life of the complainant.

(2) Everyone who commits an aggravated assault is guilty of an indictable offence and liable to imprisonment for a term not exceeding fourteen years. 1980-81-82-83,c.125,s.19.

Unlawfully causing bodily harm

269 Everyone who unlawfully causes bodily harm to any person is guilty of

(a) An indictable offence and liable to imprisonment for a term not exceeding ten years; or

(b) an offence punishable on summary conviction and liable to imprisonment for a term not exceeding eighteen months.1980-81-82-83, c.125, s. 19; 1994, c. 44, s.18

Sexual Assault

271(1) Everyone who commits a sexual assault is guilty of

(a) an indictable offence and liable to imprisonment for a term not exceeding ten years; or

(b) an offence punishable on summary conviction and liable to imprisonment for a term not exceeding eighteen months. 1980-81-82-83, c. 125, s. 19; R.S.C. 1985, c. 19 (3rd Supp), c, 10; 1994, c.44, s.19.

(2) Repealed R.S.C. 1985, c.19(3rd supp.), s.10

Sexual assault with a weapon, threats to a third party or causing bodily harm

272(1) Every person commits an offence who, in committing a sexual assault,

(a) Carries, uses or threatens to use a weapon or an imitation of a weapon;

(b) Threatens to cause bodily harm to a person other than the complainant;

(c) Causes bodily harm to the complainant; or

(d) Is a party to the offence with any other person

(2) Every person who commits an offence under subsection (1) is guilty of an indictable offence and liable

(a) Where a firearm is used in the commission of the offence, to imprisonment for a term not exceeding fourteen years and to a minimum punishment of imprisonment for a term of four years;

(b) In any other case, to imprisonment for a term not exceeding fourteen years. 1980-81-82-83, c.125, s.19; 1995, c.39, s.145.

Aggravated sexual assault

273(1) Everyone commits an aggravated sexual assault who, in committing a sexual assault, wounds, maims, disfigures or endangers the life of the complainant.

(2) Every person who commits an aggravated sexual assault is guilty of an indictable offence and liable.

(a) Where a firearm is used in the commission of the offence, to imprisonment for life and to a minimum punishment of imprisonment for a term of four years; and

(b) in any other case, to imprisonment for life. 1980-81-82-83, c.125,s.19;1995,c.39,s.146.

Meaning of consent

273(1) Subject to subsection (2) and subsection 265(3), consent means, for the purposes of sections 271, 272 and 273, the voluntary agreement of the complainant to engage in the sexual activity in question.

(2) No consent is obtained, for the purposes of sections 271, 272 and 273, where

(a) The agreement is expressed by the words or conduct of a person other than the complainant;

(b) The complainant is incapable of consenting to the activity;

(c) The accused induces the complainant to engage in the activity by abusing a position of trust power or authority;

(d) The complainant expresses, by words or conduct, a lack of agreement to engage in the activity; or

(e) The complainant, having consented to engage in sexual activity, expresses, by words or conduct, a lack of agreement to continue to engage in the activity.

(3) Nothing in subsection (2) shall be construed as limiting the circumstance in which no consent is obtained.

Spouse may be charged

278 A husband or wife may be charged with an offence

under section 271, 272 or 273 in respect of his or her spouse, whether or not the spouses were living together at the time the activity that forms the subject matter of the charge concerned. 1980-81-82-83 c.125, s.19.

Kidnapping

279(1) Every person commits an offence who kidnaps a person with intent

(a) To cause the person to be confined or imprisoned against the persons's will;

(b) To cause the person to be unlawfully sent or transported out of Canada against the person's will or;

(c) To hold the person for ransom or to service against the person's will.

(1.1) Every person who commits an offence under subsection (1) is guilty of an indictable offence and liable

(a) Where a firearm is used in the commission of the offence, to imprisonment for life and to a minimum punishment of imprisonment for a term of four years; and

(b) In any other case, to imprisonment for life.

(2) Everyone who, without lawful authority, confines, imprisons or forcibly seizes another person is guilty of an indictable offence and liable to imprisonment for a term not exceeding ten years.

(3) In proceedings under this section, the fact that the person in relation to whom the offence is alleged to have been committed did not resist is not a defense unless the accused proves that the failure to resist was not caused by threat or danger, or exhibition of force. R.S., c.c.-34, s.247; R.S.C. 1985, c.27 (1st Supp) s.39; 1995, c.39, s.147.

Abduction of person under sixteen

280(1) Everyone who, without lawful authority, abducts an unmarried person under the age of sixteen years out of the possession of and against the will of the parent or guardian of that person or of any other person who has the lawful care or charge of that person is guilty of an indictable offence and liable to imprisonment for a term not exceeding five years.

(2) In this section and sections 281 to 283 guardian includes

any person who has in law or in fact the custody or control of another person. R.S., c.c-34, s.249; 1980-81-82-83, c.125, s.20.

Abduction of person under fourteen

281 Everyone who, not being the parent, guardian or person having the lawful care or charge of a person under the age of fourteen years, unlawfully takes entices away, conceals, detains, receives or harbors that person with intent to deprive a parent or guardian or any other person who has the lawful care or charge of that person, of the possession of that person is guilty of an indictable offence and liable to imprisonment for a term not exceeding ten years. R.S., C.c-34, s.250; 1980-81-82-83, c.125, s.20.

Abduction

283(1) Everyone who, being the parent, guardian or person having the lawful care or charge of a person under the age of fourteen years, takes, entices away, conceals, detains, receives or harbors that person, whether or not that is custody order in relation to that person made by a court anywhere in Canada, with intent to deprive a parent or guardian, or any other person who has the lawful care or charge of that person, of the possession of that person, is guilty of

(a) An indictable offence and is liable to imprisonment for a term not exceeding ten years; or

(b) An offence punishable on summary conviction.

(2) No proceedings may be commenced under subsection (1) Without the consent of the Attorney General or counsel instructed by him for that purpose. 1980-81-82-83, c.125, s.20; 1993, c.45, s.5.

References

1. The Indian Penal Code, 1860, p.151.
2. *Ibid.*
3. Susan Brownmiller, *Against Our Will: Men, Women And Rape* (London)1995 p. 45.

4. P.D. Mathew, *The Law on Rape* (New Delhi) 1995, p. 3.
5. *Legal Aid Handbook 1, Domestic Violence* (New Delhi), 1992, p. 3.
6. Mathew, n. 4, p. 5.
7. Mathew, n. 6, p. 22.
8. Flavia Agnes, *The Anti Rape Campaign,* (Stree) 1993, p. 117.
9. *Ibid.*
10. *Statesman,* 15 January, 1994.
11. H.J. Antony, *Dowry Related Death,* (New Delhi) 1995, p. 1.
12. *Ibid.*
13. Agnes, n. 8, pp. 11-24.
14. *Ibid.*
15. Agnes, n. 15, p.w - 25.
16. Agnes, n.15, p. 45-27.
17. *Indian Penal Code,* p. 142.
18. Mathew, n. 4, p. 19.
19. *Indian Penal Code,* p. 211.
20. *Changing the Landscape: Ending Violence - Achieving Equality,* Executive Summary, Canadian Panel on Violence Against Women, 1993.
21. Rick Lindes, ed., *Criminology: A Canadian Perspective,* Toronto, 1993, p. 135.
22. *Ibid.*
23. Don Stuart and Ronald J. Delsie, *Leaning Canadian Criminal Law,* Toronto, 1995, p. 538.
24. Rick Linden, *Criminology: A Canadian Perspective,* Toronto, 1993, p. 137.
25. L.W. Kennedy and V.F. Sacco, *Crime Counts : A Criminal Event Analysis,*Toronto , 1996, pp. 135-136.
26. *Ibid.*
27. *Canada: Statistics on Violence Against Women,* METRAC (Toronto) 1991.
28. Excerpts from the Indian Penal Code 1860.
29. Excerpts from Martin's Annual Criminal Code 1997.

8

A Comparative Analysis of Kolkata and Toronto

The prime aim of this study is the analysis of crime in the developed and developing countries and a comparative assessment of the crime situation against women in the urban environment of two diverse regions. In India, Kolkata gives a good example of the Developing World with all the attributes such as very high population density, space constraints, and large immigrant population both from the hinterland as well as across the border, with an industrial backdrop and above all a heterogeneous population. On the other hand, Toronto, was chosen for the study as it is an apt example from the Developed World, being at the head of the Human Development Index (1993) and subsequesntly remaining at the third position in 2000. Toronto too has a large immigrant population, with a strong financial base and a multicultural population. However, one universal feature of both these diverse socio – cultural and economic backgrounds is that there is a high rate of crime against women. The two cities do not represent a unique feature, but a universal phenomenon.

The basic difference between crime studies in the Developed and the Developing World is that in the Developed countries, there is research and ample statistics to help in the improvement of the crime situation, whereas in the Developing World even basic research in the area of crime is lacking. Before going into the depth of the crime situation in the two diverse environments, it is important to study the status of women in general. It is a universal fact that the status of women is inferior to that of men in the patrarchical society. This social status of women has been sanctified by religion, society and in the family. One of the reasons for crime against women as a hypothesis used in the chapter on "Urbanization and Social Problems of Women in Cities of the World", has been:

Faster the rate of development and urbanization, the greater the crime against women

Through data from the secondary sources it is evident that population has been rapidly increasing both in the Developed as well as in the Developing part of the world. However, with escalation of population it has not necessarily led to an equal distribution of urbanization. In Europe the level of urbanization has been much higher than that of Asia and Africa. In the Developing countries urban centers have been the culmination of the migration from the villages to the larger towns and cities. This has not led to the development of infrastructure. At the same time, in the Developed world of Canada, USA, France etc. along with the growth of the urban centers there has been a positive effect on the life expectancy, literacy rates, and income levels. These have been clamped together and are known as the Human Development Index. In the Developed countries this Human Development Index is high, as in Canada (according to the UNDP Report 1996) the HDI is 0.95, while USA is 0.94 (as in table 2.5). While countries such as Pakistan and India come under the low HDI rank with values of 0.44 and 0.43 respectively. This means that in South Asia there prevails low life expectancy, low education and low levels of income.

Along with urbanization there are several problems especially in the Developing countries. The problems arises in the form of pollution, congestion, poverty and the rapid growth of shantytowns. In developing countries, the negative effect of urbanization is not as overt. There are small areas with ghetto settlements. Common knowledge is that with urbanization life becomes better due to modern amenities.

However, although in the case of women, they may have access to education and employment, status comes from the power of knowledge, economic resources and political access to power and the degree of autonomy enjoyed in the process of decision making. Women who are upwardly mobile are depend totally on their economic independence, access to education and power. While women who have least access to each of the attributes belong to a socially lower status. Another feature is that the HDI may not be coterminous to the gender - related development index. If only the gender related development index is high, then it is evident that the country has low disparity between man and women.

In chapter 3 it is evident that both in a developed as well in a developing country there is high incidence of crime. In Canada as evident from Diagram 3.5 with increase in population there is escalation in violent crimes. In Diagram 3.10 a strong positive correlation is evident between population and cases of sexual assault in cities. In other words, urbanization, which in a way is an impact of large population migration, leads to high incidences of offences against women in developed countries.

In India through the ages there has been an increase in population. In diagram 3.1, it is evident that there is a strong positive correlation between increase in population and increase in the incidence of crimes as in 1961 – 1995. An urban area is the culmination of high density of population with close proximity to industrial areas and places of employment. In urban areas, there is a higher male population, as men are more likely to move from their original place of residence to find employment. Hence, in the cities more often there are small families or single units. Few migrants know each other. Hence, there are hardly any social ties. This creates a sense of anonymity. Besides, urban life leads to high levels of stress. Hence, crime, violence and crime against women are the culmination of urban living. Life in rural areas is a close knit community, where people are under check due to social pressures and family ties. While in the urban areas, all social norms can be flouted due to anonymity. Hence, it can be concluded that faster the rate of development and urbanization, the greater has been crime against women. This feature is common both in the case of the Developed as well as in the Developing countries. However, in the case of Canada, the rate of crime against women is extremely high due to high case of reporting as the women are well aware of their legal rights due to higher levels of education. While in the case of India, due to fear of social stigma, and ostracization, women do not report cases of sexual assault and molestation etc. Reporting is far less than what actually happens behind the four walls of the home and in society.

Another hypothesis that may be compared in both countries, is that areas with higher density population and with greater urban deprivation show higher rate of total crimes against women in the city than low-density areas. In the case of less henious offences, it is evident through research that where there is higher population and more proximity to property (as in the case of property offences), there is more crime. However, in the case of crimes against women, there are various factors, which come to play in different environments and regions. In Kolkata, areas such as police divisions, which have a high density of population, do not necessarily have a high incidence of crimes against women. For example, in Kolkata, the highest density of population as in 1991 census is seen in the North Division, with the largest population and largest area space in the Eastern Division. While the highest number of incidences are in the South Division. However, in the micro study, it is evident that one police station under Eastern Division has the highest incidence of crimes against women namely Beniapukur (Sec R) in 1991 and Beliaghata (P1) in 1996. Another interesting phenomenon in the micro study is that in 1991, the largest area is under Phulbagan police station with 4.02% of the area of the Eastern Sub Division and this area also has the highest density but not the highest population. Hence, in the case Kolkata, high-density population does not necessarily have a high rate of total crimes against women.

In Toronto, the highest percentage incidence of crime is in the Central Division, the highest incidence of crime in patrol areas 2302, 3103 and 4112 in 1991 and 1996. In other words the highest incidences are in the extreme northwest corner of the Metro and in the Eastern Division. Density of population as from 1991census is evident, maximum in the Central Division. In Toronto, therefore, where there is high density of population in the macro region there is high incidence of crimes against women. In the micro level study, in the Central Division, the highest incidences of crime against women are in patrol areas of 5107 with 141 cases, followed by 133 cases in 1415 and 122 cases in 5102. In the case of density, patrol areas 5107 comes second highest in density. The overall picture however, in Division 51, where there is high incidence of crime against women, it is in the high population density areas such as in patrol areas 5107, 5106, 5105 etc.

In other words, where there is more crime against women in the developed countries, they are in areas of high population density. While in the developing countries, high incidences of crime are not necessarily co – terminus with high-density population. In other words, congestion, which leads to urban deprivation and stress in society, is more evident in the developed regions. Whereas, other socio – economic conditions such as employment status, the demographic variables of a population plays a greater role in crimes against women in developing countries.

The rate of total urban crime is more in the low rent residential areas than in the high rent residential areas within a city. The word " low residential" area has been used for those areas which have a low rent structure, there is urban deprivation, houses made of low cost building materials, pollution etc. Every city has an area with such a typical environment, whether it is in the developed world or the developing world. In Kolkata, low cost housing and low residential areas are most widespread in the Eastern Suburban Division, which was built on the marshlands. A rail line passes through the area alongside which are several small factories and workshops. The area maybe visualised as dirty, smoggy, grey with large colonies of shack type settlements. Infact, the largest bustees are clustered around this area. This area also forms the outer industrial belt of Kolkata. However, as a whole the Eastern Suburban Division has a low-density population, but there are pockets of high density where the slums or bustees are situated. As is evident from data and maps showing the incidence of crime in 1991 and 1996, the Eastern Suburban Division has the highest number of incidences. Low rent residential areas are areas of other socio – economic vice as well. The Eastern Suburban Division has high unemployment, low level of literacy and a large male non-working population. Hence, the monetary flow is also less. There are people who are idle, yet going through a lot of urban stress and strain. According to the sociological theory, of differential association, crime is a learned behaviour. In a region of vice and dilapidation, the younger generation goes through a crisis due to imbalances in resource distribution, unemployment, coupled with the awareness of anonymity in the urban area. In urban areas roles of the family and elders leads to fewer social controls and are often seen to be replaced by other institutions, resulting in the development of behavior patterns among youth that differs radically from family expectations.[1] Hence, in Kolkata, the low class residential area falls under the Eastern Suburban Division which has the highest incidence of offences such as Entally in 1981, Beniapukur in 1991, Narkeldanga in 1995 and Beliaghata in 1996. All these police stations or thanas fall under the Eastern Suburban Division. Hence, in Kolkata, the area can be easily identified.

In case of Toronto, there are no large areas of low rent residential areas. Areas, which have ethno – racial groups are most likely to be unemployed. Besides this like any other city in the world, some groups of people in the city are more likely to be living in poverty than others. Poverty is related to family structure, age, employment and education. In

Toronto, in 1991 and 1996, the incidence of crimes against women is highest in patrol areas 2302 and 3103 both in the Northwest Division. This area falls on the border of municipality of the city of Etobicoke and North York and patrol area 3103 falls in North York City. Both these areas have a high percentage of male population, a large immigrant population, with relatively low levels of educational qualifications, with a high unemployment of males above the age of 15 (as seen in table 5.6). From table 5.7, it is evident that there is a large immigrant population as well. Hence, this is an area with relatively low rent residential homes. Jane Street, which is an area of high incidence of crimes, run through patrol area 3103. Hence, it is evident that total urban crime against women is more in the low residential areas than in the high residential areas within a city irrespective of a developing or a developed country as seen in Kolkata and Toronto. However, in a Developed country due to better distribution of resources, the situation is on a much smaller scale as compared to Kolkata.

Higher the male population in a city, greater will be the number of crimes

Since the study is on crime against women, it is necessary to study the gender structure of the society. As mentioned earlier, the areas of high incidences of crime are in low rent residential areas. These areas have more immigrants, unemployment and low levels of literacy. As such no positive correlation between male population in a city vis – a – vis the incidence of crime against women has been found. However, it is evident from the micro study on the Eastern Suburban Division that where are more male non – workers there is a higher risk in crimes against women. Besides this, statistical evidence, through use of Spearman's Rank correlation shows that where there is increase in male illiteracy there are higher crimes against women. Both these coorelations show that males who are unemployed, are unskilled laborers and with low levels of literacy can be offenders than men who are employed and literate. However, this is a general statement and further research is necessary in this case. However, sociological studies have proved at several instances that men who see violence at home at a young age are more prone to be offenders of violence against women.

In the case of Toronto, from the macro study on the Central Division, it is evident that there is a positive correlation between unemployed males and the number of incidences of crimes against women. Hence, although there is no direct correlation between higher male population in a city and greater numbers of crimes against women. But, other socio – economic variables prove that areas of the city which have a poor economy, low levels of literate unemployed males are more prone to commit crimes against women which may be in the form of either domestic violence or street crimes.

Another interesting feature of this study is that certain types of crimes against women are more prominent in specific areas in a city. However, the total crimes against women are more in the urban periphery or suburbs than at the heart of the city. In fact, a large part of this study is based on this hypothesis. From the study on Kolkata, it is evident that the highest incidence of crimes against women is in the Eastern Suburban Division, which lies on the Eastern most part of the city along side, the degenerated area. Hence, in the city of a developing country, crime against women is more in the periphery than in the urban core. However, individual cases of crime are area specific. Taking a close look at the 1996 data, it is found that incidences of murder and rape are highest in the Jorasanko area, which falls in the Central Division. While cases of kidnapping are highest in Cossipore in North Division which is also an outer industrial pocket. However, in general this offence is equally distributed. On the other hand, cruelty or harassment of women is highest in Beliaghata in the Eastern Suburban Division. Cases of molestation and eve – teasing are registered maximum in the South Port area (under Port Division). Cases of attempt to murder and dowry death cases are maximum in the Eastern

Suburban Division. However, in the case of location quotient that is relative specialty of offences, cases of kidnapping is highest in the Hastings area, which is in South Division. In other words compared to total crimes in this area and compared to the city, the incidences of kidnapping is high. On the other hand harassment or cruelty of the women by husband and in-laws is amazingly high in high-rent residential areas like New Alipur, while by location quotient method, rape cases are very high in Ballygunge in South Division. By using location quotient all three grievous offences fall under the South Division.

In the case of Toronto, the highest incidences of crimes against women are in the urban periphery than at the core as in the developing country. The two highest areas of incidence are patrol areas 2302 and 3103 both according to 1991 and 1996 data. The two patrol areas are in the Northwest Division in the municipalities of Etobicoke and North York. In the case of individual offences, the highest number of incidences of crimes against women are in the form of assault, sexual assault and assault with weapon causing bodily harm and others as in table 5.3 and 5.4. In 1991 and 1996 assault cases were maximum in patrol areas 2302, sexual assault cases were registered highest in various unknown destinations in both 1991 and 1996. Assault with weapons causing bodily harm was maximum in patrol area 3101 in 1991 and unknown destinations in 1996. From this too it is evident that the major individual heads of crime are reported more in the urban periphery than the core. Therefore, further away from the city center, there are higher incidences of crimes against women.

Another interesting phenomenon used by Environmental Criminologists was to correlate time or seasonal variation of crime. Through the present study, it was possible to see that a universal phenomenon prevailed in most countries regarding the seasonal nature of crime. In Kolkata, the maximum crime during the 24 hours of a day takes place between 3:00 PM – 5:59 PM in the evening, followed by 12:00 pm – 2:59 pm. This is the time during which women are most mobile. While in the case of Toronto, the maximum number of incidents takes place between 12:00 am – 2:59 am and then 6:00 pm – 8:59 pm. Both the time periods are when the family gets together at the end of the day's work. As for the seasonal nature of crime, both in Kolkata and Toronto, highest incidents takes place during the summers. In Kolkata, there are two peak periods namely March – April and June – July. While in Toronto, the peak periods are between May – June and then again in July and August. Earlier research on the seasonal nature of crime has shown that the warm weather encourages quarrels, brawls and sex related offences. Hence, the hypothesis that there are particular seasons in a year which have the highest incidences of crimes against women. However, in case of the temporal nature of crime, the time period differs in various countries due to the work habit and other socio – cultural reasons.

Another interesting phenomenon worth mentioning in this comparative study are the laws, which prevail in the two countries. In India, which has been used as a study of a developing country, the Indian Penal Code dates back to 1861. The Supreme Court has updated various sections under the law under different clauses and verdicts. It was as late as 1983 that reforms were placed in Parliament to repeal the old rape laws and dowry laws. However as mentioned earlier, the guardians of law were not aware of as to how to use the laws on molestation and eve – teasing cases. The laws are not well classified as to what the intensity of the offence should be in the case of eve – teasing and where a case of molestation can be registered. In the rape laws too there are several lacunae as discussed in the chapter on social legislation.

However, in case of Canada, there are several laws, which fall under the classification of crimes against women. About 19 heads of crime have been taken as crimes against women. Under sexual offences, there are about seven heads of crime which fall under this category such as sexual assault, aggravated sexual assault, sexual assault with weapon, sexual interference with person less than 14 years, invite sexual touch of a person less than 14 years, incest and sexual exploitation. In Canada, because of several classifications under the law for sexual offences, a large number of cases have been registered. It is also convenient for the police to lodge offences under these well-classified laws. On the other hand in India for sexual offences other than rape, they are registered under molestation. A grievous offence gets diluted and criminals go scot free.

From the comparative study of the two countries it is evident that the nature of the study between the two countries remains the same and that women are victimised. In Canada, the victim - police – social service network is well formed. If a crime is committed, the victim can reach out to a phone and call the number 911. Within minutes, an ambulance, police and fire brigade personnel reach the spot. In India, the victims can use the number 100 which can only access the police control rooms. However, this facility is limited to urban and semi urban areas only. Toronto has several Helpline services for victims. A similar Helpline service has been started in New Delhi and Bangalore by NGO's and the police to help the victims of violence and battery. Besides this the Canadian system has social security which provides for the minimum basic existance of $1000 per person. Shelter homes in various parts of the city give refuge to women who have no place to stay. This is different from the Remand Homes or observation homes as found in India. It is necessary to create an atmosphere where the victim can be rehabilitated and not locked from the world like an accused. The Remand Homes have a jail type of environment, which could be made more congenial to cater to the needs of a traumatized victim of a rape or assault case. Some large cities in India do have family counseling centers and short stay homes; however, this should be on a uniform basis in many more cities and states and there needs to be more coordination between the police, social service institutions and health authorities.

However, the major difference between the study on the two cities is that the number of cases registered in Kolkata is not more than around 429 cases in 1996 while in Toronto, the number of cases registered in the same year has been 14267. This is more than 30 times the reported cases in Kolkata. In the Indian situation women feel reluctant to register cases related to sexual offences and harassment, due to the social stigma involved. However, in Canada, the level of awareness amongst women is far greater. With more legal awareness amongst the women and with more sensitive police personnel it will be possible to record more cases and bring the offenders to the book. However, our goal must be to build in prevention and cure of crimes against women. Through better classified laws, speedy trials and trials held in camera, the victims can be given more confidence, which could help the women to come forward with their complaints. Besides, once the police personnel with other social organizations or non–governmental organizations, bring together an awareness on the rights of women and educate women for greater levels of status, it will be possible in future to see an improvement in the situation of crime against women. At present, data from police records of both the countries is only an evidence which to only the tip of the iceberg. What happens within the four walls of the home and in the dark alleys-a lot goes unreported, and the sighs of the victim get snuffed.

Geography of space and the utilisation of that space to study a particular phenomenon of crime gives us a clear insight as to what situations, prevail, in various parts of the city in two diverse situations, one in the developing world and the other in the developed world. The debate is how and when the governments and civil society will be able to bring about a proper preventive policy on zero tolerance on crimes against women over the next couple of years, will be the big question.

Reference

1. M.B. Clinard and D.J. Abbott, *Crime in Developing Countries: A Comparative Perspective*, (1973) p. 23.

9
Conclusion

A casual overview of literature which deals with crime brings to focus studies on crime against women depicted as a social problem. They also look at the role played by the police and judiciary and the methods undertaken to crime control. However, there has been very little work on the socio – spatial aspect on crime against women and crime mapping in particular. The present study contributes significantly to our understanding of variations and nature of crimes against women. The significance of the study not only lies in the spatial aspect of crime against women in a city, but also makes the concept easy to understand with examples of case studies from two diverse backgrounds. The case studies not only show the most crime prone areas but also brings forward a comparative analysis, as to why crime against women is a universal phenomena. These socio – spatial examples provide a background as well as an understanding of urban society in general and the metropolitan situation in particular.

An overview of literature on crime against women shows that it is widespread and the urban areas are more prone to such offences. Such high levels of crime is mainly due to the awareness levels amongst women, followed by more registration of cases. Development and urbanization on the surface seem to hold the position and status of women in a positive light. But, in-depth analysis have proved that wife battery, rape, incest exists amongst the best of societies. Most social workers in both Kolkata and Toronto felt that cases of violence were more reported by the socially and economically deprived sections than women in financially and socially well off positions. The general view in this regard was the socially and economically deprived women have nothing more to lose, so they went forward with their cases. However, women who are from the higher echleons of society feel inhibited to report a case of sexual assault or wife battery as this leads to the undermining of their social position. Crimes against women in Kolkata and Toronto have several common features, yet there are differences as seen in the chapter on the Comparative Analysis between the two cities.

Through the study, it is evident that the overall position of the women in society is low. History, religion and society have undermined her position at several instances. But, it is necessary to protect the women through a well defined national policy. This protection may be through several positive preventive techniques. The strategies must bring in both individual initiaitves and institutional attempts in bringing down the crime situation.

The women's movement in India has launched several campaigns against rape, domestic violence, women being depicted poorly in the visual media as well as voiced strongly against state repression during caste and communal riots and the misuse of power by the security forces. Recently on July 15, 2004 at Manipur a young woman was raped and killed by some personnel of the Assam Rifles (a Central Police organisation). About 22 women's organisations came together and forty women staged a protest march in front of the Assam Rifles headquarters. The unique aspect of this protest march was that all the women protested naked. The patience of the people have run out and to show that the people of Manipur cannot accept this arbitary treatment further, widespread protest marches have followed. This has led to the state being paralysed and curfew being imposed for almost two weeks. There have been incidences when state run machineries use rape and torture on women to put down political uprisings. During the post-emergency period of 1977-1980, small groups of women's activists in Hyderabad, Bombay, Delhi and Madras had started taking up individual cases of custodial rape, deaths of-housewives under mysterious circumstances and excesses by the state enforcement machinery during caste/communal riots which had increased in intensity. Poor women involved in the struggles of the tribal people, the industrial working classes and the Dalit movement faced misogyny from the members of their own organisation, social ostracism and violence perpetrated by the police, military and paramilitary forces. With these kinds of experiences of individual, institutional and systemic violence, newly emerging women's groups felt the necessity to put violence against women on the political agenda. While building up systematic campaigns in diferent socio-cultural contexts and among women of different economic backgrounds and political persuasions, they had to evolve day-to-day tactics to be effective and long-term strategies to carve out more space for women to gain gender justice within the system.

From Campaigns to Political Recognition

The decade of the eighties was marked by the campaign culture in which women's groups with different priorities and ideological positions had to evolve a network amongest themselves to combat powerful patriarchal forces operating within the institution of family, state and civil society. Among the political groups and civil liberties groups, violence against women has became a hotly debated issue in the post-emergency period. Excesses by the authorities on women political prisoners had generated awareness about the question of gender violence. The democratic rights organisations had started highlighting rapes of poor and helpless women by the police in Delhi, Ludhiana and Hyderabad. Detailed reports based on first-hand information collected by the investigation teams instituted by the democratic rights and civil liberties organisations in Delhi, Bombay, Hyderabad and Kolkata resulted in petitions and public interest litigations against violence against women by powerful forces. Newly emerging women's groups learnt a lot from these organisations, but at the same time found them inadequate because they refused to highlight violence against women perpetrated by men of the oppressed community, the oppressed caste and the working classes. The issue of domestic violence created a major rift between the male-dominated progressive groups who refused to accept it as a public issue and the women's groups who came out with a slogan 'the personal is political.' While the progressive groups talked of world peace, the women's groups resorted to shouting 'peace begins at home.'

Clarity in perspective was necessary to build up campaigns against systemic violence. Issue-based study-circles, circulation of hand-written or typed copies of papers, small-groups discussions, resulted in different trends of thinking on gender violence on the following lines :

- For the liberal activists, sanctity of the individual was an issue of prime concern. Hence any citizen who was violated had to take recourse to Constitutional means of redressal for justice, by approaching the existing judicial system.

- The democratic rights organisations represented the views of the far-left groups and gave a call for direct actions which confronted the state.

- The religious and puritanical groups were perturbed by the violation of 'chastity' and the 'purity' of women.

- The feminists saw violence against women as an outcome of the subordination of women- to use it as a weapon to terriorise, intimidate and humiliate them.

On an issue-to issue basis, representatives of these four trends either came together or campaigned from their own platform. Intially, there was a tremendous aversion to dialoging with the representatives of the state apparatus-the police, the legal machinery, the Law Commission and the bureaucracy. But in course of time, they realised that there was no other way of getting redressal for the women victims or to activise the existing judicial system and to work in collaboration with the police, the courts and the medico-legal machinery.[1]

Till the domestic and international campaigns and prevention strategies on crimes against women in India gathered due to the signing of the International Bill of Rights and the different conventions such as the Convention on Elimination of all forms of Discrimination Against Women and the Convention on the Rights of the Child, Convention Against Torture and other cruel inhuman or degrading treatment or punishment. The present Human Rights Education year between 2004-2005 of the U.N. will also add emphasis on raising levels of awareness.

Perhaps the best method or mechanism is through social control. The method of social control can be executed in a three fold way:

- By increasing general awareness and sensitizing gender issues.
- By formal education
- Legal literacy programs

The Department of Women and Child Development in India has endorsed the Mexico Plan of Action (1975), the Nairobi Forward Looking Strategies (1985), The Beijing Declaration as well as the Platform for Action (1995) for appropriate follow-up. However, India ratified only a few of the conventions such as the International Bill of Rights, the Convention on the Elimination of All Forms of Discrimination Against Women.

However, there still exists a wide gap between t he aspirations and goals enunciated in the Constitution, legislation, policies, plans, programs and related mechanisms on the one hand, and the reality of the status of women in India, on the other. This has been analyzed extensively since the Report of the Committee on the Status of Women in India was placed "Towards Eqality", in 1974, and further highlighted in the National Perspective Plan for Women, 1988-2000 and the 'Shramshakti' Report, 1988.

Gender disparity manifests itself in various forms, the most obvious being a trend towards a declining female ratio in the population in the last few decades. Social stereotying and violence at the domestic and societal levels are some of the other manifestations. Discrimination against children, adolescent girls and women still persists. Consequently, the access of women (the majority of whom are in the rural areas and in the informal, unorganized sector) to edcation, health and productive resources, among others, is indequate. As a result, they remain largely disadvantaged.

India's draft National Policy for the Empowerment of Women has been drawn up against this background in the aftermath of the Beijing Conference, after a series of consultations with Members of Parliament, State Governments, non-governmental organizations, women's organizations, social activits, researchers and other experts in the country. The goal of this policy is to bring about the advancement, development and empowerment of women. This is to be achieved by changing societal attitudes and elimination of all forms of gender-based discrimination, active participation of women in all spheres of life, incorporation of a gender perpective in all policies, plans and programs, translation of de jure equality of women into defacto equality, and affirmative action, as necessary. The policy has been finalized and awaits approval of the Indian Cabinet. However, the National Perspective Plan for Women 1988-2000, which has already laid down a map towards gender equality, is being implemented. Similarly, many of the components of the National Policy are already being translated into action as programs on their own.

Recognizing that women's representation in critical numbers in higher decision bodies making bodies is essential to provide voice to women's issues and perspectives, Government had introduced a Bill in Parliament to reserve one-third of the seats for women in the national parliament and in the state legislative Assemblies, over and above the reservations already in place at the local and municipal levels.

In the recently held 13th General Elections that have just been held, all the major national parties have conciously fielded women candidates. Since gender balance in public life and in decision-making bodies is not likely to happen automatically, given the imbalances in social development, reservations of seats through democratic consensus building may well be the best way of providing this crucial gender perspective to all policies and programs in India.

An important monitoring machinery to oversee women's empowerment in India was set up by Parliament in the form of a Standing Committee on the Women in March 1997. The functions of this Committee include examining and reporting on the measures that should be taken by the Union Government for improving the status/conditions of women and considering the reporting submitted by the National Commission. for Women.

However, the litmus test is the allocaton of financial and material resources for programs for women's empowerment.

Apart from government effort for the advancement and empowerment of women the protection and promotion of their human right, the primary institutional mechanisms available to guarantee and ensure fulfillment of their rights are the courts with their strong tradition of public interest litigation, the National Human Rights Commission, the National Commission for Women, and the Standing Committee on the Empowerment of Women etc.

India is also preparing the final stages of preparation of the initial report to the CEDAW, and are participating actively in efforts to conclude on Optional Protocol to the CEDAW providing for an individual complaints mechanism in relation to the Convention.

It is more than 50 years since the Universal Declaration on Human Rights was signed, yet it is a matter of great disappointment that human rights and particularly the rights of women and children, continue to be questioned or challenged in certain quarters in the name of religion, or culture or traditions.

The method of social control has to be adopted by a national policy, taking gender issues from the back – burner to the forefront. Besides this, social organizations and the community needs to participate, for over all awareness. From mass illiteracy among women in India to sectoral unawareness in Canada, needs to be tackled. A key to control, of the weak by the strong is through lack of knowledge by one group and awareness by the other. Regular awareness workshops and camps both sponsored by the governmental bodies, educational institutions and social organizations help in creating an outreach. Gender issues can be sensitized through citizen – police workshops, holding seminars women's organizations for police personnel and widely discussing and debating women's issues relating to health, violence, education and welfare. A basic course in human rights for primary education also helps in addressing the strategic groups. There is a need for trained doctors and psychiatrists in schools to help child victims. Assistance is also necessary for those children who see violence at home. In the Victimization Survey in 1993, it was found that children who see violence at home have every possibility of becoming violent towards their spouse in the future. Hence, violence should become a part of India's Health Care policy as well.

Policies in Canada

The National Policy of Canada has taken several steps in improving the status of women. The Government of Canada is committed to ensuring that women design and participate in the processes and events that shape their lives. These commitments are an integral part of its policy towards the human development of its people and the sustainable development of the country. Attaining these goals in a world a marked by fast-pace change is both a challenge and an opportunity.

The Federal Plan for Gender Equality was prepared by the Government of Canada which is a collaborative initiative reflecting on the federal government's commitment to gender equality and represents the concerted effort of 24 departments and agencies. The first two chapter of the document set out the context for the plan and discusses the concept of equality. *The Federal Plan* identifies eight key objectives focused on improving the status of women in various dimensions. Under each objective, issues are identfied and priorities for action are outlined. These objectives are congruent with the 12 areas of action identified in the United Nations' draft *Platform for Action*, and with the United Nations' and Commonwealth's requests to institutionalize gender-based analysis in the processes of legislation, policy and program development.

Progress of Women's Rights in Canada

1916 First provinces give women right to vote — Alberta, Sackatchewan.
1918 Women are given full federal right to vote.
1920 Women are given right to be elected to Parliament.
1921 First woman elected to the House of Commons.
1928 Supreme Court of Canada decides that women are not "persons" and cannot be appointed to the Senate of Canada.
1929 British Privy Council overturns Supreme Court decision.
1930 First woman Senator.
1952 First province enacts equal pay legislation—Ontario.
1955 Restrictions on the employment of married women in the federal public service are removed.
1956 Legislation is enacted guaranting equal pay for equal work within federal jurisdiction.
1957 First woman Cabinet Minister.
1961 *Canadian Bill of Rights* is passed.
1977 *Canadian Human Rights Act* Forbids discrimination on the basis of sex and ensures equal pay for work of

equal value for women; *Canadian Labour Code* is similarly amended and provides for 17 weeks of maternity leave.

1978 *Canadian Labour Code* is amended, eliminating pregnancy as a basis for lay-off or dismissals.

1982 *Canadian Charter of Rights and Freedoms*, Section 28, is enacted —Charter guarantees apply equally to men and women.

1983 *Canadian Human Rights Act* is amended to prohibit sexual harassment and to ban discrimination of the basis of pregnancy and family or marital status.

1984 First woman Governor General.

1984 Canadian Constitution is amended to affirm that Aboriginal and treaty rights are guaranteed equally to both men and women.

1985 Section 15 of the *Canadian Charter of Rights and Freedoms* comes into effect, guaranteed equality for all Canadians before and under law and equal protection and benefit of law.

1985 Cort Challenges Program expanded to address equality rights cases.

1985 *Indian Act* is amended, restoring status and right to ban membership to Indian women who had last such status through marriage to a non-Indian.

1986 *Employment Equity Act* is introduced, applicable to Crown corporations and federally regulated business, aimed at redressing historic and systemic discrimination of "target group" populations.

1993 Guidelines on women refugee claimants are institued for the Immigrations and Refugee Board.

1994 Funding for equality test cases is reinstated as Charter Law Development Program.

1995 Gender-based anlysis of legislation and policies is adopted by the federal government.

Source: The Federal Plan for Gender Equality.

The objectives of this Federal plan are :

1. Implement gender-based analysis throughout federal departments and agencies.
2. Improve women's economic autonomy and well-being.
3. Improve women's physical and psychological well-being.
4. Reduce violence in society, particularly violence against women and children.
5. Promote gender equality in all aspects of Canada's cultural life.
6. Incorporate women's perspective in governance.
7. Promote and support global gender equality.
8. Advance gender equality for employees of federal departments and agencies.

The challenges of the future will be no less daunting than those already encountered in the past. Governments at all levels have pledged to work to ease the transition to this new order. Improving gender equality is part of government responsibility to sustain a society that values all its members and treats them with dignity and respect.

Through history it has become evident that there are few quick-fix solutions to such complex social, political, cultural and economic realities; the persistence of gender inequality underscores the need for a long-term vision.

Canada has a long history of progress in advancing women's equality. Combined efforts of governments— federal, provincial, territorial and municipal — of women's organiazations, NGOs, professional associations, academic institutions and private-sector organizations and businesses, have brought about remarkable changes over a very short period. Canada has enacted extensive civil and criminal law reforms focussed on issues such as violence against women, sexual assault, sexual harassment, child abuse and gun control; has supported NGOs dealing with equality issues; and has put in place government machinery for the advancement of women to ensure that progress toward gender equality is steadily integrated into public policy. In

Canada, there are higher enrollments and levels of graduation of women in post-secondary institutions, greater recognition of women's specific health care needs' rising levels of women's participation in the political process and greater representation of women in positions of economic power. Progress in all these areas has improved the quality of lives of women in Canada. However, poverty, inequalities stubbornly persist.

In 1995 Canada opted for the *Canadian Charter of Rights and Freedoms* which is a landmark judgement for women in Canada as this Charter made more than 150 recommendations to foster equality between women and men. 1995 is also an important year for thousands of women across the world as women, activists and government agencies congregated at Beijing, China, at the Fourth United Nations World Conference on Women. It was here that governments, reviewed the situation of women over the past decade, and adopted a global *Platform for Action* to accelerate progress toward gender equality. All U.N. member states are working towards formulating national policies to bring in the necessary changes.

Social welfare organisations have also undertaken strategies such as the City's Strategic Plan "to improve social and economic inclusion within our commnities." One of the actions identified to achieve this goal in "enhancing initiatives to address violence against women."

As the Council Committe was established to closely look into issues of violence, it was recommended that the Task Force on community Safety establish a working group specifically focused to work on woman abuse. This role complements the key goals of the Task Force: to establish the city as a leader on community safety and crime prevention and to remain current on best practices and innovative approaches; and, also respond to emerging community safety issues that impact on the City's quality of life.

The Woman Abuse Work Group represents a key opportunity for the City to take leadership on woman abuse as it impacts on Cities policies, programs and services building on current initiatives taken in these areas. It also helps in enhancing co-ordination, collaboration and the ability to share best practices with the city's community partners working in this area.

The *mandate* of the Woman Abuse Work Group is to develop strategies to achieve the following goals :

(1) to increase the profile of woman abuse issues in the City of Toronto;
(2) to strengthen the integration of woman abuse issues into City policies, programs and services;
(3) to enhance linkage between City and community partners on policies, protocols and best practices; and
(4) to strengthen the network of municipal and community services and supports for abused women and children in Toronto.

The Work Group may also consider and/or recommend strategies to address other forms of family violence.

All work done by the Woman Abuse Work Group will be within an anti-racism/oppression framework. (As amended by the Task Force on Community Safety, April 8, 2003).

Activities: The Working Group will develop a work plan to implement the following activities :

(1) designate work group members to participate in the planning committee for the annual conference supporting community co-ordination on woman abuse issues;
(2) the identification for priority in city policy a nd program areas for greater focus;
(3) the promotion and education for woman abuse issues as they relate to the City of Toronto policies, programs and services; and
(4) the identification of opportunities to strengthen the partnerships between the City and its community and institutional partners.

The other initiaitives taken by the government is the Safer Communities Initiative, headed by the National Crime

Prevention Centre (NCPC), which was launched in June 1998 as a component of the National Strategy on Community Safety and Crime Prevention. The Strategy aims to develop community-based measures to battle against crime affecting children and youth, the Aboriginal people and women. The government has committed $32 million each year to help communities to develop programs that form partnerships to prevent crime. The Safer Communities Initiative consists of four funding programs: the Crime Prevention Investment Fund, the Crime Prevention Partnership Fund, the Community Mobilization Program and the Business Acition Program on Crime Prevention.

The National Crime Prevention Center of Canada has further contributed $1,228466 to help fund 11 crime prevention projects that support efforts to increase the security of women and girls across the country.

The Crime Prevention Partnership Program supports the involvement of organizations that can contribute to community crime prevention activities through the development of information, tools and resources that facilitate commuity participation in all phases of crime prevention and this can be applied across Canada. Under a call for proposals focusing on the personal security issues of women and girls, funding of $530, 050 has been awarded to nine organizations under this program. Out of this the Canadian Women's Foundation (CWF) in Toronto, Ontario, has received $60,000 for its National Philanthropic Strategy on Violence Against Women and Girls-Research and Teen Forum. The project, in addition is working to create a database on how to prevent violence against women easily . This will also help in creating a national forum to share models an lessons learned, design a system for ongoing sharing and get input on philathropy supporting teen programs on violence against women. The three-day forum will emphasize on peer education programs, focusing on dating violence and healthy relationships.

Canadians Against Violence Everywhere, Centre for Children and Families in the Justice System of the London Family Court Clinic are few of the other project that are ongoing for preparing tools of awareness. and for looking into *exploratory investigation of the impact of maternal Incarceration—giving children a voice and creating an agenda for action.* There are several such project running successfully and giving relief to a large number of women.

Other effective strategies have gathered momentum after the virtual working group to combat violence against women was identified through a video conference in 1999 linking advocates in the field with co-sponsoring UN agencies and delegates from UN member states in the UN General Assembly to highlight the most effective strategies which are being used both at the local and at the national level. An internet working group was able to identify the five issues on women: human rights abuse of women within the family; war crimes against women; violations of women's bodily integrity; socio-economic violence in the workplace; political persecution and discrimination against women. These interaction between various groups helped in sharing of experiences which were unusual and yet successful ways in combating crimes against women.

In Australia after a bench mark survey to measure changes in the level of violence against women, Australia's overall approach to violence against women changed focus to the fact that: it is a fundamental human rights violation and that this form of violence prevents women from achieving full social and economic equality. Some recent initiatives that have been taken up by the Australian government are:

- The establishment of a national coordinated campaign to prevent and address domestic violence - the Prime Minister's Partnership Against Domestic Violence campaign where for the first time Australian governments had come together to speak out against domestic violence.

- The creation of the National Crime Prevention Programme.

- A legal reform including a national gun control legislation introduced in 1996 and a national gun buy back scheme under which several thousand firearms were surrendered.

- The continuing development and adoption of a best practice model for criminal laws dealing with violence, including those forms of violence most experienced by women.

- Laws to prohibit the trafficking and sexual exploitation of women and girls.

- Control on the portrayal of violence in the media and the internet, including through the work of the Ministerial Council on Violence in the Media.

- Innovative measures to prevent and address domestic violence through legislation and justice system and to prohibit VAW in all forms and to lessen the risk of its incidence. These reforms have laid the groundwork for a national approach to responding to and preventing violence aganist women.

In the Partnerships Against Domestic Violence **('Partnerships') campaign**

Early priority areas for *Partnership* were identified as :

- helping adults to break patterns of violence
- helping children and young people to break the cycle of violence between generations
- working with the community to educate against violence
- protection of people at risk
- information and best practice on what works in responding to and preventing domestic violence
- helping people in rural and remote communities.

National projects developed collaboratively by the Commonwealth, State and Territory governments included :

- community education
- national competency standards for workers dealing with those affected by domestic violence
- information for women with disabilities
- the effect of domestic violence on older women
- show-casing of key learnings emerging from the projects, to encourage best practice.

The second phase of *Partnerships was* launched in October 1999, helped in consolidating the key learnings from the demonstration projects and pursued the following activities:

- *Community Leadership* measures to tap into the potential of churches, charities and other major institutions by their participation on a high level taskforce that focussed on how they could play a powerful leadership role in advocating against domestic violence
- *Community Education* ($10 million): a broad national community awareness campaign to focus on key issues such as the harm done to children by domestic violence and the need for perpetrators to take responsibility for their voilence.
- The *Australian Domestic and Family Violence Clearinghouse* ($1 million) : information on domestic violence and best practice outcomes will be disseminated, complementing the drive to forge better links at policy and local service delivery levels.
- *Children affected by domestic violence* ($5 million) : focussed on prevention and early intervention work to improve the well being of children who had witnessed domestic violence. Based on results from *Partnerships* phase 1 projects, this developed appropriate and practical interventions with children and young people at risk, to reduce the intergenerational transmission of violence and better integrate policies and programs of domestic violence and child protection services.
- *Perpetrators of domestic violence* ($3 million) : built on the outcomes of the national forum on programmes for perpetrators of domestic violence convened by the Commonwealth Minister for Justice and Customs in May 1999 and provided assistance with infrastructure support, such as standards developed and evaluations.

The Beijing Declaration

But perhaps the turning point in women's movements which created a vortex for change is the coalition of women NGOs which participated , at the Beijing Summit. They were unhappy at the watered down position of the official documents, and so they issued their own NGO Beijing Declaration on 15 September 1995, the final day of the UN Women's Conference. The alternative declaration challenges governments to radically transform social, economic and political structures that oppress women and the girlchild worldwide.

In India too, the global campaign for elimination of violence against women are series of fortnight – long activities from November 25th to December 10th have been organized since 1998. Several campaigns are initiated in different parts of the country since then. However all the strategies adopted at the Beijing summit have not been fully implemented by any government.

At the Summit, the NGO's declared : "We live in a world marked by growing poverty, inequality, injustice, unemployment, environmentally destructive economic growth, war, sexism racism, xenophobia, homophobia and to her forms of discrimination and violence against women. Moreover, the intersection of gender, race and poverty create multiple burdens of discrimination for women of colour. We, NGO women of the world, rich in our diversity, have gathered along with governments in the largest global conference ever to address women's issues and the existing barriers to our achieving equality, development and peace. We believe that these goals can be realised by ending the oppression of women and girls, by women's full participation in national and international decision-making, and transforming the social, economic and political structures which underlie and perpetuate poverty, racism, inequality, injustice, unemployment, violence and war."

Till today even the United Nations obligations undertaken by its member states, on women's human rights are not yet respected, protected or promoted as inalienable, indivible and universal. Hence the women's groups called upon all governments for the following actions:

- To recognise and ensure women's equal rights to a decent standard of living, health, clean water and air, adequate food, clothing, and sanitation, safe and accessible housing, adequate social security and social insurance, education and legal aid as agreed in the International Covenant of Economic, Social and Cultural Rights.
- To take prompt action on the cancellation of multilateral debt; to enforce the accountability of international financial institutions and to ensure that all trade agreements are subject to human rights legislation, internationally, recognised labour standards and environmental protection. Economic rights are human rights.
- To end the transboundary movement, dumping and stockpiling of hazardous, toxic and radioactive wastes.
- To promote and use science and technology for peaceful purposes and people-centred, sustainable and ecologically sound development.
- To encourage, not hinder, the free expression, full participation and full access for women with disabilities in non-governmental and governmental organisations locally, nationally and internationally. To recognise and implement initiatives taken by poor and grassroots women, include them as full participants in the planning and distribution of resources.
- Not to misinterpret or impose religious beliefs or traditional practices on women in ways that deny their inalienable human rights. We also call for an end to all laws and customary practices which deny girls and women their equal rights, and deny them equal access to succession and inheritance.
- To amend their intellectual property laws so as to make indigenous women the primary beneficiaries

for the commercial use of their knowledge.

- To reject militarism in all its forms and create a culture of peace and human rights. They must redirect the $800 billion annual global military spending to peaceful purposes and convert military production to socially usefull purpose.

Governments must abolish weapons of mass destruction by banning testing, sales and stockpiling of nuclear chemical, biological, and all other weapons. The production, trade and use of all landmines must be banned. We demand that our governments work together to solve conflicts without using violence, and that they fully include women in peacemaking and conflict resolution initiatives.

- To implement their commitments to measure and value women's unwaged work and to include it in the accounting of each nation's Gross National Product.
- Dominant development models have been based upon the appropriation of resources from the South by the North and the transfer of ideas, technologies and methodologies from the North to the South.

We must build upon alternative models that curently exist in both South and North, which are based on equality, mutual respect, true participation and accountability of all women. These models must be economically and socially equitable and environmentally sound.

All development projects must take into account their effects on women, including the additonal workload imposed on women by unsustainable and inappropriate technology.

- NGO's working on women's issues call upon all people and all governments to radically reconsider and transform concepts, assumptions and structures governing social and economic life, and to take action on our recommendations. This process will require the full and equal participation of women of all races, ethnic backgrounds, religions, classes, languages, girls, young women, older women, indigenous women, grassroots women, rural women, urban women with disabilities, immigrant women, migrant women, refugee women, internally and other displaced women, women of different sexual orientation, and all other marginalised women.

They Called For

- Access for women to political structures at all levels, and equal political empowerment at all decision-making levels. Governments must support NGOs and ensure their full participation in planning and implementing all programmes and policies.
- Recognition, protection, compensation, financial and other assistance and full legal status for the millions of women and children, and the victims of nuclear and other environmental catastrophes, many of them widows or orphans who have been forced to become immigrants, migrants, refugees, internally and other displaced persons or forced into sexual slavery as a result of war, foreign occupation and political and socio-economic injustices. Every effort should be made to protect civilian population from the adverse effects of economic sanctions, which impair their human rights.
- Universally accessible, high quality, non-discrimination health care, which uses the great diversity of possibilities available in health systems world-wide rather than the present overdependence on medicine that overmedicates and patholoigises women's bodies. We require all governments to sponsor and support woman-controlled research for the prevention and cure of HIV/AIDS, to prohibit any form of discrimination of women with HIV/AIDS, and to ensure women's access to information, care, support and treatment of HIV/AIDS.
- Development and sustained use of affirmative action by both the private and public sectors of society to ensure the equality of women.

- All the media to change the present negative, exploitative and sexualised images of women and children to positive ones respecting us in all our dignity and diversity.
- Reshaping of education for all children, begining at the primary levels, to sensitise them about human rights, gender issues, and non-violent conflict resolution, stressing the need for world peace.
- Full implementation of the UN Decade for Human Rights Education and the prevention of human rights violations against women.
- New and additional financial, technical and other resources to successfully implement the plans and commitments form the Nairobi, Rio de Janeiro, Vienna , Cairo, Copenhagen and Beijing Conferences and that member states fulfill their obligations under the Convention on the Elimination of All Forms of Discrimination against Women.

The women also demanded an end to rape, and to all forms of violence, sexual exploitation and harasment of women and children. We further demand an end to the trafficking of women and children as well as sex tourism.

We seek these transformations in the spirit of service of humanity, partners with youth as agents of change, keeping our children, grandchildren and future generations in our hearts. We are convinced that as women achieve full and equal participation in all the affairs of the planet, peace will be realised, and the well-being of every individual secured. *We reaffirm that women's right are human rights.*

Social organizations both in India and Canada has been conducting legal literacy programs amongst strategic sections of women as this helps in imparting knowledge to the largest groups of citizens. In India most women are unaware of their inheritance rights, leave alone their right to live in dignity. In Toronto, immigrant and refugee women are detached from the rest of the society due to language problems. They are the worst sufferers of violence, as they remain silent about the trauma they face. The silence is due to fear of cultural stigma and for the fear that they might be deported. In language schools the immigrants not only learn English but have access to legal advice on various social issues.

By raising such concerns as torture within its campaign against Torture, Amesty International is seeking to broaden the debate about torture in India and the specific conditons-social, economic, legal and cultural-which allow the torure of women to occur and persist in the country. By focussing on the situation of dalits, "backward castes", adivasis and women who are marginalised by their economic position, the report also seeks to highlight the role of discrimination within society. The recommendations made by the report emphasizes on - not only increasing vulnerability of women to torture but reducing their chances of obtaining justice. While recognizing that violence against women in India takes many serious forms including trafficking and sexual exploitation, Amnesty International delegates limited their research to crimes of rape and other violent acts, such as assault (including stripping) which occur in the community. Amnesty International delegates also looked at the issue of violence against women in the home and the state's response to it. Amnesty International's intention through the report was to address concerns arising out of findings on the issue.

In India, non-governmental organizations have been conducting legal advice and awareness camps on a piece – meal basis at several places in the country. However, the tempo to spread legal literacy should be increased so that larger sections of women can overcome their trauma and harassment. The use of the visual and print media, especially the radio which has a large out reach in rural areas can be useful for dissemination of this type of information.

Other than legal literacy, control of crimes against women can also be taken care of through deliberate efforts like state strategies and remedies. It has been observed that laws alone cannot bring the desired changes in society unless such laws are properly implemented. For proper implementation, there must be an appropriate agency accompanied with active public participation and cooperation.

In the present Indian set – up there are many factors, which are responsible for the ineffectiveness of the laws which leads to atrocities against women. Some of the factors are out – lined as follows:

- There is evidence that there is a wide gap between enactment of laws for the development of various sections of society, especially laws for women; It is also difficult to implement the laws. Women are still unaware of the fact that laws may be enacted for them which will eventually help in their development.
- At several instances, the community has not rendered sufficient support to the women. People have been reluctant to be witnesses or act as third party complainants. In future an empowered community may take more interest in taking responsibility towards tormented women.
- The role of the police, which is most crucial in the legal system, should act in a more prompt, responsible and sensitive manner.
- Often delays in investigations especially rape and murder cases are difficult to prove as the whole case may depend on circumstantial evidence.
- Delay in criminal trials makes convictions difficult. Speedy trials are essential. Fast track courts are functioning in many parts of the country to give maximum relief to the victims.
- In Canada, time and again during the invertiews it was voiced by the NGO's and activists that the rapists were often convicted for only a few months which made the victims more vulnerable. The penalty is very little for the accused in rape cases which often prevents the victims not to report a case.
- Laws in India should be better classified especially in the case of rape and harassment cases. This will facilitate both the law enforcement agencies as well as the victims.

- Senior police officers may like to impress on the fact that there should be 100% registration of cases. Emphasis should not be played on curbing crime through manipulation of statistics.
- Besides, reporting cases of crime seems to also affect the fate of politics. Emphasis should be put on the number of cases that are registered. This pressurizes the police to "burk" down some of the crime statistics. For 100% registration, the atmosphere in a police station must be cordial. Women officers and women personnel should be posted in each police station to remove the inhibitions of the victims and their families. The police should not assume the role of terrorizing the people, but be a part of a service organisation, where the victim is the customer they need to serve.
- Regular coordination between the various social welfare organizations and the police, may make a positive impact on society. The role of the social organization is not that of interference in operational policing matters but to enhance the role of the guardians of law. A central data bank if created would benefit research work and in future investigations.
- Helpline services especially for rape victims and battered victims in trauma maybe started in every city. Often victims need sympathy and medical attention. Besides this, the law enforcement agencies must only post those personnel who are genuinely interested in the welfare of women and children. Several police officers feel that postings in human rights cells and crime against women cells are side-line postings. The role of the personnel working in these special places may be highlighted by the media. Social and cultural organisations may reward the officers at public functions.
- As part of a spatial study, probably the best method to curb crime against women is by creating atrocity – free zones for women in a city. Taking the overall

statistics, on crime against women and the demographic variables, atrocity – free zones can be created where through awareness exercises such as seminars and workshops, crime can be curtailed.

- A similar program has been introduced in Maharashtra – Chembur and Worli and Mumbai Loni Kalbhor and Chakan in Pune rural areas. These areas have been selected as pilot centers for implementation of "Pitayi muky vasahat / gaon" program. The scheme is an extension of the local committee program. Just as Neighbourhood Watch Schemes are in Toronto, this scheme can be extended over to cover protection of the women. In India too, various areas have community policing, which is used to protect property. However, this scheme can be extended for the welfare of vulnerable sections of the community.
- In the early part of 1998, the National Women Commission introduced 110 Parivarik Mahila Lok Adalats for Women. These courts are people's courts in family disputes. Such institutions can be used for the redressal and speedy disposal of cases relating to family problems especially relating to the women. In the near future, Panchayats in villages and non – governmental organizations in India can take over the functioning of such courts.
- Economic independence is a step towards prevention of atrocities of women to a certain extent. In recent years at an informal level government and various organizations have accepted the economic contribution made by the women working at home. But no real effort has been made to quantify them. A comprehensive mechanism should be evolved aiming at the economical benefit that could accrue to women working at home besides the psychological and the social acceptance of their contribution in the family. The policy may be aimed to differentiate between the same women working inside the house

and at the outer end working outside as a laborer in different capacity and fulfilling the tempo of life.

- Another method of control of violence against women may be through community control. This is where the community can have a direct involvement. These may be by creating shelter homes, organizing awareness camps; organizing safety audits as part of the scheme started by METRAC and actively helping women to participate in these deliberations by improving social barriers. Social defense mechanisms are fairly widespread in most countries in the form of family counseling centers, protection of shelter homes etc. However, such facilities are not available uniformly in any country. The various institutions which work towards welfare of women, could undertake a special study and identify the locations and voluntary organizations which could be entrusted with the task of running new Homes. Sensitization of gender issues involves drawing people's attention in making them conscious of realities that are already experienced by them. Basically, gender is the relative status of men and women in a given society. It is culture specific and many of the gender roles ascribed to men and women in our society are colored by attitudinal disposition. This social psyche, developed over a long period, have led to the institutionalized deprivation and exploitation of women.

Another method of community control is executed by a program called Municipal Strategies for public Violence Against Women, which was adopted in September 1988 by the Toronto City Council. Their main objective was to improve the quality of women's lives, and enable them to fully participate in society. This according to the Program was by:

- Better urban design/planning
- Community participation in crime prevention
- Public transit
- Better policing with the community.

Often poor urban design enables the perpetrators to commit an offence. For example a poorly lit driveway or a bus stop could be an ideal location of any street crime ranging from minor snatching to incidences of rape. According to the plan, this could be prevented by better lighting, visibility and access for help. The Women in Safe Environments Report, prepared by Women Plan Toronto and the Metro Action Committee on Public Violence against Women and Children were the first to initiate to build up a better and safer environment. METRAC introduced safety audits for concrete and practical purposes. METRAC used safety audits in the Toronto Transit Commission subway stations. Today in every subway station in Toronto there is a special zone, which is manned by close – circuit T.V. so that crime can be prevented. This is ideal for women who travel at night. Besides this METRAC conducted an audit in High Park (Toronto's largest park), in university campuses and in several towns and cities in Ontario. Today this safety audit has been used successfully in Frankfurt and some places in the USA. The safety audit may involve between 2 to 3 hours for the first audit. The audit revolves around the needs of the most vulnerable women in a community, those who may be blind, handicapped or women travelling with young children. In a typical audit attention is given to typical public and semi – public spaces, like streets, walkways, schoolyards, parking sites, parks, plazas, recreational areas and other commercial and residential areas. Safety audits guide for the *development of landuse*, such as mining landuse, i.e., including both residential and commercial places in an area.

Good lighting in public places, which should be well distributed.

Landscaping – which should not only involve enhancing the beauty, but the safety of a certain place.

Parking facilities should also have a certain amount of security, as usually these areas are isolated spots especially at night.

Internal security - especially in the residential areas. Entrances should be clearly defined and secure etc. In other words, the internal design of any complex should be safe for all individuals especially residents.

Besides this, crime prevention according to the Program (1988) for Safe City emphasized on community participation. Through a process of involvement the needs of a community can be identified, keeping in mind all the local characteristics of an area. This can be best achieved through Neighborhood Watch and Block Parents Programmes. Through these programs, crime prevention, women's accessibility to information on criminal active in the area can be achieved.

Public Transit is another area where safety of the women is necessary. Through safety audits, it was realized that the Toronto Transit Commission stops here to be planned keeping in mind that there is adequate safety in the form of lighting, public telephones etc. As for policing which was accepted as necessary for the safety of the women, it was realized that police personnel should be accountable and well represented to achieve safety programs for women. Neighbourhood Watch and Block Parent schemes were also adopted. Besides this, the police may wish to consult city planners regarding the physical sites of assaults and design for better improvement. It is human psychology that when there is police patrolling, the citizens feel safe.

However, the safety audits have emphasized on street crimes, which are far less than domestic crimes, which is difficult to detect and curb by ordinary policing techniques. However, METRAC has suggested that both human and policy practices can be audited as well. For example, at work, school, in the groups, and housing complexes etc. The questions a person can use are:

- Do you trust the people you would have to go to for help if you have been sexually assaulted?
- Would they be sensitive to your needs?
- Do you have the information that you need about sexual assaults that have happened in your neighborhood or workplace?
- Do you have a say in decisions that affect your safety?[1]

The audit may be used in the case of relationships as well. Through a set of questions, people who feel unsafe can find out whether there is any threat in a relationship or not. In the case of India too, similar audits can be used by women in each area, in schools, colleges and organizations to improve safety. Participation of the community is extremely important in curbing crimes against women.

Awareness in society has been created by schemes such as the Clothesline Project where women who have been victims have painted tee – shirts with slogans and paintings; the December 6 massacre in Montreal where 14 women were murdered has been named a National and Provincial commemoration day for women's civil, economic, cultural and political rights.

In order to check physical violence, sexual violence and other types of crimes against women, it is felt that formulating laws and clauses by judiciary will achieve no success unless proper and effective machinery is devised for enforcement of such laws. Moreover, the cooperation of the people is also essential for the effective implementation of the social welfare legislation for which awareness about such laws should be created among the masses. There must be effective investigating machinery and the investigation must automatically start whenever any crime against women is committed. The investigating officers must be especially trained in this field of the criminal justice system. The delay in the trials should be avoided and every attempt must be made to punish the guilty, while the events are fresh in the minds of the public. Further, the sentence must be tailored to meet the needs of the individual offenders and the surrounding circumstances should be taken into consideration.

Since this study entails socio – spatial variation of crime against women, emphasis has been placed on quantitative information and statistical data and its analysis. This study will help in the future deployment of police personnel in the area, which have more crime against women. Besides, various welfarian and developmental schemes for women and the family as a whole can be introduced to combat this social evil of crime against women. As agreed through out this study that an emphasis is necessary along with a national policy. However, this should not be only seen in the light of yet another social issue but crime against women should be tackled as a health issue as the state spends resources on the victim for hospitals and on medicines after assault in government hospitals. Besides, the perpetrator is not only an accused but also an individual who needs medical and psychiatric help as the victim. The woman who is battered or assaulted is a victim of the socio – economic crisis of the urban environment, which erodes family values, degrades the surroundings. But, the accused or the perpetrator is also a victim of urban lifestyle, a victim of the pressures of today's world of ambitions, rat - race that makes a person unrealistic.

Hence, the urban phenomenon of crimes against women may be taken as yet another virus which is spreading and defacing our society and which should be curtailed for the betterment of a civilisation. The best method to prevent violence is by following the code that all human beings are equal, responsible and that there should be trust and respect among all.

References

1. Ritel, Vibhuti, campaigns Against Gender Violence (1977-1993) Pencraft International, 1998.
2. *Women's Safety Audit Guide,* METRAC (1992) , p. 32.

Index

M

N

O

P